Inequalities in Geographical Space

SCIENCES

Geography and Demography, Field Director – Denise Pumain

Geography of Inequality, Subject Head – Clémentine Cottineau

Inequalities in Geographical Space

Coordinated by
Clémentine Cottineau
Julie Vallée

WILEY

First published 2022 in Great Britain and the United States by ISTE Ltd and John Wiley & Sons, Inc.

Apart from any fair dealing for the purposes of research or private study, or criticism or review, as permitted under the Copyright, Designs and Patents Act 1988, this publication may only be reproduced, stored or transmitted, in any form or by any means, with the prior permission in writing of the publishers, or in the case of reprographic reproduction in accordance with the terms and licenses issued by the CLA. Enquiries concerning reproduction outside these terms should be sent to the publishers at the undermentioned address:

ISTE Ltd
27-37 St George's Road
London SW19 4EU
UK

www.iste.co.uk

John Wiley & Sons, Inc.
111 River Street
Hoboken, NJ 07030
USA

www.wiley.com

© ISTE Ltd 2022

The rights of Clémentine Cottineau and Julie Vallée to be identified as the authors of this work have been asserted by them in accordance with the Copyright, Designs and Patents Act 1988.

Library of Congress Control Number: 2022945475

British Library Cataloguing-in-Publication Data
A CIP record for this book is available from the British Library
ISBN 978-1-78945-088-0

ERC code:
SH2 Institutions, Values, Environment and Space
 SH2_5 International relations, global and transnational governance
 SH2_11 Human, economic and social geography

Contents

Introduction xi
Clémentine COTTINEAU and Julie VALLÉE

Chapter 1. The Spatial Dimension of Educational Inequalities 1
Leïla FROUILLOU

1.1. Introduction. 1
1.2. School segregation as the central object of socio-geographical
approaches to school inequalities. 5
    1.2.1. The 1980s: from national sociological theories to localized
    approaches to educational inequalities in France 7
    1.2.2. How can we objectify the unequal distribution of students
    in the school system?. 8
1.3. The spatial dimension of educational inequalities: from policies
to trajectories 11
    1.3.1. The spatial dimension of school policies that produce
    inequalities. 12
    1.3.2. Understanding inequalities based on school placements
    and trajectories 16
1.4. Conclusion: spatial dimension of inequalities and the
interweaving of levels of analysis 19
1.5. References 20

Chapter 2. Socio-spatial Inequalities and Intersectionality 27
Negar Élodie BEHZADI and Lucia DIRENBERGER

2.1. Relationships between power relations, inequalities and space 28
2.2. Work and socio-spatial inequalities. 33
   2.2.1. Theoretical perspectives on work and space 33
   2.2.2. Professional spaces and segregation at different scales. 35
   2.2.3. Care work and assignment to private space. 38
2.3. Othering processes and spaces: the place of the other 40
   2.3.1. The dividing lines between "us" and "them" 41
   2.3.2. The space of everyday life: the home of the "others" and
the street that belongs to "us". 43
2.4. Agency and minority spaces 45
   2.4.1. Theoretical and empirical perspectives on agency. 45
   2.4.2. Space as a tool and a stake in minority struggles 46
2.5. Conclusion 49
2.6. References 51

Chapter 3. Migration, Multi-situated Inequalities and the
World Economy 61
Laurence ROULLEAU-BERGER

3.1. Toward a sociology of inequalities and migrations 62
3.2. International cities and migrant workers. 66
   3.2.1. Subalternity and the ethnicization of labor markets 66
   3.2.2. Racism at work 67
   3.2.3. The globalization of care. 68
   3.2.4. Migration and platform capitalism 69
3.3. Multi-situated inequalities and biographical bifurcations. 70
   3.3.1. Migration and multi-situated inequalities 70
   3.3.2. Inequalities and biographical bifurcations 71
3.4. Moral careers and the struggle for recognition 72
3.5. The plurality and hierarchy of transnationalisms 74
   3.5.1. Transnationalism "from above" and cosmopolitan spirit 74
   3.5.2. Transnationalism "from below" and bazaar economies 75
   3.5.3. Intermediate transnationalism and international trade 76
3.6. Forced migration, downgrading and expulsions 78
3.7. Conclusion 80
3.8. References 80

Chapter 4. The Geographical Dimension of Inequalities in Access to Employment ... 85
Philippe ASKENAZY and Verónica ESCUDERO

4.1. Introduction. ... 85
4.2. Compensatory differences between territories ... 89
    4.2.1. From the immigration model to the amenities model ... 89
    4.2.2. Empirical findings ... 90
4.3. Immobility and spatial mismatch ... 91
    4.3.1. Residential sorting and access to employment ... 92
    4.3.2. Gradients in residential immobility ... 93
    4.3.3. Commuting patterns ... 94
4.4. The importance of couples' geographic trade-offs in individuals' access to employment. ... 97
    4.4.1. A theoretically gendered space ... 98
    4.4.2. Indicators of a restricted labor market for women ... 99
4.5. Labor market networks and access to employment ... 102
    4.5.1. The empirical relevance of residential networks ... 103
    4.5.2. Networks that generate spatial inequalities? ... 103
4.6. Digital space: the abolition of geographical constraints? ... 104
    4.6.1. The emergence of online job portals and professional networking platforms ... 105
    4.6.2. Telework: a new order? ... 107
    4.6.3. Microwork: equal access but exploitation? ... 110
4.7. Conclusion ... 111
4.8. References ... 113

Chapter 5. The Perception of Inequality and Poverty in the Most Segregated, Affluent Neighborhoods ... 119
Serge PAUGAM

5.1. Studying the perception of poverty ... 122
    5.1.1. A perception that varies in time and space ... 122
    5.1.2. How do the wealthy justify their choice to reside in a segregated neighborhood? ... 124
5.2. The constitution of a moral boundary ... 127
    5.2.1. An idealized self-contained bubble ... 128
    5.2.2. A moral order within neighborhoods ... 129
5.3. Keeping out the working class. ... 130
    5.3.1. Distrust and repulsion of the poor ... 130

5.3.2. A growing feeling of insecurity in the rich neighborhoods
of Paris 134
5.4. Justifying class inequality and poverty. 136
5.4.1. The neutralization of compassion 136
5.4.2. Controlled victimization of the poor 140
5.5. Conclusion 143
5.6. References 146

Chapter 6. Modeling Inequalities in Geographical Space 151
Clémentine COTTINEAU

6.1. Introduction: different modeling formalisms for different purposes . . 151
6.2. Inequality in the distribution of economic resources and
in its spatial distribution 152
6.2.1. Lorenz/Gini, Pareto and Theil in economics: three
distinct models 153
6.2.2. Mapping socioeconomic inequalities and graphical modeling. . . 157
6.3. Statistical regression models: estimating the effects of geographic
location on inequality 160
6.3.1. Description of the models 160
6.3.2. Important results of the analysis of inequalities by
statistic models 165
6.3.3. Limitations of the analysis of inequalities in geographical
space by statistical models 167
6.4. Simulation models to explain and illustrate the dynamics of
inequalities in geographical space 169
6.4.1. Agent-based models of spatial segregation: Schelling and
its variants 170
6.4.2. Two agent-based models of the emergence of inequalities
linked to the distribution of resources in space 172
6.4.3. Three models simulating spatial relegation dynamics. 174
6.5. Conclusion 176
6.6. References 177

**Chapter 7. A Critical Reading of Neighborhood-based Policies
and their Geography** 183
Julie VALLÉE

7.1. A geography plagued by contradictions 184
7.1.1. The dual purpose of "priority" neighborhoods 184
7.1.2. Challenges of size and shape 186

7.2. Reductive policies 190
    7.2.1. A diversionary operation. 190
    7.2.2. An impoverishment of the interdependencies between
    agent and structure 193
7.3. Temporal dynamics of priority neighborhoods 194
    7.3.1. Residential trajectories 195
    7.3.2. Everyday dynamics 197
7.4. Conclusion 205
7.5. References 206

List of Authors 211

Index 213

Introduction

Clémentine COTTINEAU[1,2] and Julie VALLÉE[3]
[1] *Centre Maurice Halbwachs, CNRS, Paris, France*
[2] *Technische Universiteit Delft, The Netherlands*
[3] *Geographie-cités, CNRS, Paris, France*

The most sensitive forms of inequality today are economic and social [...]. In concrete terms, the most perceptible divisions of economic and social inequalities are projected onto the use of space [...]. Space is made up of units with certain homogeneous characteristics, nested within one another. Within each of these units there are differentiated sectors of inequality. A geography of inequalities, like any geography, is thus articulated according to multiple scales. It is as necessary to take into account the social differentiations in the occupation and control of space in a city or region as it is to measure the differences between large continental groups. (George 1981, pp. 7–8)[1]

Although the fight against inequality is an objective shared by most societies and international institutions today (it is, for example, one of the 17 United Nations

---

1. Original citation: "Les formes les plus sensibles des inégalités sont aujourd'hui d'ordre économique et social […] Concrètement, les clivages les plus perceptibles des inégalités économiques et sociales se projettent sur l'utilisation de l'espace […] L'espace est fait d'unités présentant certains caractères d'homogénéité, emboîtées les unes dans les autres. À l'intérieur de chacune d'elles se différencient des secteurs d'inégalités. Une géographie des inégalités, comme toute géographie, s'articule donc suivant diverses échelles. Il y a autant de nécessité à prendre en compte dans une ville ou dans une région les différenciations sociales de l'occupation et de la maîtrise de l'espace qu'à mesurer les écarts entre de grands ensembles continentaux" (George 1981, pp. 7–8).

Inequalities in Geographical Space,
coordinated by Clémentine COTTINEAU and Julie VALLÉE. © ISTE Ltd 2022.

Sustainable Development Goals for 2030), in retrospect this concern is a relatively recent one as it has only arisen following the establishment of democratic societies. Prehistoric societies – having not accumulated enough surplus for their members to distinguish themselves based on assets – did not see much of a difference, while pre-capitalist societies were instead analyzed in terms of homogeneous groups (classes, castes, social, ethnic, professional and religious groups) between which a "natural" inegalitarian order existed. It was only toward the end of the 19th century that greater attention started being paid to the inequalities between individuals. Indeed, it was at that time that the social and economic sciences abandoned the "representative agent" of productive groups and social classes and started to think about the lives of individuals as a legitimate object of analysis. Up until then, "[there was] no complete theory of personal distribution because there [was] no person" (Alacevich and Soci 2017, p. 36).

In geography, the analysis of inequalities is also concerned with social classes and individuals, but with a focus on space as an agent of production, of reproduction and of an expression of inequalities, and this is at different scales, as the quotation from George at the start of this chapter underlines. In this book, we are interested in inequalities between individuals in geographical space, that is, in the role geographical space has to play in revealing, maintaining and increasing or decreasing inter-individual inequalities over time. This Introduction reviews the vocabulary dedicated to the study of inequalities, analyzes the objects and subjects of inequalities that unfold in geographical space, as well as their spatial and temporal scales. It ends with a presentation of the different chapters of the book and their relationships with one another.

I.1. Back to the notion of inequality

I.1.1. *The lexical field of inequalities*

When it comes to the question of "inequality" there is a proliferation of terms with overlapping meanings. In this section, we would like to introduce and disambiguate the terms used interchangeably in common parlance in order to clarify what is meant by inequalities as they will be discussed in this book.

The combined development of capitalism and democracy in Europe created the conditions for the following paradox: at a time when societies were reaching record levels of inequality, they started promoting a liberal and meritocratic ideology that claimed fundamental equality among their members, at least from a legal point of view: this equality was later translated into the charters of northern European cities in the Middle Ages, and into the *Universal Declaration of the Rights of Man and of the Citizen* (1789) that emerged from the French Revolution: "All men are born free and equal in rights". This legal equality promoted by the bourgeois revolutions was only partial however: it notably excluded women and foreigners. Moreover, this legal equality did not include the equality of economic resources either, since the monetary remuneration from work and the distribution of resources were not integrated into the legal definition, it being understood – notably by the proponents of meritocracy – that this must be regulated by the effort made.

Beyond its legal dimension, the notion of inequality refers to questions of *hierarchies* and *disfavor*. According to Maurin (2018), "in order to speak of inequality, access to goods, services or practices must be able to be classified and valued in a hierarchical manner; otherwise, it is no longer a question of inequality, but of differences. A difference only becomes an 'inequality' when what we are talking about can be ranked in a hierarchy[2]". *Differences*, in the mathematical sense of the term, are in fact limited to describing differences in levels and values. For Lahire, the distinction between difference and inequality lies instead in the way in which the presence or absence of provision is harmful to individuals:

> For a difference to become an inequality, the social world in which the 'privileged' and the 'disadvantaged' live must be organized in such a way that the deprivation of a particular material resource, cultural good, activity, knowledge, or service constitutes a lack or a handicap. Being rich, educated and healthy is not an option to be chosen from among other possibilities. It is precisely because wealth is more enviable than poverty, that education and knowledge are more highly regarded than a lack of education and ignorance, and that good health is preferable to bad health, that it is not just a question of social differences between rich and poor, educated and uneducated, healthy and unhealthy, but of inequalities. (Lahire 2019, p. 39)[3]

---

2. Original citation: "pour parler d'inégalités, il faut que l'accès aux biens, aux services ou aux pratiques puisse se classer, être valorisé de façon hiérarchique ; sinon, il ne s'agit plus d'inégalités, mais de différences. Une différence ne devient une 'inégalité' que lorsque ce dont on parle peut être hiérarchisé".

3. Original citation: "Pour qu'une différence devienne inégalité, il faut que le monde social dans lequel vivent 'privilégiés' et 'lésés' soit organisé de telle façon que la privation de telle ressource matérielle, de tel bien culturel, de telle activité, de tel savoir, ou de tel service constitue un manque ou un handicap. Être riche, instruit et en bonne santé n'est pas une option qu'on aurait à choisir parmi d'autres possibles. C'est bien parce que la richesse est plus enviable que la pauvreté, que l'instruction et les savoirs sont mieux considérés que l'absence d'instruction et l'ignorance, et que la bonne santé est préférable à la mauvaise santé qu'il n'est

The notion of *disparity* also communicates the idea of a difference rather than a hierarchy. It applies well to certain types of geographic variation, such as levels of amenities, where the disparities observed – for example, in terms of transport infrastructure between a large city and a rural area – reflect differences in population and density levels between these two types of space, rather than a socially organized inequality in the treatment of these spaces. These differences between geographical areas can, however, become inequalities when they introduce a hierarchy between individuals according to, for example, the possibility of accessing education or medical care, and the harm that can result from living/working/studying in a space where these possibilities are greatly reduced. In the same register as difference or disparity, we find the term *diversity*. Simply referring to the co-presence of a non-hierarchical plurality of categories and situations, this term is not suited to the description of social inequalities in geographical space, in the sense that it tends to place all differences on the same level. Diversity is, however, a precondition for inequality, since a society of clones cannot distinguish or discriminate between its members. It is therefore the diversity of individuals and their characteristics (but also the diversity of the geographical spaces in which they live and which they contribute to differentiating) that constitutes a prerequisite for the processes of production, reproduction and mitigation of inequalities in geographical space.

Associated with the idea of disfavor, the idea of *injustice* can also be brought up. Since the work of Rawls (1971), inequalities between individuals have been analyzed and justified within the interpretative framework of social justice. The liberal philosopher, in line with the tradition of Rousseau's writings on the social contract, introduced the idea of compensation between citizens who are unequally endowed by nature (in terms of talents, in particular) in order to achieve a fair society. The optimal principle held by Rawls to carry out this redistribution is that of the *maximin*, that is, the maximization of transfers to improve the situation of individuals with the least resources. This idea feeds into recent thinking on *equity* (the principle of giving more to those who need it most). It can also be linked to corrective policy actions aimed at fighting inequalities, whether they concern the whole population (universal approach) or those that target certain groups or certain territories (targeted approach), with modalities or an intensity that vary according to need (proportionate universalism). In addition to the moral issues or the issues of justice between individuals with which these redistribution principles are associated, some authors also defend the idea that inequalities deserve to be combated because,

---

pas seulement question de différences sociales entre riches et pauvres, instruits et non-instruits, personnes en bonne santé ou personnes souffrantes ou diminuées, mais bien d'inégalités" (Lahire 2019, p. 39).

beyond their individual consequences, it is society as a whole that is harmed by them (see Box I.1).

Rawls' theory, which remains a key reference on the question of inequalities and redistribution rationales, can nevertheless be criticized, notably for the fact that it does not take into account the perception and feelings of the actors concerned. Thus, redistributing resources in a society may resolve material differences, but it will not cancel out the experience of humiliation and the feeling of victimization of those who have suffered from inequality (Dupuy 2003).

If all these social and moral reasons were not enough to consider the issue of inequality, it is worth noting that high levels of economic inequality can contribute to lower levels of collective well-being and economic growth for the country as a whole. This is consistent with the idea put forward by Rawls (1971) that inherent differences between individuals are neither moral nor desirable for a harmonious and collaborative society, and that redistribution between members of society is desirable so as to ensure that citizens who are unequally endowed by nature (e.g. in terms of talent) form a fair society. This idea that the difficulties encountered by one part of society are detrimental to society as a whole has been empirically studied by Wilkinson and Pickett, based on work in social epidemiology, happiness economics and sociology. In their book *The Spirit Level* (2009), they show that most of the ills generally associated with poverty – they cite low life expectancy, poor skills, mental health problems, crime and early pregnancy, among others – can also be attributed to the gap between rich and poor in the same society, i.e. economic inequality. The reason for this would be that hierarchical and rigid social stratification increases social anxiety in the population as well as the perceived threat of being downgraded: "Greater inequality seems to heighten people's social evaluation anxieties by increasing the importance of social status" (Wilkinson and Pickett 2009, p. 41). They then conclude that *inequality is not only harmful to the poorest*, but that *society as a whole suffers the consequences*. For example, by encouraging the poorest to resort to loans and mortgages to acquire houses, economic inequalities may have contributed to the subprime crisis of 2007–2008. Fitoussi and Savidan (2003) and Alacevich and Soci (2017) also make the link between high levels of inequality and threats to democracy, since the disproportionate wealth of individuals allows them to influence political campaigns and political personnel, but also to express their opinions and grievances more strongly than others. Finally, Stiglitz (2016) summarizes the channels through which *high inequality harms the entire economy*: (1) by reducing aggregate demand, and thus increasing debt to maintain the consumption levels of the poorest; (2) by reducing equality of opportunity, and thus not allowing the talents of working-class individuals to flourish; and 3) by reducing investment in common goods (e.g. public transport infrastructure).

Box I.1. *Beyond its consequences on individuals, why focus on inequality?*

Some authors thus explicitly consider the *feeling of injustice* as a medium which transforms difference into inequality. For example, we can cite Brunet et al. (1992, p. 253), who define inequality as "a difference perceived or experienced as an injustice that does not ensure the same opportunities for everyone"[4], or Bihr and Pfefferkorn (2008), who define inequality as "the result of an unequal distribution, in the mathematical sense of the expression, between the members of a society, of the resources of the latter, an unequal distribution due to the very structures of this society, and giving rise to a feeling, legitimate or not, of injustice among its members"[5] (p. 1).

The notion of inequality also implies the idea that differences acquire the status of inequalities when they are *systematic*. Indeed, it is the repetition of individual situations, associating the fact of being a woman with having a lower salary for equal skills, of living in a disadvantaged area with being in poorer health, of having a foreign-sounding name with not being able to find a job, that gives rise to the feeling of injustice for an entire group facing systematic deprivation. One of the channels through which systematic inequalities are produced is that of *discrimination*, which translates a difference in the treatment of an individual or a social group according to certain visible or supposed characteristics (race, gender, sexual orientation, disability, age, geographical origin, religion, etc.). Although discrimination can be positive (particularly in the context of quota policies aimed at reducing certain social inequalities), the default use of the term refers to the negative treatment of discriminated social categories.

In addition to being systematic, some inequalities between individuals are *systemic*, that is, they are part of the usual functioning of the system that produces them.

In other words, these inequalities are not due to chance or to an unfortunate turn of events for the individuals who suffer them: they are an integral part of the reproduction of the society that produces them. Colombi (2020) shows, for example, how the poverty of some brings prosperity to others in our societies – in other words, how the privileged existence of well-off households depends on the exploitation of the most vulnerable (for childcare, personal transport, cleaning, home delivery, etc.), since the people who make up this low-cost labor force are kept in a

---

4. Original citation: "une différence perçue ou vécue comme une injustice n'assurant pas les mêmes chances à chacun".

5. Original citation: "le résultat d'une distribution inégale, au sens mathématique de l'expression, entre les membres d'une société, des ressources de cette dernière, distribution inégale due aux structures mêmes de cette société, et faisant naître un sentiment, légitime ou non, d'injustice au sein de ses membres".

situation of dependence on these jobs for their survival. In this mechanism of social reproduction, even exceptional trajectories of social or economic mobility participate in the maintenance of the *status quo*. Jaquet uses the notion of *transclass* for this phenomenon: "Non-reproduction, in this sense, is only the perpetuation of reproduction by other means. The social order is preserved by the expulsion of an element that threatens it, that introduces disorder, because it does not conform to the ambient model"[6] (2014, p. 78).

In summary, inequalities are defined here as *differences in the distribution of valuable resources (wealth, health, education, for example), which are systematic, detrimental, experienced as injustices and fueled by discrimination practices*. However, this definition of inequality does not solve the questions addressed in the following section, namely: who are the subjects and objects of inequality?

I.1.2. Plurality of subjects and objects of inequality

I.1.2.1. Objects of inequalities

In analyses of economic inequality, the subject ("who") is often an *individual* or a household, while the object ("what") is an *economic quantity* whose distribution is studied: we are thus interested in inequalities between individuals with respect to their income or wealth (see Box I.2).

These studies of economic distribution are thus distinct from studies of poverty, that is, studies which focus on the lowest part of the distribution (Atkinson 2003). Indeed, by isolating one sub-population (the poor) from society as a whole, poverty analysis often ignores the gradients among sub-populations, their interactions and associated transfers of wealth. "While poverty may be shrugged off as a non-antagonistic issue, inequality will always, sooner or later, trigger a discussion about the structure of power and social disparities in a given society" (Alacevich and Soci, 2017, p. 15). In the field of economics, analyses of inter-individual inequalities in different countries of the world, as well as their historical evolution, have been the subject of many successful publications in the last decade (Piketty 2013; Atkinson 2015; Stiglitz 2015). This work draws on economic theory to try to explain the mechanics of inequality and reverse the trend of its historical growth.

---

6. Original citation: "La non-reproduction, en ce sens, n'est que la perpétuation de la reproduction par d'autres moyens. L'ordre social est préservé par l'expulsion d'un élément qui le menace, qui introduit le désordre, car il n'est pas conforme au modèle ambiant".

Although they are sometimes confused as being the same thing, income and wealth refer to distinct economic realities and very different levels of inequality. Indeed, wealth is much more unevenly distributed than income in general, and labor income in particular.

Income, for an individual or a household, refers to the sum of wages, interest and dividends from work and capital earned over a given year. It is the economic quantity most frequently studied in terms of inequality. Income inequality between individuals in the world has tended to decline since the 1970s, due to the significant enrichment of a large number of citizens from emerging countries (and notably from China). Thus, the global Gini index has fallen by 3.8% (from 0.662 to 0.637), the Atkinson index has fallen by 6–8%, and the ratio of the richest 10% to the poorest 10% (P10/P90) fell by almost 20% between 1979 and 2000 (Sala-i-Martin 2006, p. 384). However, income inequality has tended to increase among citizens of the same country. The inequality report by Alvaredo et al. (2018), based on their Top Income Database, shows that national income inequalities have been on the rise again since the 1980s: following a phase of significant inequality reduction in China, Russia, the United States, Canada and India following World War II, the richest 10% of these countries have collected between 40% and 60% of total annual income since 2015.

The **wealth** (or riches, i.e. gross wealth minus debts and duties) of an individual or a household is a stock of net income accumulated over time, sometimes over several generations. Although less visible (and less easily observable due to less accessible data), wealth inequality is even greater than income inequality in contemporary societies: "currently, at the beginning of the 2010s, the share of the top 10% of wealth is around 60% of national wealth in most European countries, and in particular in France, Germany, the United Kingdom and Italy. Perhaps most striking is that in all of these societies, the poorest half of the population owns almost nothing: the poorest 50% in wealth always owns less than 10% of the national wealth, and usually less than 5% [...] For this half of the population, the very notion of wealth and capital is relatively abstract"[7] (Piketty 2013, pp. 404–407).

Box I.2. *Economic inequality in terms of stock and flow: wealth and income*

---

7. Original citation: "actuellement, au début des années 2010, la part des 10% des patrimoines les plus élevés se situe autour de 60% du patrimoine national dans la plupart des pays européens, et en particulier en France, en Allemagne, au Royaume-Uni et en Italie. Le plus frappant est sans doute que dans toutes ces sociétés, la moitié la plus pauvre de la population ne possède presque rien : les 50% les plus pauvres en patrimoine possèdent toujours moins de 10 % du patrimoine national, et généralement moins de 5%. [...] Pour cette moitié de la population, la notion même de patrimoine et de capital est relativement abstraite".

The study of inequality between individuals is not limited to their economic resources. Other unequal distributions relate not to what individuals accumulate but instead to what they consume – the consumption of electricity or running water, greenhouse gas emissions, and so on (Hedenus and Azar 2005). This unequal consumption can give rise to a feeling of injustice within a given population, which is linked to wealth inequality, since consumption reflects economic means, but also to the environmental damage that this consumption brings about. Although more recent and less numerous than studies on the distribution of economic wealth, studies on the distribution of energy consumption share the same logic in that they analyze how a tiny portion of the population appropriates or consumes prized resources. In fact, inequalities go far beyond the question of income alone to extend "from education to employment, via health and leisure, etc."[8] (Maurin 2018). Drawing on work from sociology, we can also cite "cultural capital, social capital, power, prestige, health, living conditions, 'happiness', the multiple risks we are exposed to, social mobility…"[9] (Dubet 2011, §1). Drawing on work from geography, we can cite inequalities related to spatial mobility (Bacqué and Fol 2007), accessibility or the quality of living space. This book attempts to account for such a variety of inequalities and their intersection in geographical space.

I.1.2.2. *Subjects of inequalities*

The individual subjects of inequalities can be analyzed through the lens of common characteristics that contribute to the maintenance and reproduction of the inequalities in which they participate.

> Inequalities are observed between people and can therefore be grouped, for example, by age, gender, occupation (social background), etc. […] To understand inequalities is to grasp how they constitute an overall system in which factors are intertwined. You may be a woman, but you are also of a certain age, of a certain social background and of a certain skin color. Anyone who wants to observe and understand inequalities must analyze the relationships between these domains and categories of populations and unravel their respective weight. (Maurin 2018)[10]

---

8. Original citation: "de l'éducation à l'emploi, en passant par la santé et les loisirs, etc.".
9. Original citation: "les capitaux culturels, les capitaux sociaux, le pouvoir, le prestige, la santé, les conditions de vie, le 'bonheur', les risques multiples auxquels nous sommes exposés, la mobilité sociale…".
10. Original citation: "Les inégalités s'observent entre des personnes que l'on peut comparer et donc regrouper, par exemple, par âge, par genre, par métier (les milieux sociaux), etc. […]

Inequalities are multidimensional and involve both social groups and their interrelations. As a prerequisite for the measurement and analysis of inequalities – whether in terms of measuring the inequalities that affect individuals or the dynamics that (re)produce them – it is thus important to identify coherent social groups. In these analyses, the default subject of inequalities refers to the individual or the household, but there is also a second subject, that of the social group to which one refers in order to compare the position of the groups with one another. The object of inequality may be an economic quantity, the distribution of which is studied, but it can just as well be a quality (being in good health or not; having a job or not; holding a higher diploma or not, etc.) the distribution of which is analyzed among social groups. In this case, inequality emerges when the fact of being deprived of this quality (or of being endowed with it) is specific to a social group and is experienced by members of this group as an injustice or as discrimination. The comparison of average quantities can shed light on economic inequalities between population groups: for example, women's wealth is lower on average than men's wealth (Bessière and Gollac 2020). Analysis of the distributions of these quantities within groups reveals additional dimensions of inequality: for instance, the distribution of incomes is less spread out among women (and particularly among mothers, see Waldfogel (1997)) than among men (Lise et al. 2014). Similarly, the trajectory of capital accumulation differs over the life course of women and men, as Atkinson (1971) illustrates: while the most represented age group for women with wealth of more than £200,000 is 55–64 (8.5% of adults), almost as many wealthy adults are found among men in the 25–34, 35–44 and 45–54 age groups as in the 55–64 age group (between 13 and 15% of adults). Thus, Atkinson shows that wealth accumulation occurs much earlier over the life course of men than over that of women, a conclusion confirmed by Bessière and Gollac (2020).

I.2. Inequalities in geographical space

I.2.1. *Projecting inequalities in geographical space*

Starting from our definition of inequalities as being systematic, detrimental differences, experienced as injustices and fueled by discrimination practices, we must now analyze them in relation to geographical space in order to show that inequalities are inseparable from the geographical space in which they are inscribed.

Comprendre les inégalités, c'est saisir comment elles constituent un système d'ensemble où des facteurs s'entrecroisent. On est une femme, mais aussi d'un âge particulier, d'un certain milieu social et d'une certaine couleur de peau. Qui veut observer et comprendre les inégalités doit analyser les relations entre ces domaines et ces catégories de populations, et démêler leur poids respectif".

Our starting point consists of projecting these differences in geographical space: on the one hand to spatialize the differences, and on the other hand to situate the discourses, perceptions and feelings of injustice. These two aspects are closely linked, since the quantification of differences in geographical space can, depending on the case, encourage the emergence of a feeling of injustice, or result from this feeling of injustice. Highlighting the differences in resources within a city or a country thus contributes to the feeling of injustice by making the unequal situation in which a society finds itself collectively visible and public, an unequal situation that would otherwise remain a simple juxtaposition of individual and private situations. But, at the same time, it is also the injustices felt by certain individuals who systematically experience discrimination that can lead the scientific and political communities to want to objectify the deprivations of which these individuals declare themselves victims. The long-standing debate on statistics with regard to ethnicity in France is a good example: quantifying inequalities according to ethnicity or race would make it possible to objectify the discriminatory experiences of ethnic minorities, to measure their prevalence and to render the mechanisms that produce inequalities intelligible: this is a frequent demand of minority groups (and a position assumed by the American and British social sciences). However, "the reticence of French social sciences with regard to the registers of ethnicity and 'race' [refers] to the republican credo of 'indifference to differences' and [to] the desire to make cultural disparities less salient in order to unify the nation" (Simon 2008, p. 153). The definition of ethno-racial groups as statistical categories would, moreover, carry the risk of freezing these groups and institutionalizing identities.

I.2.1.1. *Spatializing difference measurements*

To spatialize differences (whether within a population or between social groups), several approaches are possible. The crudest way to do this is to compare the magnitude of differences according to administrative or political spatial units (municipalities, regions, countries, etc.). This is often done in the analysis of income inequality, when comparing the magnitude of inequality (and its evolution over time) across countries (see Chapter 6). The spatial location of inequalities can also mean identifying, locating and mapping the areas where populations subject to discrimination are systematically concentrated, whether in terms of income, employment, health, etc.

As with social groups, one may wish to group spatial units in order to create coherent socio-spatial groups, either in terms of measuring the inequalities that affect these spaces, or the dynamics that (re)produce them. These socio-spatial groups can be constructed a priori from a third indicator (e.g. political regime, population density) that may or may not include a spatial proximity constraint, or a posteriori (e.g. from measures of spatial autocorrelation) when one seeks to identify spatial units that are similar and spatially close.

The construction of these socio-spatial groups also generally relies on the statistical categories available to delineate the social groups between which certain inequalities are measured. For administrative or census data from *national statistics*, the requirements of anonymity and national synthesis often impose the geographical level of aggregation of income, education and health data of individuals. In France, for example, in the study of economic income, only income deciles are available at the commune level, while percentiles (a tenfold finer description of the distribution) are only disseminated at the regional and national levels. In the same way, when one wishes to cross-reference individual variables (e.g. access to healthcare by income level), a trade-off is often made between the fineness of the thematic classification and the fineness of the geographical level at which the data are aggregated. The compulsory *aggregation* of data therefore "smooths over" empirical knowledge on inequalities by masking local geographic disparities, which is harmful when looking for explanatory processes for inequalities, as well as when evaluating them in statistical models. However, the finest administrative unit at which aggregate data are available is not necessarily the one that should be favored in explanatory models. The choice of the scale to be used for aggregating information is a question that comes up time and again in all empirical studies with a geographical dimension, especially since the way in which the data are aggregated has a significant impact on the results of the analyses. This impact refers to the so-called modifiable areal unit problem (MAUP). This notion – proposed by Openshaw (1984) and widely taken up and discussed afterwards – underlines the sensitivity of the results of an aggregation of geographical units to the size (scale effect) and shape (zoning effects) of the units. While this sensitivity should not be ignored, it should not be considered as a bias, since the variation in the results obtained according to the spatial division adopted reflects the spatially heterogeneous and multi-scalar nature of the phenomenon studied. As such, it represents a contribution to knowledge about this phenomenon (Madelin et al. 2009). Another precaution must be taken when using aggregated data, that is, not to infer at a lower geographical level the relationship observed at the aggregated level. In doing so, one would be exposed to the so-called *ecological error*, by reasoning as if the relationships between variables observed at the group level could be transposed to the level of the individuals that make up these groups. For example, one might find a positive correlation between a city's poverty rate and its house price level. This does not mean, however, that poor people pay the highest house prices. The relationship at the aggregate level may in fact be linked to a third variable, for example, in this case, city size, which determines both – albeit independently – the poverty rate and the level of house prices.

For the analysis of inequalities in geographical space, the construction of socio-spatial groups can also make use of social and spatial data collected through *surveys* and *interviews*. These customized data sources can indeed allow researchers to obtain finer-grained, multidimensional individual data (on perceptions, in particular), as well as to follow cohorts over time (longitudinal data). However, these information-rich surveys are very time- and cost-consuming, and for this reason are mainly deployed on small samples of individuals, which often requires reaggregation of the information within larger geographic grids to obtain estimates with satisfactory statistical precision. Finally, some data also need to be reaggregated because of the non-coincidence of the geographic grids in which they are produced; for example, in France, health data in hospital perimeters, education data in academy perimeters and socioeconomic data in employment areas.

I.2.1.2. *Situating discourses, perceptions and feelings of injustice*

Spatializing measures of difference in geographical space is only one part of projecting inequality in geographical space. The feeling of injustice, the discourses and the perception of inequalities by individuals deserve to be analyzed in relation to the spaces in which they are located. "Growing spatial segregation is becoming an increasingly important factor in the constitution of the identity of social groups" (Maurin 2003, pp. 32–33). In addition to playing on the identity of social groups, the geographical dimension intervenes in a decisive way in the inegalitarian processes and in their analysis, since it orients and determines the perception, the experience and the reproduction of inter-individual inequalities.

In a major survey on the perception of inequality and injustice by French people, Forsé and Galland (2011) showed that the way in which individuals perceive the overall level of inequalities and their place in society depends in part on their social, political and demographic characteristics. In this case, they point out that "women and adults in the prime of life judge inequalities to be greater than the average French person" (Galland and Lemel 2011, p. 15), and that "the rich are more accepting of inequalities than the poor, the more educated more than the less educated, men more than women, and the elderly more than the young" (Forsé 2011, p. 35). They also found cognitive distortions when individuals placed themselves on the national income scale, as "25% of respondents incorrectly placed themselves in the lowest category," and that these distortions were particularly pronounced among high-income earners (Phan 2011, p. 70), producing the false image of a "middle-class society". Even if this survey does not account for differences in perception related to the location and spatial practices of individuals, it is possible to think that representations of society and its inequalities vary according to the social network constituted by individuals (which is bound by their daily interactions and their geographical constraints), and that the experience of inequalities is not the same between individuals depending on whether they frequent segregated, mixed, fragmented or, on the contrary, homogeneous spaces.

Space also guides the discourses that reflect and fuel stereotypes about different social classes (see Chapter 5). The same is true for the feelings of injustice that fuel political struggles. In this respect, analyses of the *gilets jaunes* (yellow vests) protests in France highlight the role of space in the perception of territorial inequalities; the inhabitants of peri-urban areas or peripheral urban areas consider themselves in turn to be the "losers" of French social policy, a feeling that polemical discourses often like to exacerbate by placing territories (and their inhabitants) in competition with one another (Epstein and Kirszbaum 2020).

Another illuminating example is what Bret (2018) calls the "Catalan paradox", in relation to the results of the 2017 Catalan independence referendum. Bret sees a paradox in the fact that the secessionists who denounce the exploitation of Catalonia by Spain (to whose budget it makes a positive contribution) are mainly located in the areas of Catalonia that are net beneficiaries of the internal redistribution of the *Generalitat*, that is, outside the metropolitan area of Barcelona (the main contributor to the regional budget). This reading emphasizes the importance of considering the geographical scale in the analysis of inequalities and territorial egos. However, it must be qualified. Indeed, the vote in favor of keeping Catalonia in Spain by those on the coast reflects less the altruism of the productive metropolis or its European interest but rather the strong presence of non-Catalan Spaniards. Moreover, Oller et al. (2020) showed that at the individual level, the most disadvantaged tended to vote against independence, while the most privileged segments of the population supported (and financed) the secessionist movement.

The geographical projection of inequalities is protean: it concerns both unevenly distributed resources and the factors of this uneven distribution and the feelings of injustice that result from it. This geographical projection of inequalities is a necessary (but insufficient) condition for political actors to take up the issue of inequalities and to give themselves the means to combat them. However, this projection is only a first step: it says nothing about the mechanisms that are at the origin of inequalities in geographical space, and does not make it possible to specify what, in these inequalities, is the result of social and spatial structures.

I.2.2. *Thinking about the spatial logics of inequalities*

While questions about the occupation, use and control of geographical space are central to understanding contemporary social phenomena in general, and inequalities in particular, there is little consensus about the status to be accorded to space (Gaudreau 2014).

Since the 1970s, *critical* and *neo-Marxist geographers* have deplored the lack of consideration for geographical space in dominant theories of social justice. Harvey (1973), for example, introduced the idea of uneven development as a direct consequence of the processes of capitalist production: according to him, globalization does not lead to a homogenization of territories but, on the contrary, to the amplification of geographical inequalities. The recurrent over-accumulation of capital is in fact temporarily resolved by the geographical displacement of investment in order to avoid its devaluation (spatial fix), whether it be to other continents and countries during colonization, or to the run-down districts of Northern cities in the form of gentrification (Smith 1996).

> This inequality, associated with intrinsic features of the capitalist mode of production, leads to oppression as sources of injustice in space (Harvey, 1996a, 1996b). Over time, critical geographers further developed Harvey's political economy by emphasizing the question of injustice, especially in the contemporary capitalist urban world. The notion of spatial justice deliberated by Ed Soja and others (Dikec, 2001; Marcuse, 2010) is a noticeable example. The term "spatial justice" refers to institutions, policies, discourse, and practices involved in formulating the organization of space, thus shaping human interactions that define (un)just geographies (Soja, 2010a, 2010b). (Israel and Frenkel 2018, p. 650)

More recently, research has analyzed how inequalities accumulate and combine to form a multidimensional whole. This cumulative process refers to the notion of intersectionality, which designates the situation of people who are simultaneously subjected to several forms of domination or discrimination in a society, or to the notion of "systemic discriminations", which designates the processes that maintain unequal social positions. Space participates in this systemic process of reproduction of power and domination, insofar as living spaces do not constitute an element that is simply added to the other factors of injustice or discrimination, but rather a factor that multiplies the force of injustice and discrimination (Hopkins 2019). Space is thus, for example, at the heart of the multi-layered and routinized forms of domination (Crenshaw 1991, p. 1245) that racialized women face in the context of their domestic or professional activities, whether in public or private places (see Chapter 2).

In the analysis of spatial reasoning on social inequalities, another field in the literature deserves to be mentioned, that of the neighborhood effects (Galster 2012) or place effects. The recent publication boom on neighborhood effects has, however, paradoxically led to an impoverishment of the meaning of space: by considering space as a simple medium whose complexity is overlooked, much of this work (generally based on multilevel regression models) has led to a compartmentalization of what is related to the individual and to space, and to a lack of awareness of their interactions and of the strategies deployed by individuals in order to take advantage of the opportunities of space or to resist its constraints. We find here the Bourdieuian criticism toward a substantialist consideration of places, which ignores the relationships between the structures of social space and the structures of physical space (see Chapter 1). This impoverishment of spatial reasoning does not, however, concern all the works devoted to neighborhood effects. Majority of it – most notably Wilson's *The Truly Disadvantaged* (1987) and his notion of the concentrating effect – has highlighted the double burden that the poorest individuals face: that of their own lack of income and that of living in a poor neighborhood. In explaining how living in a neighborhood with a concentration of poverty had a particularly negative effect on the lives of the poorest individuals, this work emphasizes that people's vulnerability to the neighborhood effects can vary according to their socio-demographic profile and their ability to cope (see Chapter 7). The social dimension of the neighborhood effects does not, however, only operate at the residential level. Recent analyses relating to the different neighborhoods that individuals frequent on a daily basis have shown that the physical distance between the facilities available and the various places of daily activities of individuals only harms socially disadvantaged individuals who do not have – unlike socially favored individuals – the opportunity or the ability to overcome the barrier of geographical distance (Vallée et al. 2021). Disentangling the importance of spatial structure versus social structure is in fact a central question when it comes to thinking about the spatial patterns of social inequalities. One can, like authors such as Di Méo (2004), explicitly want to distinguish the social from the spatial by placing them – alongside the individual – at the apex of an equilateral triangle. Other authors, however, do not adhere to this mode of representation, which may lead one to believe that there is a non-social space (see Chapter 1). This discussion finally refers to the "fetishism of space" denounced by Lefebvre (Gaudreau 2014), a fetishism into which we risk falling when we give space a reality of its own, even though it is just one of the concrete expressions of the state of social structure. It is undoubtedly to the difficulty of making social structure and spatial structure interact that we can attribute the current popularity of the term "socio-spatial" (or "socio-territorial"). The term *socio-spatial*, which is associated with inequality and suggests that the spatial is the symmetrical equivalent of the social, often conceals a theoretical and conceptual inaccuracy that extends into empirical studies (Vallée 2019). This imprecision is less marked in empirical studies of socio-spatial inequalities in the strict sense of the term, which focus, for example, on analyzing people's incomes according to their residential location (Fleury et al. 2012) – and, hence, *socio-spatial segregation*. But things become more complicated when socio-spatial inequalities concern an object that could be described as external: socio-spatial inequalities in health, socio-spatial inequalities in educational success, etc. One may then wonder whether the term socio-spatial is not being abused in studies of the spatial distribution of a phenomenon, but without the role of social structures being explicitly considered (Deboosere and Fiszman 2009), or when spatial units are used as simple containers to compare, at an aggregate level, the health profiles of the population and their socioeconomic profiles (Rican et al. 2003). In order for the mechanism being studied to qualify as socio-spatial, it is important to understand the interactions between the social and spatial dimensions, for example, by analyzing how *spatial disparities* of a phenomenon *vary across social groups* or, conversely, how *social disparities* of a phenomenon *vary across the spaces* considered (Rican et al. 2003; François and Poupeau 2008; Chen and Wen 2010; Eggerickx et al. 2018). When these interactions are explored (and the methods for doing so are diverse; see Chapter 6), it seems to us that the term socio-spatial can be mobilized on robust empirical grounds: without it, it turns out to be more of a convenient shorthand that fails to account for the interdependencies between the social and spatial dimensions of inequalities.

Other theories should also be mentioned when discussing the agent–structure couple and the place to be afforded to the spatial structure in relation to the social structure from a geographical perspective. One can think of the *structuration theory* of Giddens (1984), which makes the link between the dynamics of individual and collective structuring by emphasizing the modes of reflexive control of action that agents exercise on a daily basis, or of *the capability approach* developed by Sen (1973), which emphasizes the actual possibility of individuals to access available resources. A number of researchers, however, distance themselves from the capability approach and its liberal reading, which ultimately leaves little room for the role of social (and spatial) structures in the development of individuals' choices and, ultimately, actions (Bowman 2010).

Far from exhausting the subject, this brief overview of the work on the spatial pattern of social inequalities also raises the question of the spatial and temporal scales to which we refer when we want to analyze inequalities and their dynamics in geographical space.

I.2.3. *Spatial and temporal scales*

Inequalities between individuals unfold simultaneously at different spatial and temporal scales. It is important to distinguish between them in terms of measurement and observation, as well as in the identification of the processes that cause them and the actions that can reduce them, for the different types of inequalities. For example, some processes interact between spatial scales, which can lead to the reduction, compensation or amplification of the phenomenon studied. As an illustration, the disadvantage of living in a disadvantaged neighborhood may be partially compensated for when the neighborhood is located in a dynamic, accessible and inclusive metropolitan area or, on the contrary, it may be amplified when the neighborhood is located in a declining, highly segregated city, or when the financing of and access to public services is organized locally (as in many American cities).

I.2.3.1. *Spatial scales*

Paying attention to the spatial scales of inequalities is essential if we wish to take into account the local, family, social, economic and cultural contexts in which inequalities are inscribed (and thus avoid falling into the *atomistic fallacy*, which consists of extending the interpretation of extensive individual data to the level of an entire group or space, without taking into account the environment in which individuals evolve[11]). Although the concept of spatial scale is central to geography, its use remains polysemous. In this book, we wish to distinguish between the

---

11. The *atomistic fallacy* is frequently considered the opposite of the *ecological fallacy* (Elissalde 2018). Yet the type of error is not quite the same. The ecological error consists of inferring at a lower level what is observed at a higher (or aggregate) level. If we follow this line of reasoning, the reverse of the ecological error would be to transpose to a higher level what is observed at the lower level. If, for example, one observed that poor people are less healthy, one would conclude that the poorest countries are those where the populations are less healthy. This reasoning holds and is not strictly speaking an atomistic fallacy. Indeed, the atomistic fallacy occurs when one neglects to integrate higher level explanatory factors into a relationship. To return to our previous example, this would consist of not considering that the relationship between a person's poverty and his or her health status depends on their country (and the social protection measures and redistributive patterns implemented). The atomistic fallacy therefore concerns more the omission of higher level factors as such than the transposition of a relationship to a higher level than the one at which it has been obtained.

concepts of scale and level, favoring the use of the term *level* to describe the degree of geographic aggregation of an object, and the term *scale* to describe the geographical perimeter within which inequalities and their mechanisms are measured and analyzed. In the context of city networks, the level, for example, qualifies the type of urban definition used: municipality, morphological agglomeration or urban area; while the scale represents the horizon of interaction of cities: regional, national or global, for example (Rozenblat and Neal 2021).

But even once this distinction has been made, there is often a confusion between the geographic levels to be favored, depending on whether one wishes to measure the extent of inequalities, identify the spatial patterns at work in the reproduction of inequalities, or act to reduce the inequalities (Vallée 2019). The trade-offs related to the availability of data and the territorial political grid lead to considerable confusion about the very status of space. The basic administrative unit used by public statistics to make aggregate data available is more than just data formatting; it also has a performative value because it acts as a channel for questioning, processing and interpretations (see Chapter 7). This is illustrated by the practice of giving priority to the finest administrative unit for which aggregate data are available when it comes to analyzing spatial logics, even though these logics are *multi-scalar*. Another example of scalar confusion in the analysis of inequalities is the inclusion of "explanatory" social variables measured at the neighborhood level (such as the median income of households residing in a neighborhood), without explaining what these "neighborhood-level" variables are supposed to capture or "explain". The interpretation of the outputs of the statistical models can then be ambiguous, since these aggregated neighborhood-level variables can be thought of as indirect measures of the social status of individuals – to compensate for the lack of individual data – or as measures of the collective level of poverty in the neighborhood – to account for neighborhood effects (Vallée and Philibert 2019). The choice of geographic levels for the analysis of inequalities is in fact akin to a quest for the Holy Grail when one hopes to be able to use a single geographic level to quantify the magnitude of differences, to compensate for the lack of individual data, to quantify place effects and to promote neigborhood-based policies. By reasoning from a single geographical level (whatever the geographical scale at which one is situated), one ignores the plurality of processes operating at the level of the individual and the urban region (Petrovič et al. 2018), and even beyond: it is then a whole part of the patterns which produce social inequalities that one does not give oneself the means to understand, and against which one does not give oneself the means to act (see Chapter 7).

Attention to spatial scales is also necessary when considering the mechanisms cited in the economic literature on the reproduction of income and wealth inequalities. Indeed, it is useful to recall that prices or interest rates generally considered at the national level fluctuate in a non-random way between regions of the same country, making the behavior of households in these different regions vary. Similarly, whether it is the cost of banking services, healthy food or housing, examples abound in the literature that show that residents of poorer areas and those in minority neighborhoods tend to pay more for the same or even lower quality goods or services (Walker et al. 2010; Flood et al. 2011; Colombi 2020). On the other hand, when economists invoke the effect of inheritance or education on the reproduction of inequalities, it is worth remembering that the return on inherited capital (if it is real estate, in particular) or on education received (including the effects of peers, information circulating between families and the extent of the school curriculum taught) is not uniform across the country. Thus, inheriting a property of identical value in the center of Paris or on the outskirts of Nevers does not have the same guarantees of evolution and liquidity, and does not participate in the same way in the reproduction of wealth, symbolic capital and opportunities for heirs. As for education, François and Berkouk (2018) show that the accumulation of experience and tacit knowledge in the preparatory classes of a few high schools in large French cities (notably Paris, Lyon and Bordeaux) allows them to place a disproportionate number of their students among those eligible for the entrance exam to the "*grandes écoles*", which in turn reinforces the accumulation in these high schools of experience and tacit knowledge about how the exam works.

I.2.3.2. *Temporal scales*

The question of the geographical scale of inequalities is also inseparable from that of *time* for several reasons: first, because the analysis of the evolution of inequalities over time requires us to question the relevance of the spatial units used at each step. This is a central question that arises when we want, for example, to compare the levels of social segregation of a city over the years, even though the city's boundaries may have changed (Musterd 2005).

Moreover, taking time into account makes it possible to highlight the plurality of places with which individuals are (or have been) connected. We can thus make the connection with life-course approaches (or *biographical approaches*), which aim to provide an intersection of family, professional and residential events in time and space in order to identify the precise sequence of events (Courgeau 1985) and to highlight inequalities in access to the city according to a longitudinal and generational approach (Hedman et al. 2019; Le Roux et al. 2020). This corpus thus considers the residential strategies of individuals over the course of their lives in relation to the social position they occupy in society, for example, with regard to their access to the world of work (see Chapter 4). In this corpus, spatial mobility is still mainly studied from the point of view of residential trajectories: few links are established with the literature of time-geography (Hägerstrand 1985), which considers the daily trajectories of individuals and the inequalities that their different spatiotemporal programs of activities may generate, particularly according to gender (Kwan 1999). Yet, the cross-analysis of residential and daily trajectories could be interesting for understanding the different social and spatial positions that individuals may occupy over the course of their lives (Dubreuil et al. 2020), and the *accumulation effects* of place over time.

This temporal approach allows for a discussion of the effects of time on the relationships that individuals form with places. The work on emotions and *nostalgia* for places (Gervais-Lambony 2012) thus highlights the relationships to past spaces and times: these relationships can lead to *inertia* in place effects when some places remain significant for individuals, even if they no longer frequent them. In parallel with this inertia effect, we can also observe changes in relationships to places, either because the individual uses the same places but these change over the years, or because the changes come from changes in the individual themselves rather than in the places they frequent. In addition to the effects of time on relationships to places, the temporal dimension is important to mobilize in order to discuss the effects of time on the relationship of individuals to the social structure. In this respect, we can note that there is an inertia of the effects of the social structure since the dispositions acquired by the socialization of an individual in a defined social space last in time, even if the individual is in a different social space (see the notion of *hysteresis*, developed by Bourdieu). Finally, some individuals experience multi-situated trajectories when they are simultaneously inscribed in distinct places within which they occupy different social positions. This is the case of transnational migrants, studied by L. Roulleau-Berger in Chapter 3.

Finally, an interest in the temporal scales of inequality means being interested in the *temporal dissonance* that can affect the representation that individuals have of the level of inequality existing within their geographical space, as shown by Chauvel (2003) in relation to the gap between class consciousness and inequality in France since the Industrial Revolution. He notes that it often takes several decades and generations for class identities to adjust to the intensity of inequalities, which creates a gap between the reality of social structuring and its representation. Thus, the structuring of French society into very unequal classes (in the first half of the 20th century) contributed to the creation of a strong class identity in the following decades, even as this structuring was breaking down. The representation of a "classless" society was, however, renewed from the 1980s onwards, at the very moment when inequalities began to increase again.

Although the spatial and temporal scales of inequality have so far been presented and discussed separately, they are in fact closely linked. As soon as we become interested in the dynamics of inequalities, we cannot ignore the importance of the trajectories (residential, daily, social) of individuals, as well as the trajectories of geographical spaces (whether at the level of neighborhoods, cities, countries, etc.). *Inequalities are in motion in time as well as in space*, and the same is true for the factors that participate in their (re)production. This double articulation of the spatial and the temporal is, in fact, inherent to any analysis of inequalities in geographical space. From a methodological point of view, however, the study of this spatiotemporal dimension requires overcoming a certain number of obstacles, linked as much to the availability of data as to the methods to be used to cross the spatial and temporal dimensions and to model the dynamics of inequalities in geographical space over time (see Chapter 6). From a theoretical point of view, the introduction of the temporal dimension into the reflection on social and spatial structures is proving fruitful, as shown by the notion of *rhythmanalysis*, developed by Lefebvre (1992) to emphasize that repetitions and rhythms are not foreign to the production of space, or the notion of *regionalization* introduced by Giddens (1984) in his theory of structuring. Giddens, like Gombin (2014, p. 5):

> [...] thus considers that routine, everyday social practices are not only inscribed in space-time, but contribute to form particular regions in space-time which, in return, structure and constrain (as well as allow, according to the rationale of double structuring) these social practices. If this conceptualization, notably inspired by Simmel's *time-geography* [...] (from whom he borrows this idea that it is reciprocal human action that generates the space which, in return, makes action possible) [...] and by Elias [...] seems at first sight simple, it actually opens interesting perspectives to social science research attentive to the spatial and temporal dimensions of social processes.

Introduction xxxiii

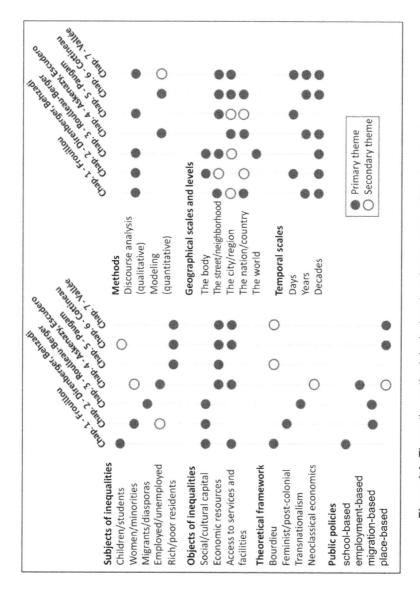

Figure I.1. *Thematic, methodological and scalar coverage of the book's chapters. For a color version of this figure, see www.iste.co.uk/cottineau/inequalities.zip*

I.3. Coverage of the book

In this book, we cannot claim to be exhaustive in our approaches, scales and methods on all the inequalities and individuals concerned.

We have therefore chosen to maximize the overall diversity of approaches by assembling chapters that each go into greater depth on one object of inequality, or one approach, or one method, by applying it to several scales or geographical contexts. The advantage is that we have been able to invite authors to deal with subjects in which they are specialists, while hopefully providing a complementarity of views throughout the book.

The distribution of chapters by theme, method and scale is summarized in Figure I.1.

I.3.1. *The subjects (the "who"?)*

The book offers specific insights into four categories of inequality issues. In Chapter 1, L. Frouillou addresses inequality between schoolchildren, students and their families within the school system. In Chapter 2, L. Direnberger and N.E. Behzadi focus on gendered and racialized characteristics of individuals in public and work spaces. In Chapter 3, L. Roulleau-Berger focuses on the inequalities experienced and managed by migrants in their host and transit societies. Finally, P. Askenazy and V. Escudero study inequalities in access to employment in the geographical space of the "Northern" economies (Chapter 4). The following chapters are cross-cutting with periodic focuses on certain categories of individuals.

I.3.2. *The objects (the "what"?)*

In the different chapters, individuals are analyzed according to their unequal possession of or access to resources. Chapter 1 deals with the social, economic and cultural capital that differentiates families and children. Chapters 3 and 4 deal with jobs. Wealth is addressed in Chapter 5, where S. Paugam analyzes the perceptions of poverty and the justifications of inequalities by the most privileged individuals. Wealth is also the subject of inequality, which is addressed from the perspective of modeling by C. Cottineau in Chapter 6. Finally, Chapters 2 and 7 focus on inequalities in access to certain spaces and services, the first in relation to migration experiences, and the second in the context of public policies to reduce inequalities, as analyzed by J. Vallée.

I.3.3. *Theoretical frameworks*

In terms of theoretical frameworks, some of them apply particularly well to the study of certain objects of inequality, as is the case with Bourdieu's constructivist approach in the study of educational inequalities (Chapter 1). In the same way, feminist and post-colonial approaches, as well as intersectional theory, allow us to shed light on the patterns of gender, class and race inequalities (Chapter 2). The transnationalism approach could do the same in the study of migrants (Chapter 3). On the contrary, neoclassical economic approaches are confronted by the authors of Chapter 4 with empirical observations to describe and explain the persistence of geographical inequalities in access to employment.

I.3.4. *Public policies*

Most of the thematic chapters deal with the issue of public policies, either to analyze their effects on one aspect of inequality (Chapters 2 and 3), or to assess their performance in reducing inequality (Chapters 1 and 7). In particular, school, migration, territorial and employment policies are addressed in this book.

I.3.5. *Methods*

One chapter of the book is dedicated to the presentation of a set of methods for analyzing inequalities in geographical space. Chapter 6 presents in detail three families of models: graphic and cartographic models, statistical models and simulation models. Chapter 5 is based on a field survey of wealthy residents of the inner cities of Paris, Sao Paulo and New Delhi. Finally, Chapters 2 and 3 refer to qualitative studies, while Chapter 4 is based on quantitative analyses.

I.3.6. *Geographic scales and levels*

The geographical levels mobilized in the book go from the level of bodies, inscribed at the heart of the power relations (re)producing inequalities (Chapters 2 and 3), to the level of the neighborhoods considered as units of public action, whether as neighborhood-container or neighborhood-agent (Chapter 7). The geographical scales at which inequalities are analyzed vary from the domestic and professional space to the street (Chapter 2) and the neighborhood (Chapters 1, 5 and 6). Some chapters refer to urban and regional processes, especially in relation to labor markets (Chapter 4) or housing (Chapters 6 and 7). The state and the nation are frameworks for analyzing school (Chapter 1) and economic (Chapters 4 and 6) systems, while the transnational approach developed by L. Roulleau-Berger in Chapter 3 considers the world as the most relevant scale for analyzing migration-related inequalities.

I.3.7. *Temporal scales*

The scales of analysis in the book are divided into three temporalities: that of the day to address the effect of daily interactions on perceptions, discourses and power relationships between individuals in the geographical space (Chapters 2, 5 and 7); that of the year to evaluate the effect of school, political and economic organizations on the dynamics of inequalities in the medium term (Chapters 1, 4, 6 and 7); and that of the decade to account for the dynamics of the reproduction of inequalities in most chapters.

Each chapter of this book has been iteratively evaluated by the two coordinators of the book. The chapters written by the book's coordinators were also carefully reviewed by Denise Pumain, Leïla Frouillou, Philippe Askenazy and Lucia Direnberger (Introduction), Lena Sanders (Chapter 6) and Renaud Epstein (Chapter 7). The two coordinators would like to thank them, along with the authors of the different chapters, as well as Bernard Bret for the intellectual exchanges to which the writing of this collective work gave rise.

I.4. References

Alacevich, M. and Soci, A. (2017). *A Short History of Inequality*. Agenda Publishing, Newcastle upon Tyne.

Alvaredo, F., Chancel, L., Piketty, T., Saez, E., Zucman, G. (eds) (2018). World Inequality Report 2018. Belknap Press and Harvard University Press, Cambridge, MA.

Atkinson, A.B. (1971). The distribution of wealth and the individual life-cycle. *Oxford Economic Papers*, 23(2), 239–254.

Atkinson, T. (2003). Inégalité, pauvreté et État-providence : un point de vue européen sur le débat autour de la mondialisation. In *Comprendre les inégalités. Revue de philosophie et de sciences sociales*, Fitoussi, J.-P., Savidan, P. (eds). Presses Universitaires de France, Paris.

Atkinson, A.B. (2015). *Inequality: What Can be Done?* Havard University Press, Cambridge, MA.

Bacqué, M.H. and Fol, S. (2007). L'inégalité face à la mobilité : du constat à l'injonction. *Revue suisse de sociologie*, 33(1), 89–104.

Bessière, C. and Gollac, S. (2020). *Le genre du capital : comment la famille reproduit les inégalités*. La Découverte, Paris.

Bihr, A. and Pfefferkorn, R. (2000). *Le système des inégalités*. La Découverte, Paris.

Bowman, D. (2010). Sen and Bourdieu: Understanding inequality. Social Policy Working Paper, University of Melbourne, The Brotherhood of St Laurence, Melbourne.

Bret, B. (2018). Spatial justice and geographic scales. *JSSJ Justice Spatiale/Spatial Justice*, 12, 1–14.

Brunet, R., Ferras, R., Théry, H. (1992). *Les mots de la géographie*. La Documentation française, Paris.

Chauvel, L. (2003). Inégalité, conscience et système de classes sociales : les contradictions de l'objectivité et de la subjectivité. In *Comprendre les inégalités*, Fitoussi, J.-P., Savidan, P. (eds). Presses Universitaires de France, Paris.

Chen, D.-R. and Wen, T.-H. (2010). Socio-spatial patterns of neighborhood effects on adult obesity in Taiwan: A multi-level model. *Social Science & Medicine*, 70(6), 823–833.

Colombi, D. (2020). *Où va l'argent des pauvres*. Payot/Rivages, Paris.

Courgeau, D. (1985). Interaction between spatial mobility, family and career life-cycle: A French survey. *European Sociological Review*, 1(2), 139–162.

Crenshaw, K. (1991). Mapping the margins: Intersectionality, identity politics, and violence against women of color. *Standford Law Review*, 43, 1241–1299.

Deboosere, P. and Fiszman, P. (2009). De la persistance des inégalités socio-spatiales de santé. Le cas belge. *Espace populations sociétés*, 1, 149–158.

Di Méo, G. (2004). Une géographie sociale dans le triangle des rapports hommes, sociétés, espaces. *Bulletin de l'Association de géographes français*, 81(2), 193–204.

Dubet, F. (2011). Régimes d'inégalité et injustices sociales. *Sociologies* [Online]. Available at: https://doi.org/10.4000/sociologies.3643.

Dubreuil, A., Vallée, J., Shareck, M., Frohlich, K. (2020). L'évolution des espaces d'activité lors de la transition vers l'âge adulte (Montréal, Canada). *Revue jeunes et société*, 5(1), 71–98.

Dupuy, J.-P. (2003). Inégalité, hiérarchie, humiliation et ressentiment victimaire. In *Comprendre les inégalités*, Fitoussi, J.-P., Savidan, P. (eds). Presses Universitaires de France, Paris.

Eggerickx, T., Léger, J.-F., Sanderson, J.-P., Vandeschrick, C. (2018). Inégalités sociales et spatiales de mortalité dans les pays occidentaux. Les exemples de la France et de la Belgique [Online]. Available at: https://doi.org/10.4000/eps.7800.

Elissalde, B. (2018). Erreur écologique [Online]. Available at: https://hypergeo.eu/erreur-ecologique/.

Epstein, R. and Kirszbaum, T. (2020). Ces quartiers dont on préfère ne plus parler : les métamorphoses de la politique de la ville (1977–2018). *Parlement[s], Revue d'histoire politique*, 30(3), 23.

Fitoussi, J.-P. and Savidan, P. (2003). La démocratie à l'épreuve des inégalités. In *Comprendre les inégalités*, Fitoussi, J.-P., Savidan, P. (eds). Presses Universitaires de France, Paris.

Fleury, A., François, J.-C., Mathian, H., Ribardière, A., Saint-Julien, T. (2012). Les inégalités socio-spatiales progressent-elles en Île-de-France [Online]. Available at: https://metropolitiques.eu/IMG/pdf/MET-Geographie-cites.pdf.

Flood, D., Hancock, J., Smith, K. (2011). The ATM reforms – New evidence from survey and market data. *RBA Bulletin, March*, 43–49.

Forsé, M. (2011). La hiérarchie perçue et souhaitée des rémunérations. In *Les Français face aux inégalités et à la justice sociale*, Forsé, M., Galland, O. (eds). Armand Colin, Paris.

Forsé, M. and Galland, O. (eds) (2011). *Les Français face aux inégalités et à la justice sociale*. Armand Colin, Paris.

François, P. and Berkouk, N. (2018). Les concours sontils neutres ? Concurrence et parrainage dans l'accès à l'École polytechnique. *Sociologie*, 9(2), 169–196.

François, J.-C. and Poupeau, F. (2008). Les déterminants socio-spatiaux du placement scolaire. *Revue française de sociologie*, 49(1), 93–126.

Galland, O. and Lemel, Y. (2011). Jusqu'à quel point la société française estelle jugée inégalitaire ? In *Les Français face aux inégalités et à la justice sociale*, Forsé, M., Galland, O. (eds). Armand Colin, Paris.

Galster, G. (2012). The mechanism(s) of neighbourhood effects: Theory, evidence, and policy implications. In *Neighbourhood Effects Research: New Perspectives*, van Ham, M., Manley, D., Bailey, N., Simpson, L., MacIennan, D. (eds). Springer, Dordrecht.

Gaudreau, L. (2014). Espace, temps et théorie du capital chez Henri Lefebvre et Marx. *Cahiers de recherche sociologique*, 2013(55), 155–176.

George, P. (1981). *Géographie des inégalités*. Presses Universitaires de France, Paris.

Gervais-Lambony, P. (2012). Nostalgies citadines en Afrique du Sud [Online]. Available at: https://www.espacestemps.net/articles/nostalgies-citadines-en-afrique-sud/.

Giddens, A. (1984). *The Constitution of Society: Outline of the Theory of Structuration*. University of California Press, Berkeley, CA.

Gombin, J. (2014). Contextualiser sans faire de l'espace un facteur autonome. La modélisation multiniveau comme lieu de rencontre entre sociologie et géographie électorales [Online]. Available at: https://doi.org/10.4000/espacepolitique.3066.

Hägerstrand, T. (1985). *Time-geography: Focus on the Corporeality of Man, Society, and Environment. The Science and Praxis of Complexity*. United Nations University Press, New York.

Harvey, D. (1973). *Social Justice and the City*. Johns Hopkins University Press, Baltimore, MD.

Hedenus, F. and Azar, C. (2005). Estimates of trends in global income and resource inequalities. *Ecological Economics*, 55(3), 351–364.

Hedman, L., Manley, D., van Ham, M. (2019). Using sibling data to explore the impact of neighbourhood histories and childhood family context on income from work. *PLoS One*, 14(5), e0217635.

Hopkins, P. (2019). Social geography intersectionality. *Progress in Human Geography*, 43(5), 937–947.

Israel, E. and Frenkel, A. (2018). Social justice and spatial inequality: Toward a conceptual framework. *Progress in Human Geography*, 42(5), 647–665.

Jaquet, C. (2014). *Les transclasses, ou la non-reproduction*. Presses universitaires de France, Paris.

Kwan, M.-P. (1999). Gender and individual access to urban opportunities: A study using space-time measures. *Professional Geographer*, 51(2), 210–227.

Lahire, B. (ed.) (2019). *Enfances de classe. De l'inégalité parmi les enfants*. Le Seuil, Paris.

Le Roux, G., Imbert, C., Bringé, A., Bonvalet, C. (2020). Transformations sociales de l'agglomération parisienne au cours du XXe siècle : une approche longitudinale et générationnelle des inégalités d'accès à la ville. *Population*, 75(1), 71.

Lefebvre, H. (1992). *Éléments de rythmanalyse : introduction à la connaissance des rythmes*. Syllepse, Paris.

Lise, J., Sudo, N., Suzuki, M., Yamada, K., Yamada, T. (2014). Wage, income and consumption inequality in Japan, 1981–2008: From boom to lost decades. *Review of Economic Dynamics*, 17(4), 582–612.

Madelin, M., Grasland, C., Mathian, H., Sanders, L., Vincent, J.-M. (2009). Das "MAUP": Modifiable areal unit – Problem oder Fortschritt? *Informationen zur Raumentwicklung*, 10, 645–660.

Maurin, L. (2003). Portrait d'une France inégale. In *Comprendre les inégalités*, Fitoussi, J.-P., Savidan, P. (eds). Presses Universitaires de France, Paris.

Maurin, L. (2018). *Comprendre les inégalités*. Observatoire des inégalités, Tours.

Musterd, S. (2005). Social and ethnic segregation in Europe: Levels, causes, and effects. *Journal of Urban Affairs*, 27(3), 331–348.

Oller, J.M., Satorra, A., Tobeña, A. (2020). Privileged rebels: A longitudinal analysis of distinctive economic traits of Catalonian secessionism. *Genealogy*, 4(1), 19.

Openshaw, S. (1984). *The Modifiable Areal Unit Problem*. Geo Books, Norwich.

Petrovič, A., Manley, D., van Ham, M. (2019). Freedom from the tyranny of neighbourhood: Rethinking socio-spatial context effects. *Progress in Human Geography*, 44(6), 1103–1123.

Phan, D. (2011). Stratification sociale perçue : une société de "classe moyenne". In *Les Français face aux inégalités et à la justice sociale*, Forsé, M., Galland, O. (eds). Armand Colin, Paris.

Piketty, T. (2013). *Le capital au 21ème siècle*. Le Seuil, Paris.

Rawls, J. (1971). *A Theory of Justice*. Clarendon Press, Oxford.

Rican, S., Jougla, E., Salem, G. (2003). Inégalités socio-spatiales de mortalité en France. *Bulletin épidémiologique hebdomadaire*, 30–31, 142–145.

Rozenblat, C. and Neal, Z.P. (eds) (2021). *Handbook of Cities and Networks*. Edward Elgar, Northampton.

Sala-i-Martin, X. (2006). The world distribution of income: Falling poverty and... convergence, period. *The Quarterly Journal of Economics*, 121(2), 351–397.

Sen, A. (1973). *On Economic Inequality*. Oxford University Press, Oxford.

Simon, P. (2008). Les statistiques, les sciences sociales françaises et les rapports sociaux ethniques et de "race". *Revue française de sociologie*, 49(1), 153–162.

Smith, N. (1996). *The New Urban Frontier: Gentrification and the Revanchist City*. Psychology Press/Routledge, London.

Stiglitz, J.E. (2016). Inequality and economic growth. *The Political Quarterly*, 86, 134–155.

Vallée, J. (2019). Les effets de lieu au quotidien. HDR, Université Paris 1 Panthéon-Sorbonne, Paris.

Vallée, J. and Philibert, M. (2019). V comme Voisinage. In *Abécédaire en géographie de la santé*, Fleuret, S., Gasquet-Blanchard, C., Hoyez, A.-C. (eds). Éditions Matériologiques, Paris.

Vallée, J., Shareck, M., Kestens, Y., Frohlich, K.L. (2021). Everyday geography and service accessibility: The contours of disadvantage in relation to mental health. *Annals of the American Association of Geographers*, 112(4), 931–947.

Waldfogel, J. (1997). The effect of children on women's wages. *American Sociological Review*, 62(2), 209–217.

Walker, R.E., Keane, C.R., Burke, J.G. (2010). Disparities and access to healthy food in the United States: A review of food deserts literature. *Health & Place*, 16(5), 876–884.

Wilkinson, R. and Pickett, K. (2009). *The Spirit Level: Why Greater Equality Makes Societies Stronger*. Penguin Books, London.

Wilson, W.J. (1987). *The Truly Disadvantaged: The Inner City, the Underclass, and Public Policy*. University of Chicago Press, Chicago, IL.

1

The Spatial Dimension of Educational Inequalities

Leïla FROUILLOU
CRESPPA-GTM, Université Paris-Nanterre, France

1.1. Introduction

Educational inequalities can be understood as a specific type of social inequality, in that they involve institutional systems that play a crucial role in the construction of social trajectories. Meritocratic ideology, which goes hand in hand with the idea that each pupil should have access to the best possible education, can thus justify practices of differentiation (adapting curricula, creating streamed classes, suggesting school orientations corresponding to the "skills" of each pupil, etc.). As inequalities are always associated with a school *system,* the history of these systems plays a decisive role in understanding the ways in which socially differentiated schooling trajectories are constructed and justified. As Felouzis (2009, §3) reminds us, "each national education system constitutes a response to the universal and recurring problem of inter-individual inequalities linked to social stratification". Using the French system as a starting point and comparing it with elements describing other school systems, this chapter shows how geographical approaches can contribute to an understanding of educational inequalities.

This question is far from obvious, since the spatialization of social issues can present an obstacle to the analysis of the mechanisms producing inequalities (Tissot and Poupeau 2005). Indeed, the use of spatial categories – such as the neighborhood, priority education zones or schools in the Paris suburbs – can reinforce "a homogenizing vision of populations that are *irreducibly different*" (*ibid.*, p. 8).

Inequalities in Geographical Space,
coordinated by Clémentine COTTINEAU and Julie VALLÉE. © ISTE Ltd 2022.

Moreover, for Tissot and Poupeau, this spatialization "leads to thinking about the situation of the most segregated territories independently of overall mechanisms" (*ibid.*, p. 5). How then can we construct a geographical approach that does not spatialize social issues, and that makes it possible to grasp the mechanisms of production of social inequalities at and/or through school[1]? It seems to us that the concept of spatial dimension which we define in line with the work of Veschambre and Ripoll (Ripoll and Veschambre 2005; Veschambre 2006) makes it possible to avoid the pitfalls of the spatialization of social issues while also taking into account mechanisms which would otherwise be invisible.

This concept is part of a Bourdieusian reading of the social world, the key features of which are presented in this introduction. The theory of reproduction (Bourdieu and Passeron 1970) describes the school as a product of the social world and as a way of maintaining its structures. Social hierarchies are reproduced from one generation to the next through their transmutation into school hierarchies. While the school presents itself as indifferent to social differences, it legitimizes a relationship to the world and to culture which is specific to the dominant classes (relationship to the written word, to speech, to authority, the "legitimate culture" of the arts and letters, etc.). In this approach, the exceptional trajectories of social mobility, whether upward or downward, contribute to enriching the meritocratic ideology of school, without calling into question the reproduction of social positions[2]: "The relative leeway of the school game enables the reproduction of social positions – in complete invisibility" (Palheta 2012, p. 326). This conception is often presented as being opposed to Boudon's individualistic approach, in which individuals make cost/benefit trade-offs at each school level. The Boudonian reading of trade-offs describes the social filtering operated by the school system, but understands it as resulting from social stratification, without the school's autonomy in producing social inequalities. The Bourdieusian reading, on the contrary, emphasizes the active role of the school system in the production of inequalities, through reproduction mechanisms (guidance councils, assignment mechanisms, school mapping, etc.) on which the school system is based. We revisit these later in the chapter.

The Bourdieusian approach, which can be qualified by its author as structuralist constructivism or constructivist structuralism (Bourdieu 1987, p. 147), describes the

---

1. By "school" we mean the educational system, which implies considering different levels (primary, secondary, post-secondary, higher education), sectors (private, public) and a wide variety of social agents (teaching and administrative staff, pupils, students, etc.).
2. In the Bourdieusian relational perspective, we are interested in social positions relative to a social space, and not in the social conditions of existence: having a baccalaureate (high school diploma) does not have the same social meaning today as in the 1960s.

positions (and trajectories) of social agents in a social space structured by capital (economic, cultural, social and symbolic). The proximities between agents outline social groups, or even social classes. The link between the individual action of the agents and the objective social structures is made by the *habitus*, which is the result of the incorporation by the agents of the system of norms, practices and dispositions associated with their social position. This approach makes little room for space in the geographical sense[3], and even underlines the errors[4] made by an observation of "physical" space detached from a reading of social structures (Ripoll 2013): "One can only break with the false evidence, and with the errors inscribed in the substantialist thought of places, if one proceeds to a rigorous analysis of the relations between the structures of social space and the structures of physical space" (Bourdieu 1993, p. 250). We find here the limits related to the spatialization of social problems, stated in the introduction following the works of Tissot and Poupeau.

The work of Veschambre and Ripoll allows us to place the Bourdieusian theory in a geographical approach based on a dimensional definition of space. According to Veschambre (2006), the term "spatial dimension" spread slowly from the 1970s onwards in French social geography. For proponents of the dimensional approach, space spans society like time: it is not as aligned with society as the term "socio-spatial" would have us believe. Space as a dimension then allows us to "reveal the social construction of the inequalities by and faced with the material and ideal relationships with space" (Ripoll and Veschambre 2005, p. 481). Thus, "the spatial dimension not only raises the question of forms of inequality that have remained in the shadow of statistics, but it also questions all of the processes that (re)produce social conditions and positions, and therefore social relations" (Ripoll and Veschambre 2005, p. 467). Space is "an inherent *dimension* of social relations: the social is *always already* spatial" (Ripoll and Tissot 2010, p. 5). Ripoll and

---

3. Bourdieu sometimes underlines geographical variations (the difference between Paris and other places, for example). In a late text, entitled "Effects of Places", he clarifies the relations between "social space" and "physical space" on a theoretical level, the latter being a "reified social space" functioning as a social catalyst: "The gathering in the same place of a homogeneous population in dispossession also has the effect of redoubling the dispossession, notably in matters of culture and cultural practice" (Bourdieu 1993, p. 261).
4. See in particular the notion of the screen effect, which shows that observation at certain scales masks social structures: "This properly social delimitation is specified by the effects of spatial delimitation in that agents are always (more or less) attached to a locally based social space, the position in this space (village, neighbourhood, set of classmates, colleagues, etc.) tends to obscure the position in the global space of the familiar subspace which can be experienced as a microcosm of the social world as a whole (with its dominants and its dominated, etc.)" (Bourdieu 1984, p. 15).

Veschambre (2005) show that we can analyze the spatial dimension of different types of capital: properties (holdings, concentration and location of surfaces) objectify the spatial dimension of economic capital and living spaces objectify the spatial dimension of social capital. It is also possible to work on the spatial dimension of the conditions of accumulation and use of social resources through concepts such as mobility or the capital of autochthony, which is the way in which "inscription in local social networks can generate real resources for the working classes" (Ripoll and Tissot 2010, p. 6). This dimensional approach of space allows us to analyze the effects of places "without empowering them, to identify unevenly distributed relative advantages without making a new spatial capital" (Ripoll 2013, p. 371).

Drawing on the Bourdieusian analysis of the three states of cultural capital (1979), which distinguishes between the objectified state (cultural goods, such as paintings, books), the institutionalized state (school titles, status), and the embodied state (*habitus* or disposition of agents), Ripoll shows that "space [...] exists (at least) three times: in things in the material sense, but also in institutions and in heads" (2013, p. 377). The materiality of the social world constitutes the most obvious state of the spatial dimension: it refers to things, thus to bodies, architectural elements or landscapes, localizations and displacements. But the spatial dimension allows us to link these material elements to the representations of social agents (what is close or accessible, familiar or even appropriate places, places from which one feels excluded, etc.) and to institutional functioning (administrative networks, action zones and perimeters defined by public policies). Understanding the spatial dimension through the three states of cultural capital thus helps us not to forget that space runs through institutions and representations and helps us to avoid reducing it to its materiality or to locations.

This approach is particularly interesting for understanding schools because cultural capital plays a crucial role in the school field and in social reproduction. Indeed, school qualifications (diplomas) are one of the ways of objectifying cultural capital. The place of other types of capital in the field of education depends on the system observed and the period. In France, for example, economic capital has historically played a less central role in educational trajectories than cultural capital, insofar as the public and free system forms the structure of a large majority of the primary and secondary educational field, including the most prestigious establishments, which are in the public domain. The current role of economic capital is, however, in dispute because the increase in school competition reinforces residential strategies or the choice of private schools, which presuppose families having sufficient financial resources. In Helsinki, for example, the very strong correspondence between school sectors and student catchment areas makes residential mobility one of the only strategies that families can use to change schools (Bernelius and Vilkama 2019), and this requires economic capital.

The spatial dimension allows us to grasp school inequalities through the prism of this Bourdieusian reading, attentive to the different kinds of capital and their states. Thus, measuring the unequal distribution of pupils implies a reflection on the *materiality* of school segregations (location of pupils, staff and schools). The latter cannot be understood without at the same time considering *institutional* issues (the administrative network that often constitutes the framework for statistical measurements of disparities, the specificities of schools), or the *representations* of this school social space, which are always spatial, that political and professional actors, or students and their families, make of themselves, and which contribute to structuring their trajectories in the school space. To this end, this chapter first focuses on school segregation as a synthetic object of socio-geographical approaches to school inequalities (section 1.2), and then looks at public policies and school trajectories as elements of understanding school inequalities that need to be approached in their spatial dimension (section 1.3).

1.2. School segregation as the central object of socio-geographical approaches to school inequalities

By analogy with urban segregation, work on "school segregation" focuses on the unequal distribution of students in schools. Barthon (1998a) defines school segregation as the spatial concentration of disadvantaged pupils, which results at least in part from a distancing in a hierarchical school space, which can generate inequality of access to school goods and lead to school captivity. Work on school segregation thus encounters *measurement* issues (variables used to define groups, and scales of analysis of the concentration of these groups in classes, schools, departments, etc.) and analyses of the *mechanisms* for producing these differentiations, as well as their effects on school trajectories. Since the term "segregation" has negative connotations, it implies highlighting an institutional "distancing" that causes inequality or social exclusion (van Zanten 1996). Some definitions specify the ways in which these inequalities are produced, expressing inequality in access to resources and in the contexts of socialization: "Segregation distributes groups in unequal spaces in terms of resources, and at the same time distributes them in spaces where the configuration of the groups in co-presence, which contributes to defining the conditions of local sociability, is variable" (Oberti et al. 2012, p. 74).

This unequal distribution of social groups in schools can be objectified, depending on the national context, the time period and the data available, on the basis of variables describing the social origin of pupils (parents' occupations, income, etc.), their migratory or racial origin and their academic results. For example, rescarch on school segregation shows that French secondary school populations are distinguished according to social origin (often objectified by the parents' socio-professional category), "ethnic" profile (the migratory trajectory of the parents and/or the student) and school characteristics (marks, grades, results) (Felouzis 2003a). These different variables describing school populations go hand in hand – "ethnic, academic, and social segregation are clearly correlated with each other" (Merle 2012, p. 17) – which "justifies the generic use of the term 'school segregation'" (*ibid.*, p. 18). School trajectories (established on the basis of socially differentiated school "successes", but also of socially differentiated orientations, even at equivalent school grades for pupils) gradually transform social position (objectified by the social origins of parents and their migratory trajectory) into school capital. The school variables thus gradually absorb the variables linked to social position when describing students' trajectories statistically, which explains the correlation between these variables (social origin, academic skills, migratory origin) and the need to consider them together.

This unequal distribution of students is partly related to the form of the school system considered. Indeed, a comparison based on the PISA 2003 survey (Felouzis 2009) shows that the strongly differentiated distribution of students according to streams or schools may reflect the strong correlation between social origin and academic skills in some countries. This is the case in Hungary, Germany, Turkey, Belgium, Austria and the Czech Republic, where there is an unequal distribution of students across the different streams of the education system. In Brazil and Indonesia, this unequal distribution is linked to the institutions rather than to the differentiation of the educational tracks themselves. In other countries, the school systems are more unified (a single curriculum is offered) and there is little difference at the school level, which goes hand in hand with less pronounced social inequalities, for example in Poland, Iceland, Norway and Finland. Intermediate situations, however, underline that the relationship between the more or less unified structure of the education system and the production of socially based educational inequalities is not mechanical, but involves other factors: "The United States and Great Britain have low indices of social and academic segregation [i.e. varying social origins and academic levels among students in different streams or schools] while having high social inequalities [i.e. a strong correlation between individual academic levels and trajectories and social origins, author's note]" (Felouzis 2009, §18). In the United States, the long history of research on school segregation stems from the role played by schools in the racial desegregation movement that began in the 1950s. Indeed, Coleman's 1966 report, "Equality of educational opportunity", considered not only the role of social class or "race" in student achievement but also regional disparities and institutional effects.

Another way of presenting the geographical diversity of school systems and their more or less differentiated character is to consider a gradient in which Finland (which has a mainly public and uniform system, based on a sectorization leaving little choice to families) is compared to Chile (which has a mainly private and differentiated system, where school strategies are central), paying particular attention to systems whose differentiation brings into play a confessional dimension, as in Germany, Belgium, Scotland or the Netherlands (Boterman 2019).

1.2.1. *The 1980s: from national sociological theories to localized approaches to educational inequalities in France*

In France, research on educational inequalities has long focused on the link between social class (or social stratification/mobility) and educational success (Bourdieu 1966). At the end of the 1990s, Barthon (1998b) noted a rich conceptual and theoretical debate on school segregation in France, but it was not until the 1980s that the "urban dimension" (sometimes referred to as the "spatial dimension") of school inequalities was considered (Léger and Tripier 1986). Since then, research in France has shown that school choice could be reflected in residential strategies that affected real estate prices, for example in Paris (Fack and Grenet 2009), or that peri-urban municipalities could use the school map as a tool to attract certain social classes (Charmes 2007). Most analyses consider the "urban dimension" (van Zanten 2001; Oberti 2005, 2007b) in the sense of "context", while others, from a more geographical perspective linked to spatial analysis (François and Poupeau 2005), construct a "school space" marked by discontinuities (administrative networks), polarities (gradients, high points, center–periphery organization) and flows (student mobility).

School segregation often raises questions about the relationship between city and school: How do urban discontinuities and differentiations translate into inequalities in access, recruitment or academic success? And, conversely, how do schools contribute to the reproduction of spatialized inequalities in cities? Few researchers, however, explain the theoretical status of space or the spatial dimension in the construction of school inequalities, with the terms "space", "geography" and "spatial dimension" being used as quasi-synonyms in some analyses, in the same way as the terms "urban", "city" or "residential". It seems to us that the dimensional approach put forward in the introduction makes it possible to grasp this subject of school segregation without reifying space (i.e. without attributing to it a role that is independent of social structures), and without reducing it to material locations (a fortiori "urban" ones), by expressing the latter with institutional elements (school map), or strategies of both students and schools.

1.2.2. *How can we objectify the unequal distribution of students in the school system?*

Working on school segregation implies highlighting a differentiation of learning contexts, and then looking at the mechanisms and effects of this unequal distribution of pupils (and staff). How can we objectify these school segregations?

The emergence of this socio-geographic research object[5] as school segregation is partly due to changes in school systems. Taking France as an example, the massification of education and the social generalization of access to the secondary level of the lycée (high school, students aged 15–18) from the 1980s onwards have gone hand in hand with a strengthening of distinctive school behaviors in the middle and upper classes, which are marked by segregation between baccalaureate streams and/or between establishments (Merle 2012) "in [a] context of strong stigmatization of working-class and immigrant spaces" (Oberti 2005, p. 15). The former exclusion of children from working-class backgrounds has now been replaced in part by their relegation to stigmatized fields (Bourdieu and Champagne 1992). This deferred elimination is constructed not only through a hierarchy of streams but also through mechanisms of self-elimination of the students with the least capital (dropping out or academic failure). The spatial dimension of this relegation and the diversification of the school system are visible in particular through school policies, which are spatialized in France with the priority education zones (ZEPs) set up in 1981, and local education contracts, or local education plans, which contribute to the institutional differentiation of schooling contexts (Rouault 2005). The French priority education policy "aims to correct the impact of social and economic inequalities on educational success by strengthening pedagogical and educational action in schools and establishments in the territories with the greatest social difficulties", according to the website of the Ministry of National Education (consulted on June 29, 2020) and can thus be read as a "re-translation of the social question into territorial categories" (Tissot and Poupeau 2005, p. 7). With these

---

5. As Oberti (2005) notes, geographers play an important role in this "spatial turn" in French research on educational inequalities (Rapetti 1990; Renard 1990; Augustin 1993; Hérin 1993a; Hérin et al. 1994; François 1996; Rhein 1997; Barthon 1998b). Hérin thus emphasizes early on the relevance of a geographical approach to educational inequalities: "The training of young people, in an education system that is nevertheless well centralized, is strongly marked by the diversity of local and regional contexts" (1993b, p. 145).

changes in the education system, the differentiation of schooling contexts is becoming a central theme in French research in the sociology of education, as illustrated by van Zanten's *L'École de la périphérie* (2001). This movement corresponds to that observed in other countries: school segregation is now a lively area of research, as illustrated by a recent special issue of *Urban Studies* (Boterman et al. 2019)[6].

In France, this research highlights the construction of local hierarchies in secondary (Oberti 2005) and post-secondary education (Frouillou 2017). These configurations are inscribed in urban history and the social division of space, and therefore go beyond the strict framework of school. Rhein shows from school flows in the Paris region that there is "a genealogy of different types of establishments [that] highlights the links between structures of the school apparatus and the pattern of social division of space" (1997, p. 65). In concrete terms, as opposed to schools whose educational offer was centered on technological and vocational courses, general education lycées were located in the old, bourgeois town centers of the Paris region. The 1970s and 1980s saw the construction of lycées in more working-class communes, which had been left out until then despite their demographic growth and their place in the urbanization of the Parisian metropolis (Rhein et al. 1999). This contrasts with the more abundant and diversified school offer in the "beaux quartiers" (upmarket districts).

This historical perspective can be supplemented by a synchronic analysis of the differentiated configurations of secondary education, understood as local micro-hierarchies by certain authors (Oberti 2005). The structure of the educational offer (public and private share, diversification of courses of study, density of schools, etc.) and its inclusion in a residential area sometimes marked by strong segregation thus define competitive school spaces that require localized approaches (Broccolichi and van Zanten 1997). However, as Merle explains, "the social transformations of urban and peri-urban space raise the problem of the relevant territorial scale for measuring urban or school segregation phenomena: commune, group of communes, département, or region" (2012, p. 103). This question of scale invites researchers to define neighborhoods in order to think about issues in school, neighborhoods that are not clearly delineated, unlike administrative grids, because "the immediate environment of each school may partially cover that of neighboring schools" (François and Poupeau 2008b, p. 98).

---

6. As the authors point out (*ibid.*, p. 3056), "the intertwining of school system segmentation and residential segregation has become even more crucial for understanding the socio-spatial mechanisms of social reproduction and intergenerational social mobility".

Work on school segregation thus distinguishes several levels in the differentiation of students' schooling contexts. The class effect may involve both the role of the teacher and the school's policy on grade levels and/or options (Moignard 2007), which may be reflected spatially in the school by the segregation of certain classes, such as Segpa classes (adapted general and vocational education sections), which, in France, take in students aged 11–15 with major learning difficulties (Caro et al. 2010). Blanchard and Cayouette-Remblière (2011) point out that while questions about the choice of pathway and options are old, those about school choice are more recent in France. Indeed, with the work on school segregation, it is the level of the school (especially at collège, or middle school) that is most often mobilized (Ballion 1991; Broccolichi and van Zanten 1997; Oberti 2007b; van Zanten 2009). This "desire to break with macro-sociological analyses and to reflect on the productivity of the school on the basis of local specificities" (Cousin 1993, p. 401) brings together several lines of analysis: from the effects of the place of schooling on students' trajectories (social selection, academic selection and socialization) to the identities constructed by the schools, and even to the implementation of strategies for recruiting students and/or staff (Delvaux and van Zanten 2006). The school is thus considered "one of the most relevant places for understanding schools today" (Cousin 2000, p. 139). The other levels of analysis make it possible to broaden the context of schooling by including it in the local micro-hierarchies mentioned above (communal and supra-communal scale), in administrative meshes such as the départements, academies or regions, where significant inequalities in educational success can be highlighted (Broccolichi et al. 2006; Caro et al. 2010), or finally on a national scale, with surveys such as PISA (OECD) making it possible to compare the weight of social inequalities at school in the different education systems.

Research often involves empirically objectifying these school segregations. Ly and Riegert (2015) show, for example, that intra-school segregation, that is, segregation between school classes in French collèges (for children aged 11–15) hardly varies between départements and is mainly related to academic performance. On the contrary, inter-school segregation, which is highly correlated with social origin variables and academic results, varies greatly between départements. Inter-school segregation according to students' social origin is particularly strong in urban départements with metropolitan areas, "firstly because the collèges reflect residential segregation more accurately, and secondly because a situation of competition arises, leading to the emergence of 'desirable' collèges and collèges 'to be avoided'" (*ibid.*, p. 5). The study by Oberti et al. (2012) on the effects of the relaxation of the school map in the Paris region confirms that school segregation is greater than residential segregation, due to the difference in the distribution of young populations compared to the general population and school practices (avoidance, private sector, etc.).

School segregation can thus be read as an accentuated reflection of residential segregation, especially in collèges, and it is particularly strong in the private sector. This complex link between residential and school segregation calls for localized approaches at the level of neighborhoods or districts, such as the one developed by Audren (2012) which focused on Marseille collèges, making it possible to grasp local configurations with regard to the policies and strategies of the students, which is the subject of the next part of the chapter.

Thus, the spatial dimension of educational inequalities crystallizes in school segregations because the latter draw a hierarchical school space, where local configurations and the scale of analysis are crucial to grasp the ways in which learning contexts are differentiated. Boterman et al. (2019, p. 3057) thus speak of educational landscapes, "formed where national, regional and local regulations and policies are combined with historically developed geographies of education" (Boterman et al. 2019, p. 3057). But understanding these processes of segregation between courses, classes or schools implies going beyond the debate on measurement or indices[7] to articulate two complementary perspectives on the mechanisms at work. The first is related to current policies, which promote free school choice and thus the establishment of school markets. The second concerns school "choices", based on questions of school mobility or avoidance, and the effects of different schooling contexts (classes, schools, departments, academies, etc.) on students' trajectories. Taking into account the spatial dimension of these two perspectives is the subject of the next part of the chapter, and this makes it possible to reason more generally about the spatial dimension of educational inequalities without restricting them to the urban areas where this segregation is strongest.

1.3. The spatial dimension of educational inequalities: from policies to trajectories

An understanding of the mechanisms of production of school segregation allows us to reflect on the spatial dimension of school policies as well as on the construction of the trajectories of agents, students and staff in this hierarchical school space.

---

7. These methodological debates, which are common to studies of urban segregation, concern: the type of index used (and therefore their mathematical properties of decomposition, monotonicity or comparison), the variables and modalities used (which social groups are compared, which breakdowns of the social structure) and the geographical scales of analysis (national, regional, departmental, and the size of the units whose social, educational and racial recruitment are being compared).

1.3.1. *The spatial dimension of school policies that produce inequalities*

Public policy plays a vital role in understanding school segregation. For example, it is important to understand the recruitment processes of schools. In the Netherlands, both schools and parents have a high degree of autonomy in the choice of school and the admission processes, but this does not invalidate the role of residential segregation in the unequal distribution of students according to their migratory origin and social class (Boterman 2019). In France, this institutional aspect refers rather to the "school map", which still largely organizes catchment areas for primary and secondary schools. The term "school map" refers to much more than just the allocation of students: it is a "set of measures aimed at defining the public school offer and dealing with the educational demand of families" (van Zanten and Obin 2010, p. 3). It was set up in France in the early 1960s and suggests a territorial division associating each school with a recruitment area and the means to accommodate it. This forward-looking instrument for managing educational resources, set up in a context of increasing school enrolment, later became an instrument for promoting social diversity in schools (Fack and Grenet 2009). In primary schools, the management of student assignments is the responsibility of mayors. In secondary schools, a distinction must be made between the assignment procedures for collèges and those for lycées. Since 2004, the drawing up of the sectorization of lower secondary schools has been the responsibility of the general councils, while the inspectors of the academy remain competent a posteriori for the assignment and de-allocation procedures (Barrault 2012). At the lycée level, the greater diversity of educational opportunities (e.g. vocational) implies that students can deviate from a strict school map. School sectors (called "districts") often include several schools (Fack et al. 2014).

The "relaxation" of the school map in French secondary schools has gone through several stages since the 1980s. In 2007, the use of exemptions was made public and official in a context where several years of low birth rate had created a large number of available places, which were unequally distributed according to the academies and schools. The right of families "to choose between the local school and any other where places are available" was affirmed (van Zanten and Obin 2010, p. 38), and a list of prioritized criteria (disability, medical care, scholarships, special schooling, siblings, proximity to home) was established for accepting exceptions if they exceeded capacity. However, the introduction of a socioeconomic criterion (scholarships) has not resulted in a significant reconfiguration of school recruitment. For example, for the start of the 2009 school year in the sixth grade, "applications granted to scholarship students represented only 9.2 percent of waivers for France as a whole (13.7 percent for the Paris Academy), while waivers granted to students wishing to follow a particular pathway – most often a language option that would allow them to avoid the collège assigned to them according to the school map – represented 12% of waivers granted (40.1% for the Paris academy)" (Merle 2011, p. 39). More generally, there is a relative permanence of previous management methods: "The resistance of the school map to change is at once political, technical and social" (Barrault 2012, p. 125). Local administrative officials retain a margin of action (van Zanten and Da Costa 2013), notably through the weighting of priority criteria for exemptions. Above all, "maintaining the priority given to students in the school sector has [...] authorized only a limited number of waivers, especially to the most attractive collèges, insofar as the capacity of the establishments has remained the same" (Oberti et al. 2012, p. 141).

Despite these continuities, the relaxation of the French school map reflects a policy of promoting "free choice" in education, which has been reflected since the mid-2000s in the implementation of assignment management systems that reconfigure the production of inequalities in access to secondary and higher education. The 2007 reform coincided with the generalization of the Affelnet application to all academies in 2008. It is an algorithm that allows students to be prioritized according to their preferences, their academic record, their scholarship status and their geographic proximity. The weighting varies by academy (Fack et al. 2014). In Paris, Affelnet corresponds to the establishment of "a regulated school choice system" (*ibid.*, p. 33). The status of scholarship holder is taken into account, but the weighting leaves an important place, in addition to the criterion of geographical belonging to the district, to the criterion of academic results (van Zanten and Obin 2010; Merle 2011; Fack et al. 2014). In higher education, the Admission post-Bac national assignment system was generalized to all the Academies in 2009, sometimes replacing regional systems of sectorization of university assignments, such as Ravel (automated census of students' wishes), which offered "sector" universities in Île-de-France between 1990 and 2008 for baccalaureate holders from the region in order to limit the demographic pressure on Parisian institutions (Frouillou 2016). This post-Bac admission system, which originated in engineering schools and preparatory classes, was replaced by Parcoursup at the start of the 2018 academic year. This system generalizes selection processes based on applications to all French higher education programs, whereas in the past, a large proportion of university programs were accessible with the baccalaureate, without evaluation and ranking of all applicants (Frouillou et al. 2019). The French assignment system thus emphasizes the continuity between secondary and post-secondary education in the promotion of "free choice" at school, with academic results playing a crucial role when the courses applied for are full.

The segregative effects of the design of school sectors have been highlighted by French researchers (Rouault 2005; Dubet and Duru-Bellat 2006). In the Paris academy, for example, the sectorization of public secondary schools "ratifies the separation brought about by the social division of residential space" (François 2007, p. 205). But several studies also point to the accentuation of inequalities in the distribution of pupils following the relaxation of the school map. In secondary schools, research has shown an increased hierarchy of schools (especially in collèges), which is more or less pronounced depending on the context (more or less diversified school offer) and the scale of analysis for segregation measures (Merle 2011; Oberti et al. 2012).

> In Paris, but also in regional capitals such as Bordeaux and Lille, the privileged collèges have become gentrified; the disadvantaged collèges have hardly benefited, if at all, from the overall gentrification of the population of large metropolises. The research highlights a phenomenon of relative, or even absolute, ghettoization for the most disadvantaged schools, which results in the loss of staff and the loss of students from privileged backgrounds. (Merle 2011, p. 47)

The increased importance of academic results, combined with a priority criterion for scholarship recipients, goes hand in hand with segregation between schools that is more closely linked to students' academic backgrounds than to their social origin. Affelnet has thus contributed to the increased stratification of Parisian lycées according to academic results, even if the scholarship bonus has made it possible to limit segregation according to social origin (Fack et al. 2014). More generally, the principle of liberalizing school assignments has led some researchers to denounce the "trap of free school choice" (Oberti 2007a), a "free choice" that is in fact socially situated, as we shall see in the following section.

The spatial dimension of sectorization policies seems obvious. The introduction of assignment systems in secondary and post-secondary education, which make these institutional boundaries more flexible, does not, however, erase this dimension: the priorities set out in the algorithms often retain a spatial character, as the Education Code partly constrains assignments on a geographical basis. Moreover, the selection practices of certain programs are based on geographic criteria, as Orange (2010) has shown, for example, for the "higher technician" sections. This allows us to propose a synthetic approach to grasping the spatial dimension of school institutional logics that produce inequalities. It can be analyzed, again using the French system as a starting point, through two complementary elements: on the one hand, the definition of the perimeters or the location of certain policies, measures or projects (priority education, boarding schools of excellence, social opening measures, school projects, etc.) and, on the other hand, the spatial dimension of the orientation processes and procedures.

The first element invites us to work on the *institutional* differentiation of learning and teaching contexts. In the French university sector, this differentiation can easily be highlighted by the progressive autonomization of institutions (Musselin 2001). Recent reforms (LRU 2007; Fioraso 2013; ORE 2018; LPR 2020) have reinforced the autonomy of universities and encouraged them to develop attractive (and distinctive) training offers. The differentiation of universities goes hand in hand with "complex processes of multilevel territorialization of higher education and research" (Benninghoff et al. 2012, p. 12). As in French secondary education, institutions, which can refer to a site, a branch, or the institution to which these sites are attached, are now relevant units of analysis: "In the university, as elsewhere, 'context makes a difference'" (Felouzis 2003b, p. 213). The incentive to enable increased modularity of courses contributes to this differentiation of institutions. This concerns post-secondary education, but also secondary education, where modularity and the promotion of "free choice" have been reflected in the recent reform of the baccalaureate (2019), with general courses of study being replaced by a more individual choice of specialties and an increased share of continuous assessment. In general, the differentiation of pathways from secondary to post-secondary education is a crucial element of the spatial dimension of educational inequalities as it contributes to the structuring of quasi-markets of schools, where schools are in competition and must develop strategies around their educational offer and recruitment (Felouzis et al. 2013). The way in which school systems are financed is also part of the analysis of this differentiation and does not completely overlap with the distinction between the public and private sectors: in Denmark, the Netherlands and Spain, the private sector is largely financed by the state (Boterman et al. 2019).

The second element of a general analysis of the spatial dimension of educational inequalities linked to institutions lies in the functioning of the orientation process. Research highlights a "channeling of school aspirations", which is not only achieved through a selection of the courses of study presented to students (brochures, invitations to professionals, open days, career forums, etc.) but also through more or less individualized monitoring of the construction of wishes by students, depending on the school (van Zanten 2015). The construction of the space of possibilities for further study is thus differentiated according to class and school, with STS (advanced vocational courses), for example, often presented as a logical continuation for students in technological streams in lycées where these higher education programs are present (Orange 2010). The algorithmic procedures of the allocation systems, although rarely made public, can then reinforce these institutional links through geographical priorities or the practices of recruitment committees that take into account the applicants' schools of origin. The consideration of schools in the orientation process thus plays a role in the construction of educational trajectories, which also make it possible to read this hierarchical school space.

1.3.2. *Understanding inequalities based on school placements and trajectories*

Many French studies focus on school "choices" (Ballion 1991; Barthon, Oberti 2000; Oberti 2007a; van Zanten 2009; Beaud 2011; Ben Ayed 2011; Blanchard and Cayouette-Remblière 2011; Œuvrard 2011; Poullaouec 2011; Orange 2012). A comparison of studies of school choice in different national configurations (Wilson and Bridge 2019) shows a link between high levels of school segregation and systems that promote family school choice, in countries with "*open enrollment*" systems, such as England and Chile, but also in countries with sectorization and the opportunity to opt-out, such as the United States. Socially situated, these school "choices" are based on families' and students' more or less detailed knowledge of the school system, or on an unequal capacity to resist institutional injunctions, for example, in the French case, to refuse a vocational orientation (Palheta 2011) or to reclassify an academic difficulty as a medical problem (Garcia 2013), or finally, on mechanisms of self-exclusion that concern the working classes in particular (Poullaouec 2011).

School "choices" make it possible to grasp the spatial dimension of school inequalities because the options and streams are, as we have seen, unevenly distributed between schools (Œuvrard 2000). The term "choice" poses a problem in a Bourdieusian approach, which favors an understanding of the structures or mechanisms linked to the construction of educational trajectories rather than a reading that assumes a relative freedom of choice for individuals, a reading that, as we have seen, echoes the policies of relaxing sectorization and diversifying educational paths. Talking about school "placements" makes it possible to grasp the practices and representations of pupils and families, which can be expressed in terms of "choices", "trade-offs", "strategies" or "constraints" with other approaches. The term "placement" is thus part of a "practical sense" that reflects a "dynamic and open-ended logic" of the social world rather than a mechanistic one (Bourdieu 1994, p. 5). Placements then describe the objective arrangement of social practices without assuming conscious calculations. This adjustment through "practical sense" constitutes for the ruling classes "a decisive advantage whenever the 'sincerity' and 'naivety' of the 'vocation' or the 'conversion' are part of the tacit conditions of occupation of the position, as in the case of the artistic professions" (Bourdieu 1974, p. 14).

School placements, limited or favored by the institutional functioning described above, always have a spatial dimension: it is a question of (re)positioning oneself in the school field, which we have seen is spatially hierarchical. We can define a sense of school placement: "Rather than 'schooling choices', placement practices are the product of an incorporation of the conditions of existence, integrating local offers in terms of housing, culture and education, public services, but also the possibilities of doing without public services by resorting to 'private' services. Linked to the volume of capital possessed by families and to the structure of the distribution of cultural and economic capital in the areas under consideration, school placement thus requires a form of 'mobility capital' offering families the ability to orient themselves in hierarchical school spaces" (François and Poupeau 2008b, p. 104).

Some placements can be read a posteriori as schooling circuits (Broccolichi and van Zanten 1997), in other words, recurrent flows between certain primary, secondary or higher education establishments. Other school placements result in mobility between schools and are the subject of much research. School avoidance can be defined as "the group of practices by families who send their children to a school other than the one in their catchment area" (François 2002, p. 308). It includes both transfers to other public schools and enrollment in the private sector (Ballion 1982; Léger and Tripier 1986; Ballion 1991; Broccolichi 1995; Broccolichi and van Zanten 1997; van Zanten 2001; François and Poupeau 2004). François and Poupeau show the importance of neighborhoods in the avoidance strategies of students and their families, which must be placed not only socially but also spatially in a local configuration of the educational offer (distance/accessibility to training), because "the spatial inscription of social inequalities reinforces the social sorting exercised by the educational system" (François and Poupeau 2008b, p. 112). Finally, taking into account the spatial dimension strengthens the understanding of school placements: "The variables of social affiliation appear to be all the more efficient in predicting students' avoidance practices when larger spatial scales are taken into account [...] In the end, the more spatial variables are integrated, the more the importance of social variables is revealed" (François and Poupeau 2008a, p. 156).

A doctoral study (Frouillou 2017) on university segregation in the Ile-de-France region at the turn of the 2010s highlights the collective logic of the placements corresponding to entry into higher education. Their spatial dimension is formed around the lycée, a place that partly defines the spaces of possible further education because of the institutional channeling of aspirations and the role of peer groups in the construction of school "choices". More precisely, this work highlights a sense of university placement, which can be read in relationships to studies (which are also relationships to places of study), in strategies of avoidance or symbolic requalification of a university such as Paris 8 Vincennes-Saint-Denis, one of the fields of investigation. This "practical sense" allows students to adjust to the Francilian university space. It stems from an internalization of material (location of university sites and accessibility) and institutional constraints (modes of assignment, selectivity of institutions, reputation, etc.). The meaning of placement is constructed according to the social position of students, defined according to the structure and volume of capital (cultural, economic, social, symbolic). The spatial dimension of this social position refers to residential location, inclusion in institutional perimeters (academy), and representations of distances (which can, for example, lead a university to be "too far" both spatially and socially). While economic capital seems to be secondary in the construction of the sense of university placement in relation to high school enrollment (which defines access priorities in the Admission post-bac system, and often corresponds to peer groups), it may be more decisive in the construction of other strategies for entering higher education (private schools, guidance coaches, private preparation for competitive exams, renting a studio apartment to be closer to the place of study, etc.). This example shows that the spatial dimension of educational inequalities can be grasped at the level of pupils or students, by inscribing their "choices" in institutional contexts, whose constraints are always both material and embodied.

Taking a dynamic look at the sense of placement means reintroducing time as a complementary dimension to space in order to understand school inequalities on the basis of the trajectories of students and schools. These trajectories highlight the construction of the sense of school placement, and therefore the learning processes associated with the dispositions to orient oneself in finely hierarchical school spaces. Indeed, the longitudinal approach makes it possible not only to reveal inter-institutional trajectories that show hierarchies, with the most academically endowed pupils or students often joining institutions that correspond to their academic characteristics (Frouillou and Moulin 2019) but also to grasp the importance of time in the construction of school placements. Retrospective analysis shows the importance of avoidance attempts, repetition of grades and moves in the construction of placements at each stage of an educational trajectory, thus deconstructing the often implicit linearity of pathways as we imagine them (Frouillou 2017). More quantitative surveys make it possible to question the link between school segregation and educational trajectories. Oberti and Savina (2019) thus link a typology of collèges in the dense urban area of Paris with the results obtained by students (these results then allow for relatively easy access to certain courses of study or schools), based on the "Scolarité 2009" database and the results of the Brevet between 2006 and 2012. They show that, regardless of their social origin, students perform better if they are enrolled in a privileged rather than an underprivileged school, and this is particularly true for boys from underprivileged backgrounds. But the effect of school type on academic performance is not the same across the board: there is an advantage in attending a disadvantaged school in Paris rather than in the suburbs, and a clear disadvantage in attending a disadvantaged school in an advantaged suburb such as the Hauts-de-Seine. This may be linked to local patterns of school competition (avoidance of private schools, greater or lesser stigmatization of disadvantaged schools, etc.), or to hidden variables that reveal the importance of the spatial dimension (do the Parisian working classes reflect the same social positions as the working classes living in another more or less privileged area of the Parisian suburbs?)

Finally, while the spatial dimension of students' placements and educational trajectories seems essential for understanding the construction of inequalities in a system that promotes "free choice", it is necessary to shed light on the trajectories of staff working in the field of education with this approach that is sensitive to mobility, places and contexts of education. In France, the spatial dimension of national education staff assignment systems, which complements approaches focused on the public, constitutes a lively avenue of research, which could be included, for example, in the perspective of a recent contribution on the inter-academic algorithm that manages secondary school teacher assignments (Terrier et al. 2019).

1.4. Conclusion: spatial dimension of inequalities and the interweaving of levels of analysis

While school segregations are a crucial object for understanding the spatial dimension of school inequalities, these inequalities are not limited to residentially segregated urban contexts. The dimensional approach provides a theoretical framework for understanding the articulation between institutional, material and embodied aspects of school inequalities, which are always spatial. Analyses in terms of opportunities, mobilities, placements or local configurations thus make it possible to renew the theories of reproduction considering a national school space, by showing the consequences in terms of inequalities of recent policies favoring a differentiation of the educational offer and a "free choice" of school. The space approach thus makes it possible to understand not only the *form of* school inequalities by documenting the distribution of students and schools and its evolution over time, linked to residential issues, but also to bring out the *mechanisms* of production of these inequalities by highlighting discontinuities (academic network or sectorization), material (accessibility of schools) and symbolic (stigmatization, channeling of school aspirations, etc.) and mobility understood as school placements (avoidance, assignments, etc.). These elements intersect with a critical analysis of public policies and a comprehensive reading of the trajectories of students and staff.

Empirically, the spatial dimension of school inequalities can be understood at different scales, which raises questions about school data, often produced for administrative purposes, and their availability for research (geolocation of student databases, for example). The reflection on the relevant geographical scales for thinking about school inequalities is thus crucial and depends in part on the areas of competition between schools, whose basis is more or less local depending on the level (primary, secondary, higher education), the institutional constraints (sectorization) and the resources of students and families. Recent work on child socialization and its consequences in the construction of inequalities (Lahire et al. 2019) invites us to link research on socialization (relationship to the body, to the written word, to time, to authority, etc.), the construction of pedagogical practices (Bonnéry 2011), with research on the differentiation of learning and teaching contexts, in order to understand how the inequalities in trajectories that mark school systems today are concretely constructed, in classes, in schools, in families and in groups of peers – in other words, in specific areas of a hierarchical and segmented school space.

1.5. References

Audren, G. (2012). Dynamiques scolaires et recompositions socio-territoriales : quels impacts sur la ségrégation à Marseille ? *Géographie, économie, société*, 14(2), 147–170.

Augustin, J.-P. (1993). La ville, la scolarisation et l'inégalité des chances. *Espace populations sociétés*, 2, 355–364.

Ballion, R. (1982). *Les consommateurs d'école : stratégies éducatives des familles*. Stock, Paris.

Ballion, R. (1991). *La bonne école : évaluation et choix du collège et du lycée*. Hatier, Paris.

Barrault, L. (2012). Les résistances de la carte scolaire. *Politix*, 98(2), 109–127.

Barthon, C. (1998a). Espaces et ségrégations scolaires : l'exemple des enfants d'immigrés dans les collèges de l'Académie de Versailles. PhD Thesis, Université de Poitiers, Poitiers.

Barthon, C. (1998b). La ségrégation comme processus dans l'école et dans la ville. *Revue européenne de migrations internationales*, 14(1), 93–103.

Barthon, C. and Oberti, M. (2000). Ségrégation spatiale, évitement et choix des établissements. In *L'école, l'état des savoirs*, Van Zanten, A. (ed.). La Découverte, Paris.

Beaud, S. (2011). Par delà les choix scolaires : les rapports de classes. *Revue française de pédagogie*, 175(2), 77–80.

Ben Ayed, C. (2011). À qui profite le choix de l'école ? Changements d'établissement et destins scolaires des élèves de milieux populaires. *Revue française de pédagogie*, 175(2), 39–57.

Benninghoff, M., Fassa, F., Goastellec, G., Leresche, J.-P. (eds) (2012). *Inégalités sociales et enseignement supérieur*. De Boeck, Brussels.

Bernelius, V. and Vilkama, K. (2019). Pupils on the move: School catchment area segregation and residential mobility of urban families. *Urban Studies*, 56(15), 3095–3116.

Blanchard, M. and Cayouette-Remblière, J. (2011). Penser les choix scolaires. *Revue française de pédagogie*, 175(2), 5–14.

Bonnéry, S. (2011). D'hier à aujourd'hui, les enjeux d'une sociologie de la pédagogie. *Savoir/Agir*, 17, 11–20.

Boterman, W.R. (2019). The role of geography in school segregation in the free parental choice context of Dutch cities. *Urban Studies*, 56(15), 3074–3094.

Bourdieu, P. (1966). L'école conservatrice. Les inégalités devant l'école et devant la culture. *Revue française de sociologie*, 7(3), 325–347.

Bourdieu, P. (1974). Avenir de classe et causalité du probable. *Revue française de sociologie*, 15(1), 3–42.

Bourdieu, P. (1979). Les trois états du capital culturel. *Actes de la recherche en sciences sociales*, 30(1), 3–6.

Bourdieu, P. (1984). La représentation de la position sociale. *Actes de la recherche en sciences sociales*, 52(1), 14–15.

Bourdieu, P. (1987). *Choses dites*. Éditions de Minuit, Paris.

Bourdieu, P. (1993). Effets de lieu. *La misère du monde*, 249–262.

Bourdieu, P. (1994). Stratégies de reproduction et modes de domination. *Actes de la recherche en sciences sociales*, 105(1), 3–12.

Bourdieu, P. and Champagne, P. (1992). Les exclus de l'intérieur. *Actes de la recherche en sciences sociales*, 91(1), 71–75.

Bourdieu, P. and Passeron, J.-C. (1970). *La reproduction : éléments pour une théorie du système d'enseignement*. Éditions de Minuit, Paris.

Broccolichi, S. (1995). Orientations et ségrégations nouvelles dans l'enseignement secondaire. *Sociétés contemporaines*, 21(1), 15–27.

Broccolichi, S. and van Zanten, A. (1997). Espaces de concurrence et circuits de scolarisation. L'évitement des collèges publics d'un district de la banlieue parisienne. *Les annales de la recherche urbaine*, 75, 5–17.

Broccolichi, S., Ben Ayed, C., Trancart, D. (2006). Les inégalités socio-spatiales d'éducation. Processus ségrégatifs, capital social et politiques territoriales. Report, Ministry of National Education, the Ministry of Research and DATAR, Paris.

Caro, P., Rouault, R., Cassan, D., Hérin, R. (2010). *Atlas des fractures scolaires en France : une école à plusieurs vitesses*. Éditions Autrement, Paris.

Charmes, É. (2007). Carte scolaire et "clubbisation" des petites communes périurbaines. *Sociétés contemporaines*, 67(3), 67–94.

Cousin, O. (1993). L'effet établissement. Construction d'une problématique. *Revue française de sociologie*, 34(3), 395-419.

Cousin, O. (2000). Politiques et effets-établissements dans l'enseignement secondaire. In *L'école, l'état des savoirs*, Van Zanten, A. (ed.). La Découverte, Paris.

Delvaux, B. and van Zanten, A. (2006). Les établissements scolaires et leur espace local d'interdépendance. *Revue française de pédagogie. Recherches en éducation*, 156, 5–8.

Dubet, F. and Duru-Bellat, M. (2006). Carte scolaire : la fin d'un tabou. *Le Monde* [Online]. Available at: https://www.lemonde.fr/idees/article/2006/09/08/carte-scolaire-la-fin-d-un-tabou-par-francois-dubet-et-marie-duru-bellat_811039_3232.html.

Fack, G. and Grenet, J. (2009). Sectorisation des collèges et prix des logements à Paris. *Actes de la recherche en sciences sociales*, 180, 44–62.

Fack, G., Grenet, J., Benhenda, A. (2014). *L'impact des procédures de sectorisation et d'affectation sur la mixité sociale et scolaire dans les lycées d'Île-de-France*. Institut des Politiques Publiques, Paris.

Felouzis, G. (2003a). La ségrégation ethnique au collège et ses conséquences. *Revue française de sociologie*, 44(3), 413–447.

Felouzis, G. (2003b). *Les effets d'établissement à l'université : de nouvelles inégalités ? Les mutations actuelles de l'Université*. Presses Universitaires de France, Paris.

Felouzis, G. (2009). Systèmes éducatifs et inégalités scolaires : une perspective internationale [Online]. Available at: https://journals.openedition.org/sociologies/2977#notes.

Felouzis, G., Maroy, C., van Zanten, A. (2013). *Les marchés scolaires : sociologie d'une politique publique d'éducation*. Presses Universitaires de France, Paris.

François, J.-C. (1996). Discontinuités dans la ville l'espace des collèges de l'agglomération parisienne, 1982–1992. PhD Thesis [Online]. Available at: http://cybergeo.revues.org/1851.

François, J.-C. (2002). Évitement à l'entrée en sixième et division sociale de l'espace scolaire à Paris. *L'Espace géographique*, 31(4), 307–327.

François, J.-C. (2007). La carte scolaire en ses contours. La métropole parisienne. *Centralités, inégalités, proximités*, 185–207.

François, J.-C. and Poupeau, F. (2004). L'évitement scolaire et les classes moyennes à Paris. *Éducation et sociétés*, 14, 51–66.

François, J.-C. and Poupeau, F. (2005). De l'espace résidentiel à l'espace scolaire, les pratiques d'évitement scolaire en Île-de-France. Ministry of National Education and DATAR, Paris.

François, J.-C. and Poupeau, F. (2008a). *Le sens du placement : ségrégation résidentielle et ségrégation scolaire*. Raisons d'agir, Paris.

François, J.-C. and Poupeau, F. (2008b). Les déterminants socio-spatiaux du placement scolaire. *Revue française de sociologie*, 49(1), 93–126.

Frouillou, L. (2016). Admission post-bac : un "libre choix" sous contrainte algorithmique [Online]. Available at: http://www.jssj.org/article/admission-post-bac-un-libre-choix-sous-contrainte-algorithmique/.

Frouillou, L. (2017). *Ségrégations universitaires en Île-de-France : inégalités d'accès et trajectoires étudiantes*. Observatoire de la vie étudiante éditions/La Documentation Française, Paris.

Frouillou, L. and Moulin, L. (2019). Les trajectoires socialement et spatialement différenciées des étudiants franciliens. *Formation emploi*, 145(1), 7–28.

Frouillou, L., Pin, C., Van Zanten, A. (2019). Le rôle des instruments dans la sélection des bacheliers dans l'enseignement supérieur. La nouvelle gouvernance des affectations par les algorithmes. *Sociologie*, 2(10) [Online]. Available at: http://journals.openedition.org/sociologie/5543.

Garcia, S. (2013). *À l'école des dyslexiques : naturaliser ou combattre l'échec scolaire ?* La Découverte, Paris.

Hérin, R. (1993a). La formation scolaire : les dimensions géographiques de l'inégalité des chances. *Espace, populations, sociétés*, 11(2), 343–354.

Hérin, R. (1993b). Y a-t-il une façade atlantique de la formation scolaire et universitaire ? *Norois*, 157(1), 137–153.

Hérin, R., Rouault, R., Veschambre, V. (1994). Atlas de la France scolaire : de la maternelle au lycée. Centre d'études régionales et d'aménagement, Montpellier.

Lahire, B. (ed.) (2019). *Enfances de classe. De l'inégalité parmi les enfants*. Le Seuil, Paris.

Léger, A. and Tripier, M. (1986). *Fuir ou construire l'école populaire ?* Méridiens Klincksieck, Paris.

Ly, S.T. and Riegert, A. (2015). Mixité sociale et scolaire, ségrégation inter- et intra-établissement dans les collèges et lycées français. Study, CNESCO, Paris.

Merle, P. (2011). La carte scolaire et son assouplissement. Politique de mixité sociale ou de ghettoïsation des établissements ? *Sociologie*, 2, 7–50.

Merle, P. (2012). *La ségrégation scolaire*. La Découverte, Paris [Online]. Available at: http://www.sudoc.fr/160866162 [accessed May 25, 2012].

Moignard, B. (2007). Le collège comme espace de structuration des bandes d'adolescents dans les quartiers populaires : le poids de la ségrégation scolaire. *Revue française de pédagogie. Recherches en éducation*, 4(158), 31–42.

Musselin, C. (2001). *La longue marche des universités françaises*. Presses Universitaires de France, Paris.

Oberti, M. (2005). Différenciation sociale et scolaire du territoire : inégalités et configurations locales. *Sociétés contemporaines*, 59–60, 13–42.

Oberti, M. (2007a). Le piège du libre choix scolaire. *Mouvements*, 52, 145–152.

Oberti, M. (2007b). *L'école dans la ville : ségrégation, mixité, carte scolaire*. Presses de Science Po, Paris.

Oberti, M. and Savina, Y. (2019). Urban and school segregation in Paris: The complexity of contextual effects on school achievement: The case of middle schools in the Paris metropolitan area. *Urban Studies*, 56(15), 3117–3142.

Oberti, M., Préteceille, E., Rivière, C. (2012). Les effets de l'assouplissement de la carte scolaire dans la banlieue parisienne. Report, Presses de Sciences Po, Paris.

Œuvrard, F. (2000). La construction des inégalités de scolarisation de la maternelle au lycée. *L'école, l'état des savoirs*, 311–321.

Œuvrard, F. (2011). Quels choix ? Pour quelle école ? *Revue française de pédagogie*, 75(2), 73–76.

Orange, S. (2010). Le choix du BTS. Entre construction et encadrement des aspirations des bacheliers d'origine populaire. *Actes de la recherche en sciences sociales*, 183(3), 32–47.

Orange, S. (2012). Interroger le choix des études supérieures. *Genèses*, 89(4), 112–127.

Palheta, U. (2011). Enseignement professionnel et classes populaires : comment s'orientent les élèves "orientés". *Revue française de pédagogie*, 175(2), 59–72.

Palheta, U. (2012). *La domination scolaire : sociologie de l'enseignement professionnel et de son public*. Presses Universitaires de France, Paris.

Poullaouec, T. (2011). Choix du destin et destin du choix. *Revue française de pédagogie*, 175(2), 81–84.

Rapetti, D. (1990). Disparités sociales et retards scolaires en milieu urbain : l'exemple des collèges du Grand Nantes en 1985. *Espace, populations, sociétés*, 8(1), 159–162.

Renard, J.-P. (1990). Aspects de la préscolarité en France. *Espace, populations, sociétés*, 8(1), 63–71.

Rhein, C. (1997). De l'anamorphose en démographie. Polarisation sociale et flux scolaires dans la métropole parisienne. *Les annales de la recherche urbaine*, 75, 59–69.

Rhein, C., Le Pape, A., Grosbras, P.-A. (1999). Division sociale de l'espace et inégalités de la scolarisation. Report, LADYSS, Paris.

Ripoll, F. (2013). Quelle dimension spatiale des structures sociales chez Bourdieu ? Localisations résidentielles et jeux d'échelles. In *La distinction, trente ans après la distinction de Pierre Bourdieu*, Coulangeon, P., Duval, J. (eds). La Découverte, Paris.

Ripoll, F. and Tissot, S. (2010). La dimension spatiale des ressources sociales. *Regards sociologiques*, 40, 5–7.

Ripoll, F. and Veschambre, V. (2005). Sur la dimension spatiale des inégalités : contribution aux débats sur la "mobilité" et le "capital spatial". In *Rural-urbain. Nouveaux liens, nouvelles frontières*, Arlaud, S., Jean, Y., Royoux, D. (eds). Presses Universitaires de Rennes, Rennes.

Rouault, R. (2005). Les dimensions spatiales de la scolarisation, entre espaces prescrits et parcours choisis. *Espace populations sociétés*, 3, 355–366.

Terrier, C., Combe, J., Tercieux, O. (2019). Améliorer la mobilité des enseignants sans pénaliser les académies les moins attractives ? *Administration Education*, 163(3), 91–101.

Tissot, S. and Poupeau, F. (2005). La spatialisation des problèmes sociaux. *Actes de la recherche en sciences sociales*, 159(4), 4–9.

Veschambre, V. (2006). Penser l'espace comme dimension de la société. Pour une géographie sociale de plain-pied avec les sciences sociales. In *Penser et faire la géographie sociale. Contribution à une épistémologie de la géographie sociale*, Séchet, R., Veschambre, V. (eds). Presses universitaires de Rennes, Rennes.

Wilson, D. and Bridge, G. (2019). School choice and the city: Geographies of allocation and segregation. *Urban Studies*, 56(15), 3198–3215.

van Zanten, A. (1996). Fabrication et effets de la ségrégation scolaire. In *L'exclusion, l'état des savoirs*, Paugam, S. (ed.). La Découverte, Paris.

van Zanten, A (2001). *L'école de la périphérie : scolarité et ségrégation en banlieue*. Presses Universitaires de France, Paris.

van Zanten, A. (2009). *Choisir son école : stratégies familiales et médiations locales*. Presses Universitaires de France, Paris.

van Zanten, A. (2015). Les inégalités d'accès à l'enseignement supérieur. *Regards croisés sur l'économie*, 16(1), 80–92.

van Zanten, A. and Da Costa, S. (2013). La gestion de la carte scolaire dans la périphérie parisienne. Enjeux, dynamiques et limites de la gouvernance éducative locale. *Éducation et formations*, 83, 99–107.

van Zanten, A. and Obin, J.-P. (2010). *La carte scolaire*, 2nd edition. Presses universitaires de France, Paris.

2

Socio-spatial Inequalities and Intersectionality

Negar Élodie BEHZADI[1] and Lucia DIRENBERGER[2]
[1] *University of Bristol, UK*
[2] *Centre Maurice Halbwachs, CNRS, Paris, France*

The way in which space constructs and is itself constructed by social power relations is at the heart of several theoretical currents that have profoundly renewed sociological and geographical approaches. By power relations, we mean here structurally asymmetrical relationships, essentializing social groups and thus producing inequalities between social groups. The characteristics attributed to social groups are generally treated as immutable and arising from natural differences (Guillaumin 2016) between social groups. These include social power relations based on gender as well as on race, ethnicity, sexuality and class. These power relations are characterized by a specific unequal relationship: that of appropriation, which results in the exploitation of the body in general, and labor power in particular (Guillaumin 2016). The concept of "social power relations" is not necessarily asserted as such by all the authors we quote. Nevertheless, beyond the question of inequalities, what they have in common is that they underline the existence and the importance of structural asymmetries based on exploitation and/or oppression.

This chapter presents three main theoretical currents that enable us to think about the links between power relations, inequalities and spaces.

The first part of this chapter (section 2.1) presents three currents that feed into the reflections on socio-spatial inequalities and the interweaving of power relations:

feminist analyses, queer approaches and postcolonial perspectives. These three currents are converging in contemporary academic work. This chapter also draws on a central concept which was initially developed through critical race studies and which has significantly influenced and transformed all three theoretical approaches: the concept of intersectionality (Davis 1983; Crenshaw 1989, 1991; Hill Collins 2000; Yuval-Davis 2006; Hill Collins and Bilge 2016). This section discusses both Anglophone and Francophone theoretical bodies of work, which are often considered separately.

Following this initial theoretical part, this chapter proposes three themes to grasp the socio-spatial processes at work in power relations. Section 2.2 is devoted to the division of labor. Space gives structure to the production of socio-professional inequalities at different scales, and the processes of domination at work at a given scale have effects on inequalities at other scales. The following section (section 2.3) deals with the nation and processes of othering. Space is used by the majority group to produce the othering of minority social groups. In other words, the assignment of minorities to otherness – which is reflected in the attribution of minorities to dangerous, threatening and violent behaviors, or even as oppressed and incapacitated – is co-constructed by the "assignment to a territoriality" (Hancock 2008). Finally, we show in the last section (section 2.4) that space is a crucial issue for restoring *agency*, that is, the capacity of minorities to act. Indeed, individual and collective attempts to deal with, negotiate, contest and subvert the relationships of domination and socio-spatial inequalities are notably realized through the creation of places, flows and mobilities with a view to achieving greater social and spatial justice.

These themes, mainly based on the French context, do not of course exhaust the subjects on which feminist analyses, queer approaches and postcolonial perspectives have profoundly renewed knowledge – and the very way knowledge is produced. These three themes do not claim to be exhaustive in their consideration of the articulations of social relations and socio-spatial inequalities. On the contrary, the epistemological positioning chosen insists on the need to take into account the social, historical, economic and political context of the production of social relations of class, gender and race. Finally, this chapter draws on readings by geographers, while leaving room for approaches from other disciplines, recognizing that contemporary geography draws on largely multidisciplinary perspectives.

2.1. Relationships between power relations, inequalities and space

In the 1970s, innovative feminist analyses emerged in different academic spaces. In France, the pioneers of materialist feminism, Christine Delphy, Nicole-Claude

Mathieu, Paola Tabet and Colette Guillaumin, revisited the concept of "class", derived from Marxist theories, to analyze the production of a class of women. They thus pointed out the exploitation of women's work in the service of the patriarchy, interwoven with a capitalist economy. The assignment of women to the domestic space is a central element of this exploitation, which leads more broadly to the oppression of women in this feminist materialist analysis (Abreu 2017). Feminist research in geography would go on to analyze this construction of the dichotomy between private and public space. Jacqueline Coutras' pioneering Francophone work conceptualizes women's "spatial duty", involving the reproduction of the home and containment around domestic space (Direnberger and Schmoll 2014). During the same period, the work of feminist geographers in the UK and the USA criticizes the masculinism of geography in English-speaking countries in the construction of knowledge, and in particular the exclusion of women in the production of geographical knowledge (Monk and Hanson 1982). They denounce the normalization of the idea of universal knowledge based on a dominant scientific rationality in the quantitative geography of the time (Oberhaueser 2002). Like feminists in France, geographers in the UK and the United States analyzed the dichotomy between private and public (McDowell et al. 1984).

Thus, feminist and gender studies have shown that space and scale are not neutral from the point of view of social gender relations. They deconstruct the supposed immutability of spatial categories such as the public/private dichotomy and show that, within this context of gender hierarchies, men and women do not have the same access to, or uses of, different spaces (Hancock 2002; Marius and Raibaud 2013; Blidon 2019). Because of the assignment of women to the domestic space and the male violence they experience in various spaces, women are indeed constrained in their occupancy of places and spaces. The freedom to move around, to enter or leave a space is at the heart of many feminist assertions. For their part, lesbian geographies contest their "natural" invisibility in the city (Cattan and Clerval 2011). As Karine Duplan summarizes, "they pave the way for new ways of understanding space, for new ways of producing spaces, which are more informal, less territorialized and less visible, with ephemeral and shifting localizations" (Duplan 2012, §19).

Queer studies, based on postmodernism and feminist theories, introduce a new turn in the consideration of gender in socio-spatial dynamics. Based on the pioneering work of philosopher Judith Butler and Jack Halberstam, a researcher in literature and gender studies, queer studies challenge the heteronormativity of society, which is based on the woman/man dichotomy. Instead, they take into account "the proliferation of alternative genders and sexualities" (Dupont and Prieur 2012; Prieur 2015). They thus expose the imposition of a binary and heterosexual gender norm. Cha Prieur asserts the need to take into account alternative femininities and masculinities, such as "female masculinities, male femininities, queers, trans FtoM [Female to Male] and MtoF [Male to Female], drag queens and drag kings. I didn't want us to forget all these in-betweens who, by interfering with the complementarity of masculinity and femininity, destabilize them, deconstruct them and allow us to take a critical look at gender and sexuality norms" (Dupont and Prieur 2012, §19). Queer geographies then set out to "study places and communities that resist different kinds of normativities (indicative of power relations and domination) and see through what political, social and cultural actions they carry out" (Prieur 2015, §16).

Another theoretical trend that helps us understand power relations is postcolonial studies. Postcolonial theories emerged in the 1980s, mainly in the American and British academic space. They have been pursued by researchers from ex-colonized societies, or under Western hegemony, such as Frantz Fanon, Homi Bhabha, Edward Said and Partha Chatterjee. Postcolonial theories are not uniform but what they have in common, despite their diversity, are their analyses of forms of imperialism and colonialism (Young 2003). Postcolonial studies in geography (Blunt and Rose 1994; Sidaway 2000; Blunt and McEwan 2002; Jazeel 2014; Woon 2015; Radcliffe 2017) have focused on "the links between representations of space, practices of space, identities, territories, and powers", and have set out to "reconsider the question of spatiality as it relates to colonial power" (Blais 2009, p. 146). In the analysis of colonial situations and moments, these works were interested in "the production of geographical knowledge, colonial representations and imaginary geographies of space", but also in "geographies of contact, conquest, colonial administration, diasporas and migrations" (*ibid.*, p. 147) by questioning the production of spaces and their social effects in a colonial situation. As Hélène Blais summarizes, "there is a general agreement in these approaches that spatiality is linked to practices of domination" (*ibid.*) and includes both a discursive and material dimension. Postcolonial studies in geography also analyze how colonization affects spaces long after independence, and how colonial mindsets are maintained in a neoliberal capitalist order within societies. This body of work has also analyzed social and political mobilizations within (ex-)colonized societies, as well as the processes of subjectivation of (ex-)colonized individuals, thus bringing (ex-)colonized subjects back to the fore.

These approaches nurture a fruitful critical dialog around power relations. We would like to highlight three contributions of the confluence between feminist, queer and postcolonial theories.

First, on the epistemological level, these three theoretical currents have emphasized the importance of situatedness and reflexivity in the production of knowledge. The consideration of situatedness and reflexivity is exercised on two dimensions. The first is that of the individual who produces academic knowledge (Haraway 1988). The producers of geographical knowledge, that is, geographers, are not free from any power relation or social hierarchy. Feminist, queer and postcolonial theories have thus contributed to making this positionality of geographers explicit and have shown that it has an effect on the very definition of spaces and its analyses (Rose 1993). The inequalities in the spaces of knowledge production are based on a relationship of dichotomies such as man/woman, white/racialized, cis-heterosexual/queer, on the one hand, and intellect/body, reason/emotion, culture/nature, public/private, center/periphery, visible/invisible, universal/individual, on the other hand. It is then a question of reclaiming the situatedness of knowledge production (Haraway 1988), that is to say situating in terms of power relations the experiences that produce both minority and majority knowledge. By being reflexive, geographers can thus shed light on how knowledge is situated. The second dimension captured by the work of taking situated knowledge and reflexivity is the academic discipline itself, that is, geography as an institution (re)producing power relations, and thus a system of exploitation, oppression and inequality (Rose 1993; Jazeel 2012, 2014). As Florence Deprest summarizes, much Anglophone work has analyzed how geographers have contributed to the imperial and colonial dominations of European metropolises, producing, in particular, "geographical knowledge and imaginaries as instruments of symbolic oppression and social control in colonial contexts" (Deprest 2014, p. 275). This expertise of geographers relied in particular on processes of categorization of populations and territories, and on environmental determinism, which served to legitimize and administer the European colonial enterprise (*ibid.*, p. 275). The (re)production of social hierarchies and inequalities through discipline did not cease after official independence. Recent work in the geography of English-speaking countries rethinks the link to this imperialist past through the prism of decolonial theories, questioning the feasibility of a political project of decolonizing knowledge, curricula, research practices and methodologies in the present (Pualani Louis 2007; Daigle and Sundberg 2017; Esson et al. 2017; Radcliffe 2017; de Leeuw and Hunt 2018; Craggs 2019; Ferretti 2019).

Second, many feminist, queer and postcolonial theories underscore the need to work on the interweaving of social relations of power on the basis of sex as well as gender identity, sexuality, race, class, ethnicity, caste and religion in specific configurations and contexts. Yet it is mostly feminist intersectional theories, as we pointed out at the beginning of this introduction, that have made a major contribution to these analyses. The concept of intersectionality, coined in American academia by legal scholar Kimberlé Crenshaw (1989, 1991), comes from black feminism, a current of thought notably supported by authors like Gloria T. Hull, Barbara Smith, Audre Lorde, bell hooks, and by collectives such as the Combahee River Collective, some of whose texts are brought together in collective works such as *All the Women Are White, All the Blacks Are Men, But Some of Us are Brave* or *This Bridge Called My Back*, published in 1982 and 1981, respectively. As the latter shows, black feminism was in dialogue early on with Latina, Asian and Indigenous feminists living in the Americas, who also questioned white feminism and the belief in the homogeneity of the female class. Together, they participated in the development of a *Third World Feminism* that sought to make visible and politicize the experiences of racialized women. In this context, critical race studies and the concept of intersectionality have also entered into dialogue with other postcolonial feminists, particularly their critiques of the way in which some Western feminisms represent Southern women by constructing the idea of the "third world woman" to be saved by white women (Mohanty 1988). For the postcolonial feminist theorist Chandra Talpade Mohanty (1988), Western feminism homogenizes "third world" women, those from Africa and Asia, from "developing" countries. The creation of this category of third world women erases the diversity of experiences and reproduces the idea of ignorant Southern women, victims of gendered oppressions rooted in family and tradition, in contrast to Western women who are educated and have freedoms with regard to their movements and sexuality. According to the feminist author, the creation of this hierarchy is a colonialist act. The scientific uses of intersectionality in France were first nurtured by the translated texts of American black feminist theorists and focused on what was happening in America. Whether in the scientific or political realm, these texts represent a compass on the interweaving of gender, class and race (Larcher 2018). For several years, research has contributed to centering the intersectional gaze on the French post-imperial context and enhancing the visibility of feminist, anti-imperialist, anti-racist, anti-colonial and anti-capitalist political thought developed by minority women, particularly black women (Germain and Larcher 2018). In particular, this research has drawn attention to the writings of Jane and Paulette Nardal, Gerty Archimède, Roberte Horth and Awa Thiam, but also collectives such as the *Unions des femmes communistes* in La Réunion, and the *Coordination des femmes noires* in Guadeloupe and Martinique. The concept of intersectionality is mobilized in these works, on the one hand, to make visible these minority voices in the political and social space, obscured by the major feminist movements, or by the translations of American authors; on the other hand, to contribute to the history of (ex)colonized women's movements in the French imperial context. These issues are all the more important given that critical studies of race and intersectionality are largely disqualified as a theoretical approach and tool for understanding social relations in France (Belkacem et al. 2019). In French geography, over the past 15 years, reflections on the interweaving of gender relations have been deployed in multiple fields: migration studies (Chaïb 2008; Moujoud 2008, 2012; Arab 2009; Schmoll 2020), violence against women (Lieber 2016), sexual and gender minorities (Prieur 2015; Arab et al. 2018), urban politics (Hancock and Lieber 2017) or racism and processes of exoticization and othering (Hancock 2008, 2011; Najib 2019).

Third, space is also a site where intersectional inequalities are produced, reproduced and contested (as will be developed later on in this chapter). Far from being isolated in the understanding of inequalities, however, the notion of space is also linked to another central geographical notion: "scale". Inequalities are constructed, deconstructed and contested at different scales: from the global to the domestic, via the local and the national. The consideration of power relations between men and women also leads to the consideration of previously ignored scales, such as the domestic space, the space of everyday life and bodies. These different scales of power have been taken into account in the study of the relationship between men and women. They are connected, and the understanding of inequalities often requires an exploration of their relationships: the global, in fact, is co-constructed by the local, and the lived and embodied experience of inequalities is intimately linked to the changes taking place at other scales (Marchand and Runyan 2000; Nagar et al. 2002). The work of deconstructing the private/public socio-spatial dichotomy, whose boundaries are shifting and reconfigured according to the social, political and economic context, is thus central to feminist and gender studies within geography. Beyond the work on "the position of women", this deconstruction work challenges the very conceptualizations of space and "allows us to envision a new structure of territorial occupancy focused on the fluidity of everyday connections" (Duplan 2012, §15). Women's bodies are a central scale in these feminist geographies. They allow us to take seriously the coercion, fear and violence that structure power relations between different groups (Fluri 2009; Dixon 2011, 2015; Pain and Staeheli 2014; Hyndman 2019).

2.2. Work and socio-spatial inequalities

2.2.1. *Theoretical perspectives on work and space*

Feminist, queer and postcolonial productions in geography have made important contributions to understanding how ideologies and experiences of work produce inequality, violence and exclusion (Hanson and Pratt 1995; Lawson 1999; McDowell 1999; Oberhauser 2002; England and Lawson 2005; Wolkowitz 2006; Wright 2006; Behzadi and Direnberger 2020). One of the major contributions of feminist geographers has been to highlight the gendered spatial division of labor that forms the basis of the capitalist and patriarchal system (McDowell et al. 1984).

Indeed, they have shown how, in Western and industrial societies, the notion of work was associated with paid, male work in the public sphere, while women's unpaid work in the domestic sphere was devalued and excluded from the definition of work itself. Marxist and materialist feminists have played a crucial role in critically analyzing the dichotomies of home/work, paid/unpaid work, public/private sphere, productive/reproductive work and the exclusions that these binary visions produced (Dalla Costa and James 1972; Vogel 1983; Gimenez 1998; Gimenez and Vogel 2005). In particular, they highlighted the way in which women's unrecognized labor in the home constituted a central mode of production in the organization of the capitalist economy (Vogel 1983; Delphy 1998; Gimenez 2005). Reproductive labor, defined to include (1) biological reproduction; (2) reproductive labor power; and (3) care (Teeple Hopkins 2015), is indeed, according to feminists, an integral part of a system that rests on the exploitation of women's bodies and the appropriation of their labor for capitalist accumulation and expansion (Federici 2004).

More recently, and following the growing interest in transnational analyses, feminist analyses of care have studied the power relations between the North and the South (see Chapter 3). Care covers activities that take care of the "needs of others", such as domestic work, care, education and support. It therefore involves the material, physical, relational, emotional and moral capacities of the people who perform it (Borgeaud-Garciandía et al. 2020, p. 13). It is organized according to an international division of labor characterized by its commodification in the North and South, and an exploitation of women from ex-colonial societies, which makes it possible for States to avoid investment in social protection systems (Borgeaud-Garciandía et al. 2020).

This national and international division of productive/reproductive labor is based on essentialist arguments about bodies. In this perspective, size, strength, fertility, sexuality, validity, intelligence and ability are all mediums for gender, class and racial hierarchies that determine who can do what kind of job and their position in the professional hierarchy. Men and women who do not respect these hierarchies by participating in forms of work that run counter to social expectations are considered as "not being in their place" or "out of place" (McDowell 1999; England and Lawson 2005; Behzadi 2019). Some of these workers are even constructed as abject and/or dirty (Tyler 2011; Simpson et al. 2012). Authors working on this issue have also more recently focused on the role of the body in experiencing these inequalities and exclusions, but also in resisting them (Wright 1997; McDowell 1999; Nagar et al. 2002; England and Lawson 2005). Bodies are disciplined by work, while embodied work practices constitute a site for micro-political struggles (McDowell and Court 1994; Dyer et al. 2008; McDowell 2009; McDowell et al. 2007). The following sections illustrate these theoretical discussions with empirical analyses on the French metropolitan territory. In section 2.2.2, we show how access to professional spaces is structured by gender, class and racial inequalities. In section 2.2.3, we focus on care work, which is massively assigned to women who are most affected by discrimination in the labor market and by administrative precariousness.

2.2.2. Professional spaces and segregation at different scales

The inequalities experienced by minority social groups are reflected in a socio-spatial segregation in professional spaces, which is organized at different levels: from the city to the neighborhood, and even within a single building. This segregation at work is understood here as the product of a (post)colonial economic, political and social order. The industrial development of the countries of the North is based on an international division of labor that spatially inscribes the relations of production, notably through imperial and colonial enterprises. This is true of the distribution of economic activities, of the circulation of goods but also of the mobility of people, on which we reflect in more detail (see Chapter 3). In fact, in ex-colonial European societies in general, and in France in particular, the industrial and economic development of the 1960s and 1970s was made possible by the importation of workers, especially from ex-colonized societies whose economies had been ravaged by colonization. From the 1960s onwards, the importation of labor from the Maghreb, sub-Saharan Africa, the West Indies, Reunion, and French Guiana increased (Sayad 1999; Ndiaye 2009). Foreign workers and workers from (post)colonial immigration[1] were recruited into professional sectors marked by their onerous working conditions and were assigned to positions at the bottom of the professional hierarchy (Ndiaye 2009, p. 74).

Since the 1950s, the construction sector has been an employment sector that has made use of the abundance of foreign labor, particularly from post-colonial immigrants. There was also a long-standing use of foreign labor in the metallurgy sector, but this intensified from the end of the 1960s. The automobile industry was another particularly important sector for migrants in the 1970s, in connection with the increase in production rates and the fragmentation of work, which led to an increase in the number of specialized workers (Pitti 2008, pp. 98–99). Since then, the geographical distribution of migration in metropolitan France has partly reflected

---

1. We define persons descended from postcolonial immigration by the fact that they are assigned to an otherness, repositioned as different, in the view of republican ethnocentrism. The latter thus separates the Others, people from postcolonial immigrations, from "Us, the recognized citizens, children of the fatherland or those assimilated to a white genealogy" (Boubeker and Hajjat 2008, p. 13).

the distribution of the industries that primarily use this labor force: large urban centers for the construction industry, and the Île-de-France, North and East of France for the metallurgical and automotive industries.

However, the French/foreign labor dichotomy does not exhaust these professional socio-spatial segregations. Professional and spatial hierarchies are built on logics of ethno-racial assignments that divide and hierarchize French citizens. From 1963 to 1982, the Bureau for the Development of Migration (Bumidom) organized the emigration of approximately 160,000 women from Reunion, Martinique and Guadeloupe to mainland France (Paris 2020, p. 357). This labor force was directed to the professions of domestic service, hospital workers, community workers and laborers, according to France's needs (Ndiaye 2009, pp. 69–70). The goal was to provide French nationals for the lower ranks of the civil service, particularly in the then expanding service sector (Ndiaye 2009, pp. 69–70). It was also to regulate the demographics in the West Indies, and to counteract social protest movements. Migration was thus a political management tool of an imperial center with respect to its margins.

As Black immigrants, as early as the 1960s, women from Reunion and the Caribbean spoke of the difficulties associated with racism in the workplace: "The acerbic or paternalistic remarks of colleagues referring to them as blacks, that is, as idle people who prefer to party and nap" (Ndiaye 2009, p. 70). As we will see later, this situation was not without individual resistance. As a result of the economic crisis, but also because of the racism suffered, there was a weakening of migration from the West Indies in the 1990s.

While foreign workers of a postcolonial immigrant background are still over-represented in the construction sector and in particularly devalued jobs (Jounin 2009), there was a socio-professional diversification of people of a postcolonial immigrant background in concurrence with the economic crisis of the 1980s and 2000s: intermediate professions, managers and professionals, students, etc. (Ndiaye 2009, p. 75). This diversification did not, however, result in a reduction in socio-spatial inequalities in the 2010s, as research on the cleaning, restaurant and hotel sectors has shown.

Employment and working conditions in the hotel–café–restaurant sector are generally unattractive. This is a more feminized sector: although the proportion of women in the sector's workforce has declined, it remains higher than in the French economy as a whole (48.9% versus 43.4% for the period 2006–2008) (Pinna 2013, p. 23). Young employees with few qualifications and little experience are also very present. From the point of view of gender relations, a "dual market" of employment can be observed within this sector itself: "A relatively more qualified market, access to which is reserved more for men, on the one hand, and a 'transitional labor market' in which the positions are low-qualified, female and open to inexperienced employees, on the other" (Pinna 2013, p. 23). Low-skilled jobs are unevenly distributed between white and racialized people. This division of labor has direct effects on the spatial organization of occupational locations. Thus, there is spatial segregation from what is visible or invisible from the clients' point of view: men from post-colonial immigrant backgrounds are recruited to work as dishwashers and cleaners in communal areas, while non-white women are assigned to clean rooms. Generally speaking, racialized people tend to be relegated to back-office positions, that is, positions in which employees do not come into contact with the clients, or do so as little as possible, and must remain inconspicuous. The demand for invisibility of the tasks, and of those who do them, leads to difficult working hours: shift work, adapted daily according to the customers' reservations, etc. Front-office positions, which are visible work, are better paid, valued by managers and clients alike, and often allow for greater autonomy in carrying out tasks. They are primarily assigned to white employees, especially in the luxury hotel industry. Thus, as Pinna shows, "the organization of work and the rigid boundary between front and back office follow a gendered and ethnic division of labor" (Pinna 2013, p. 25).

This division between back-office and front-office can also be found in restaurant chains serving less privileged social classes. From a participant observation as a waitress in a French chain restaurant in a working-class neighborhood of Paris, Marie Mathieu also notes "the more general invisibility of racialized kitchen employees [...] the vast majority of whom are men of Malian and Senegalese origin – who, outside of the times dedicated to staff meals, cannot circulate in the restaurant and remain hidden from the view of customers during their work hours" (Mathieu 2019, p. 18). The bar and kitchens appear to be masculine spaces, while the dining room is assigned to women, and this feminine professional space imposes particularly difficult constraints on body visibility. Consequently, it is the female workers' bodies themselves that become a territory of struggle between economic exploitation and resistance. In the welcome booklet given to the waitresses, "eye, cheek, lip and nail make-up according to extremely precise rules" is imposed, as well as a "neat and elegant" hairstyle, the wearing of "flesh-colored tights in the summer – black in the winter" and of "plain, black, closed shoes, such as pumps with heels of at least 3 cm", as well as jewelry. This construction of the body suggests "a model of feminine elegance marked by social class", at a distance from a popular femininity with no pretense of luxury restoration (Mathieu 2019, p. 19). To conform to these standards, women's bodies suffer (muscle and joint pain, blisters, being cold). Even though waitresses' pay is low, the costs incurred to look the part are significant: the purchase of clothes, shoes, and makeup products, the use of hairdressing and beauty services (manicure, waxing). Moreover, it relies on work time that is invisible: the time to change clothes in the workplace, sometimes several times a day, but also the consumer's time in stores to buy the necessary professional equipment (Mathieu 2019). The "work of formatting bodies extends the professional activities of appearance to the domestic sphere and calls into question the boundary between professional and personal time-spaces" (Mathieu 2019, p. 25). We then observe an extension of the professional space into "spaces considered the most private, such as bathrooms" (Mathieu 2019, p. 17). This extension implies free labor in the home – laundry and ironing of work clothes in the "extension of activities associated with their position as women in the family" (Mathieu 2019, p. 26). But this production of female bodies is even more burdensome for racialized waitresses. Indeed, the imposed femininity is a femininity that relies on a valorization of whiteness. On the one hand, more white women are hired into these menial front office positions. On the other hand, the characteristics associated with non-whiteness – "big" hair or hair that is not straight – are then particularly sanctioned and require a "heavier daily workload to fit the chain model" (Mathieu 2019, p. 28).

The segregations of class, gender, race and nationality thus shape the geography of work, the division between the visible and the invisible, and draw a space saturated with power relations from the widest scales of the international division of labor to the most intimate scales of the conformation, exploitation and resistance of bodies at work.

2.2.3. *Care work and assignment to private space*

Women have long been sidelined in the analysis of the links between migration and the division of labor in Francophone research. When they have been mentioned, the focus on female migrants arriving as part of a family group has obscured many other situations, such as women arriving alone and being deprived of papers and rights, for example (Chaïb 2008; Moujoud 2008). Moreover, research on women has long favored an evolutionary approach that supports "the idea of a linear change in the situation of migrant women [...] [establishing] from the outset a contrast between the societies (or sometimes the 'cultures') of departure and arrival" (Moujoud 2008). In this analysis, arriving in France mechanically represents an improvement, access to "modernity". However, migration and employment policies have assigned the work of migrant and racialized women to low-skilled, low-valued and low-paying jobs in France (Bentouhami 2017). While care work is a professional activity that can be performed within the public space (in state institutions and private companies), it is very often performed in the private sphere (in the homes of employers). Thus, the assignment to domestic work reinforces the gendered opposition between public and private spaces.

In France, migrant and racialized women have historically been assigned to domestic and care work. This assignment has been organized by the State within the framework of Bumidom: when migration from Reunion to France was at its height, in 1975, women represented 53% of migrants (Paris 2020, p. 382). This migratory system applied to Reunion had three main objectives: to reduce the fertility of the Reunionese population (which the French state considered problematic at the time), to stifle anti-colonial movements and to provide a workforce for service jobs, in particular those of domestic workers, housekeepers, hospital workers or community workers. Thus, "in practice, women from Reunion and the Caribbean have been massively assigned to 'dirty jobs', literally 'dirty work', involving the use of their own labor" (Paris 2020, pp. 393–394). Whether as a "ward girl" in a hospital or as a domestic worker, they perform the same tasks: preparing meals, serving, feeding, caring for, washing people, making beds, cleaning rooms and washing dishes. The migrants from the West Indies and Reunion would take care of the bodies in the metropolis, mostly white, and the dirt that these bodies produce in socially and economically devalued jobs. For Myriam Paris, West Indian and Reunionese immigration thus constitutes "an important step in the racialization of domestic work in France" (Paris 2020, p. 395).

Even today, many racialized women work in the care sector as nannies, housekeepers and care assistants (Moujoud 2012; Ibos 2016; Damamme et al. 2017). In addition to being assigned to the domestic space, migrant women face extremely precarious working conditions. Many of them do not have a residence permit, which prevents them from accessing labor law and, more generally, many social rights. By mobilizing Abdelmalek Sayad's conceptual framework on the different "ages" of male migration, Nasima Moujoud shows, for example, that Moroccan domestic workers in France have very different socioeconomic profiles. Yet, "exclusion from rights unites them" (Moujoud 2018, pp. 277–278) and their living and working conditions as domestic workers are very poor. They are poorly paid or not paid at all, many have their passports confiscated by their employers, are poorly housed, and are separated from their relatives against their will. Moreover, fear of the police, because of their legal situation, forces them to rarely leave or remain confined to the space where they work and/or live. Many of them (re)marry in order to escape undocumented status, but marriage often results in assignment to domestic labor, "which includes sexuality and control of forms of subjectivity because they are women and undocumented" (Moujoud 2018, p. 284). Thus, migrant women implement individual strategies and convert their social ties into bonds of solidarity, both to escape undocumented status and domestic labor, and thus the confinement that division of labor and migration policies impose on them (Moujoud 2018).

A significant amount of feminist research has for a long time shown that public spaces (the space of the professional world, social and political life, social networks, and leisure) are open in a way that is advantageous to men, and the "private spaces of everyday life" (the space of the home, the family, the school, the supply of provisions, the neighborhood) are assigned to women (Hancock 2002; Marius and Raibaud 2013). Through these examples, we observe that the division of labor reconfigures the production of private and public spaces. The partial substitution of racialized women for white women in private spaces does not challenge the private/public dichotomy. The continuity of white middle- and upper-class men's socio-spatial privileges has, for the most part, remained unchanged.

2.3. Othering processes and spaces: the place of the other

The processes of othering are based on various ideologies, one of which is Orientalism, whose analysis by Edward Said constitutes a founding work of postcolonial theories. Edward Said defines Orientalism as a "style of thought based on the ontological and epistemological distinction between the 'East' and (most often) the 'West'" (Said 1980, p. 15), which is part of an enterprise of European domination (Said 1980).

In this analysis, territory is one of the fundamental elements of Orientalism. Indeed, otherness is particularly inscribed in a spatial distance: "All we have to do is draw these borders in our minds, and they become 'them' and their territory and mentality are designated as different from ours" (Said 1980, p. 70).

Articulated in various but central ways with Orientalism in (ex-)colonial societies, national ideology is also an ideology that rests on a process of othering. National ideology is based on the idea of the nation as an "imagined community" (Anderson 1983), that is, a symbolic and material construction that organizes connections, distances and exclusions between individuals and social groups. Here again, it is based on socio-spatial distributions and a double dividing line: one that forms the border with the outside of the national community and one that hierarchizes individuals and social groups within the national community itself, thus creating a "double process of othering" (Jarry-Omarova and Marteu 2013).

In the 2000s, feminist geopolitics (Fluri 2009; Dixon 2011, 2015; Pain and Staeheli 2014; Hyndman 2019) fed into these debates by shifting the attention toward certain neglected actors, actresses and objects, which are nonetheless at the heart of geopolitical stakes: women, children, immigrants, asylum seekers, prisoners, the everyday, the home, the body, the intimate, the emotional. It is indeed a question of revisiting the conventional repertoire of geopolitics – the nation, but also the State, borders, security, militarism, etc. At the same time, feminist geopolitics proposes new objects of analysis such as trauma, violence, terrorism and security through theoretical and methodological approaches that capture their complexity in the "materiality of everyday life". It is within this everyday life that bodies, subjectivities, practices and discourses become the centers of geo-political conflicts (Dixon and Marston 2011).

In the following sections, we focus precisely on developing the way in which, in specific cases, the various processes of othering mobilize spatial imaginaries and create hierarchies that are fundamental to experiences and subjectivations. We first observe the way in which (1) lines of division are constructed to build and contrast "us" versus "them", then (2) how these lines of division are translated into everyday spaces.

2.3.1. *The dividing lines between "us" and "them"*

Manifesting the hierarchies between groups and between societies, the lines of division between "us" and "them" are built on "territorial assignments – because the social representations concerning persons or groups are accompanied by spatial representations, concerning the spaces associated with these 'dominated' groups or persons" (Hancock 2008, p. 117). Gender is a major issue in this production of dividing lines. In the war against terrorism launched by the U.S. administration in 2001, European and North American powers have set themselves up as guarantors of the defense and protection of women's rights in predominantly Muslim societies. The "suffering of women" is thus a discursive pattern mobilized by international organizations and conservative and liberal political forces in the United States to legitimize military intervention (Eisenstein 2004). The discourses and representations of women in the context of the "war against terrorism" thus mobilize Islam as a distinctive feature; Muslim women are said to experience specific suffering. It is thus, through the prism of religion and/or culture, that the problems of women in predominantly Muslim societies are often evoked, erasing the diversity of these societies, as well as the power relations at work. On the one hand, violence against women is described as specific to these societies; on the other hand, the values of freedom, emancipation and self-determination of women are spatialized in the United States and Europe (Bahramitash 2006; Mahmood 2008; Kian 2010; Abu-Lughod 2013). This "suffering of Muslim women", which in theory deprives them of any capacity for action, justifies humanitarian aid and military intervention (Daulatzai 2006; Abirafeh 2009).

A similar process is at play for sexual minorities. As Alexandre Jaunait, Amélie Le Renard and Élisabeth Marteu summarize, respect for the rights of minorities, defined as "the vanguard of democratic modernity [...] allows us to oppose a European and Western 'us' that protects sexual minorities to a non-Western 'them' newly characterized by a homophobia and sexism thought of as cultural. The rhetoric of sexual democracy thus participates in the production of external and internal borders, altering at the same time, in a block mentality, a set of countries considered as non-democratic – mainly so-called 'Muslim' countries" (Jaunait et al. 2013, p. 10). This "homonationalism" also translates spatially into the control of people's mobility and the strengthening of borders. Indeed, these discourses are also mobilized by anti-migrant actors, allowing for a distinction between "good" and "bad" migrant women (Arab et al. 2018), with this designation implying selection, thus promoting the restriction of mobilities of people from spaces constructed as inherently hostile to sexual minorities.

The dividing line between "us" and "them" thus separates groups located in different territories, but also within a territory or national space (Hancock 2008). In France, cities and working-class neighborhoods are spaces that are particularly stigmatized, thought of and administered through political (see Chapter 7) and media categories that "[carry] [...] the risk of obscuring the mechanisms of domination, whether economic, social or racist", and which thus help to lay "the foundations for a despondent view" (Tissot and Poupeau 2005, p. 8). By closely interweaving populations ("immigrants", "young people from immigrant backgrounds", etc.) and spaces ("suburbs", "housing estates", "sensitive neighborhoods", etc.), these categories produce "a homogenizing vision of populations that are *irreducibly different*" (*ibid.*). Thus, there is a "double assignment" of a social group to a territoriality and an identity, characterized by immigration, underqualification and unemployment both in public policy and media (Hancock 2008, p. 118). This double assignment is also characterized by a use of gender, as shown by Marion Dalibert's work on the media coverage of the association *Ni putes ni soumises* (NPNS) [*Not prostitutes not dominated* in English]. In 2003, the actions of NPNS, in particular the march of the women of the districts for equality and against the ghetto, had the consequence of putting sexism "on suburban housing estates" into the media and on the political agenda. The media framing of this movement is not so much about the movement itself or its actions as it is about the "sexism of the suburbs": "Journalists have merely staged a collective victim, 'non-white' teenage girls and young women, against a culprit, the 'young boys of the suburbs'" (Dalibert 2013, §3). This framing, operated both by journalists but also by the government – Prime Minister

Jean-Pierre Raffarin announced measures to fight sexism "in the suburbs" – contributes to interweaving the public problem of the suburbs and ethno-racial minorities forged since the 1980s with the older imaginary of the "Arab man" as a sexual aggressor (Guénif-Souilamas 2006; Dalibert 2013; Shepard 2017). In this framing, white women and men are not mentioned as either victims or perpetrators of this violence. Similarly, other spaces (such as school, university, professional, media, political, cultural fields, etc.) are not described as spaces that produce violence against women. Fueled since the 2000s by multiple controversies around "gang rapes", "polygamy", "forced marriages" (Dagistanli and Grewal 2012), or the situation of sexual minorities (El-Tayeb 2012), this framing feeds the othering of "the suburbs". In turn, it represents a "racialized rhetoric of otherness that sketches a hollow image of a France attentive to women's rights and intransigent in matters of homophobia" (Fassin 2009, p. 49).

Seen exclusively through the prism of oppression and alienation, sexual and gender minorities can only emancipate themselves by accessing European modernity. This framing reduces their possibility of subjectivation as women or queer people, and conditions their presence in "host societies" to the expression of a sense of gratitude (El-Tayeb 2012, p. 80; Arab et al. 2018). The inscription of such framing in a spatial imaginary is not a French specificity. The city of Amsterdam, for example, is built on an opposition between the "modern gay identity" of the city center and those who are deprived of access to the city center, consigned to homophobia and a conservative culture (El-Tayeb 2012). On the one hand, there is the center, characterized by its picturesque architecture, so-called "metrosexual" culture, multicultural markets, liberal drug laws and international tourism – which also caters to a gay clientele. On the other hand, there are working-class neighborhoods like Bijlmer and Slotervaart, with cheap rent and substandard housing, massively occupied by non-white people, especially young and poor migrant workers, who embody a violent and dangerous otherness for the gay or heterosexual, local or international traveler.

2.3.2. The space of everyday life: the home of the "others" and the street that belongs to "us"

The processes of othering are rooted in the spaces of everyday life, whether in professional activities, as we have already seen, or in domestic activities. The professional segregation of people from the West Indies and Reunion who arrived under Bumidom between the 1960s and 1980s (mentioned in the previous section) was accompanied by large-scale access to small, often dilapidated housing in the working-class neighborhoods of Paris (from the 18th arrondissement to the 11th and

20th arrondissements, along Porte de Clignancourt-Barbès-Stalingrad-Oberkampf), as well as in the large suburban housing projects (Ndiaye 2009, p. 70). At the same time, African migrants also had difficulty finding decent housing, both in low-income housing projects and in the private market. Many families were housed in cramped and unsanitary apartments. The residential segregation of black people in France is thus based on professional segregation, through low salaries, but also on specific mechanisms of racial discrimination in access to housing (Célestine 2018, pp. 63–64). Black people are not the only racialized people to experience this segregation, as the situation of other social groups analyzed in this chapter shows. Indeed, many female Moroccan domestic workers in the 1980s and 1990s lived and grew old in *chambres de bonnes* (maids' rooms) in Paris (Moujoud 2008). Thus, processes of othering structure even the intimate spaces of the home, both for minority groups and for the majority group, which tends to benefit from a more diversified and better maintained housing stock.

Public space is also a major stake in the construction and reaffirmation of social race relations. This everyday violence and its link to national politics are particularly apparent in national contexts, where Muslim populations are minorities (Schenk et al. n.d). In Paris, Islamophobia is analyzed as a spatial organization that distinguishes spaces and places, such as the city center and the suburbs, private and public spaces, means of transportation and public institutions (Najib 2019; Najib and Hopkins 2019; Najib 2020). This socio-spatial violence is also gendered: women, because of their real or assumed affiliation to Islam, appear to be the main victims of Islamophobia in public space, whether in terms of discrimination or physical aggression (Najib 2019; Hancock and Mobillion 2019). Muslim women are more exposed to violence, discrimination and inequality in "socially valued" spaces, better served in terms of public services and more attractive in terms of access to employment, whereas they are less exposed in working-class neighborhoods and cities (Najib 2019, p. 22), which are more marked by unemployment and difficulties in accessing public services and housing. Moreover, according to facts recorded in 2015, 64% of Islamophobic acts suffered by women took place in a public institution, such as a town hall, school or hospital (Najib 2019, p. 21). If Islamophobia affects women in particular in their relationship to state institutions, it is because the legal framework and debates that have fueled the regulation of veils have fostered stigma, discrimination and violence against Muslim women (Hancock and Mobillion 2019). They are constructed as "guilty victims" who do not belong to the French national community. The Islamophobia that women experience in unequal access to public space and, with it, in access to social rights and public services thus constructs a second-rate citizenship for women who are French nationals, while it contributes to barriers and even disenfranchisement for foreigners.

2.4. Agency and minority spaces

2.4.1. *Theoretical and empirical perspectives on agency*

Minorities do not remain impassive when confronted with the relations of domination and their socio-spatial effects. To designate the diversity of positionings when faced with this situation, feminist theories have revised the concept of agency. By relying on poststructuralist theories while going beyond them, Judith Butler (1988, 1990) has redefined the notions of gender, sexuality and agency through her conceptualization of performativity. Opposing biological or purely cultural readings of gender, Butler argues that gender is the effect of a system of power produced by discourse(s) as well as realized/experienced through a series of ritualized and embodied acts. Because performance never repeats something identically, it produces an "incorrect copy" that also opens up spaces of subversion and resistance to gender norms and heteronormativity.

In the 1990s, increasing attention was given to the question of bodies in the social sciences in general, and in geography in particular. The body was conceptualized as a site of renegotiation and resistance, an approach that has been deepened by more recent theories that have sought to rematerialize processes of subjectification. Feminist geographers have emphasized how discursive constructions define socio-spatial and embodied inequalities (Nast and Pile 1998). At the same time, corporeal feminists have emphasized the importance of the "material weight" of bodies (Longhurst 2001, p. 5). The body, they argue, is the primary source of knowledge, experience and resistance. Bodies are not inert supports on which power relations are inscribed. Instead, they are "lived, embedded in systems of meaning and representation" (McDowell and Sharp 2014, p. 4), constructed through a history of gendered and ethnoracial hierarchies (McKittrick 2006). It is also through bodies that certain forms of resistance emerge.

Postcolonial and/or Southern authors have also contributed to relocating and contextualizing the notion of agency. The very foundations of the concept of agency have thus been revisited. Saba Mahmood, for example, develops a critique of the liberal vision of agency, which would systematically associate this concept with the idea of freedom and resistance, and proposes to reconceptualize agency as a "capacity for action within structures of subordination" (Mahmood 2006, p. 33), an embodied capacity that must always be contextualized. Agency, then, does not always mean resistance, and the ability to act is not always a quest for freedom as Western societies define it. This redefinition of agency has thus made it possible to take seriously the strategies of minority women, which do not come under the heading of an explicit collective struggle against patriarchy and racism, without regarding them as passive and unconscious victims of the relations of domination. In this perspective, Carmen Teeple Hopkins and Kawtar Najib analyze the strategies of veiled women in urban spaces, and the work of identifying safe spaces that sexist and Islamophobic violence in public space requires (Najib and Teeple Hopkins 2020, p. 105). Indeed, the Islamophobia that women experience has daily consequences for their socio-spatial mobility in predominantly non-Muslim countries. They must then reinvent new mobilities to avoid potential situations of discrimination and violence (Najib and Teeple Hopkins 2020, p. 453). The neighborhood of residence often represents a space where they feel confident and less exposed to Islamophobic acts. Some veiled women explain that they do not go to the center of Paris where they feel more exposed to violence, more stigmatized and less comfortable than in the suburbs. In their daily lives, many of them therefore favor spaces and activities in their immediate environment (Najib and Hopkins 2019, p. 105).

Sociologist Hanane Karimi analyzes the "agency deployed [by veiled Muslim women] to escape the conditions of employability that involve the invisibilization of religious expression in the case of an increasingly diffuse duty of religious neutrality" (Karimi 2020, p. 108). In a context where they "experience several types of intertwined discrimination, including sexism, racism and Islamophobia, with a strong impact of social class on their academic and professional pathways" (Karimi 2020, p. 111), they develop strategies to "try to escape from discrimination through entrepreneurship" (Karimi 2020, p. 115). Self-entrepreneurship, practiced in their homes, allows them to access a status without wage subordination, to wear the veil at work and to increase household income (Karimi 2020). While this choice – the least disadvantageous one – presents a number of advantages for these women, it accentuates the difficult reconciliation between work and family (Karimi 2020, p. 122) and the confinement of veiled Muslim women to the space of the home, "despite their desire for social mixing and escaping from the social enclaves by which they are subsequently constrained" (Karimi 2020, p. 122).

Thus, taking into account the agency of these women makes it possible to show that socio-spatial segregation is not the result of minority people or their supposed behavior linked to a culture of origin (Moujoud 2008), or to a religion, but rather of the majority because of the racism and sexism that structure public and professional spaces.

2.4.2. *Space as a tool and a stake in minority struggles*

In social movements, space is seized as "a privileged means of struggle", and as a "stake of struggle between social groups" (Hmed 2009, p. 222). In other words, it is a matter of creating spaces of struggle to carry out the social, political and economic project, and to propose a conception of space that is carried by social movement. We find these two spatial stakes in the collectives of racialized women who mobilize to improve their living and working conditions and denounce the inequalities they suffer. In the context of the framing of the West Indian and Reunionese population by the French authorities through Bumidom, West Indian and Reunionese women have created spaces to fight against this policy and its social, economic and spatial consequences. Here, we take the example of the mobilizations of Reunionese women through the Women's Group of the *Union générale des travailleurs réunionnais* (UGTRF), in France, analyzed by Myriam Paris. These women activists expressed themselves from 1979 onwards in a newspaper entitled *Combat réunionnais*. They explained the need to unite among themselves to denounce colonialism, imperialism and capitalism. In their own words, they created "a place to fight", "a place where we will listen to our voices". Together they could "open up space" and make these places "liberated territories" (Paris 2020, p. 373). This space thus aims to make visible what was invisible, both their position as women among Reunionese women, and as Reunionese women among women. In this space, they could share their experiences, which allowed them to criticize sexism, racism and imperialism, and to make demands. Access to greater social and spatial mobility was at the heart of these demands: whether it was through the refusal of women's assignment to the domestic space – that of the family (as a daughter, mother, wife) and that of the employer (as a domestic worker and caretaker). While they aspired to greater recognition of their work and a more important place in the Reunionese mid-communist space (Paris 2020, pp. 373–375), they spoke out in particular against the state management of the socio-spatial segregation of which they were victims. This criticism is deployed on a global scale – through the criticism of national migration policies – but also on local scales – through the criticism of the "pre-training" centers reserved for migrants supervised by the Bumidom. Among these centers, the one in Crouy-sur-Ourcq, in Seine-et-Marne, which was in operation from 1965 to 1983, was the object of numerous denunciations by the Women's Group of the UGTRF in the *Combat réunionnais*. Isolation and confinement were the terms by which they described their conditions of "training" for domestic service. Based on testimonies that described the center as a prison, the UGTRF Women's Group denounced the deprivation of spatial and social mobility, but also the stigmatization of black women's bodies, designated to dirtiness and laziness (Paris 2020, pp. 405–406).

More than 30 years later, space remains a crucial issue for activists who suffered and denounced the oppression they experienced as black women in France in the 2010s. It is also one of the goals of the Afrofeminist collective Mwasi, which "demands an 'intersectional' approach to the violence and oppression black women experience" (Larcher 2017, p. 118). They challenge the lines that separate "Black" and "European" through the notion of Afropeanity, which constructs the legitimacy of a presence of Black people in French society (Larcher 2017, p. 105). To construct these reflections, they organize segregated spaces. Deliberate segregation emerged in the 1960s, during the U.S. civil rights movement, to create a space of struggle by and for black people (Delphy 2017). The spaces allow dominated social groups to express themselves, think, share and organize without the presence of the dominant group (Delphy 2017). Initiated by Mwasi in July 2017, the Nyansapo festival hosted three single-sex, Black women-only workshops in private spaces. The creation of these single-sex spaces sparked violent controversy on social networks and in the French media: "In the name of anti-racism and against 'anti-white racism,' calling for the maintenance of 'republican order,' the authority of universalism and even feminism, and even science, one voice after another condemned [this] festival en bloc" (Larcher 2017, p. 103). These spaces are thus particularly contested, including when they are temporary and in private spaces.

While creating spaces between minorities is a crucial issue, so is blocking off public space as minorities, as demonstrated by the performance *30 nuances de Noir(es)...*, a musical and immersive show, which took place in the gardens of the Cité internationale universitaire de Paris (Larcher 2017, p. 99). A score of Afrodescendant women walked around to embody "a true public ode to the diversity of morphologies and black and mixed-race femininities" (Larcher 2017, p. 98). This performance was part of the Necessary Horizons festival, which invited the audience to "think about the city of today and tomorrow" as "the space we share in concrete and sensitive ways". Anchored in this project, Sandra Sainte Rose's performance allowed for a double questioning: the "Eurocentric norms of beauty and femininity [...] [that] traverse social space and underpin access to opportunities and places" (Larcher 2017, p. 99), on the one hand, and the concealment of black women in public space, on the other hand.

Another presence that is revealed in the public space through activist actions is that of sexual minorities in working-class neighborhoods, who are assigned to otherness. This is one of the objectives of *Femmes en lutte 93*, a women's collective whose actions take place in Saint-Ouen, Saint-Denis and Aubervilliers (Hanane et al. 2014). Since 2010, this collective has been mobilized in the feminist struggle and is aimed at making the actions of struggling working-class women visible: "We wanted to popularize women's struggles, whether in the workplace, in the public space, in the private space, or at the international level" (Hanane et al. 2014, p. 82). During the debate on "marriage for all", the lesbian feminists in the group took the initiative by creating a "four-page LGBT publication to address this issue in the neighborhoods" (Hanane et al. 2014, p. 82). In this text, they set out to deconstruct the following prejudices: "There are no LGBT people in working-class neighborhoods, and anyway [...] if you say you are LGBT and you are in a working-class neighborhood, you are dead". From testimonies, they nuance these representations and assert a reality that is often hidden: "LGBT people exist, and just because they are not in official LGBT associations in the neighborhoods doesn't mean that they are not in collectives, that they don't exist. They are in the neighborhoods, at work, in lots of places, and to say that they don't exist because they don't organize collectively, that's not true" (Hanane et al. 2014, p. 8). This desire to make gender and sexual minorities in working-class neighborhoods visible is also shared by the organizers of the *Marche des fiertés en banlieue*, which took place in Saint-Denis on June 9, 2019. Slogans such as *"Banlieusard-e-s et fier-ère-s"* [Suburban and proud], *"Le périph' n'a pas arrêté le sida"* [The suburbs didn't stop AIDS], *"Nos quartiers ne sont pas des déserts LGBTQI+"* [Our neighborhood has LGBTQI+ people, too]. During the speeches that closed the march on the square of the town hall of Saint-Denis, *Femmes en lutte 93* denounced the stigmatization of working-class neighborhoods by the instrumentalization of homophobia: "Our primary homophobe is not our neighbor in the working-class neighborhoods. The worst homophobe in France is the French State". They justify this assertion by the gentrification of working-class neighborhoods, the lack of public services (housing, schools, daycare centers), the deportation of undocumented migrants, migration policies, racism, police violence, capitalism, France's colonial policies and military interventions abroad, which also, and especially, affect LGBTQI+ people. They demand the regularization of all undocumented people and freedom of settlement, access to housing for all, access to assisted reproductive technology for all women and "the police out of our lives, out of our neighborhoods". Like other types of "feminism on the margins", they use "an expanded definition of women users of public spaces and a reflection on the varying definitions of safety and the related definition of violence that moves away from the dominant idea" (Hancock and Lieber 2017, p. 22). They, who define themselves as "the margins among the margin", also assert an empowerment of LGBTQI+ issues by inner-city women themselves. Like Afrofeminists, they are mobilizing to assert that those who experience socio-spatial inequalities are the ones most able to effect social and spatial transformations to end segregation and assignment of identity and space for greater social justice.

2.5. Conclusion

This chapter has made it possible to restore the links between the social relations of gender and race, and their interweaving with inequalities in geographical space, drawing on the concept of intersectionality initially developed by critical race studies. In this chapter, we have focused on three theoretical currents and their role in understanding socio-spatial inequalities: feminist analyses, queer approaches and postcolonial perspectives, as well as their contributions to knowledge production in Francophone and Anglophone geography. The first part of this chapter traced the origins of these theoretical currents, and identified three common contributions to the geography of inequalities: (1) first, an epistemological contribution linked to the consideration of situated points of view and a recognition of the importance of reflexivity; (2) an understanding of the way in which social relations are interwoven through the prism of intersectionality; (3) a recognition of the importance of space and scale in understanding the production, reproduction and contestation of (resistance to) inequalities. We then break down this theoretical reading into three central themes, supported by examples in the French context: first, the question of work, then the question of the production of otherness at the national level, and finally, the question of agency of minorities.

An intersectional analysis of work, influenced by feminist, queer and postcolonial theories, allowed us to highlight the way in which hierarchies of gender, class and race, rooted in a colonial past, structure the division of labor in metropolitan France. Section 2.2 presented analyses of occupational hierarchies built on ethno-racial assignments – for example, through the over-representation of foreign workers in certain occupational categories, such as the construction sector, and precarious employment conditions in the feminized hotel sector, the control of the bodies of racialized people and their relegation to invisible spaces in the same sector. Research on care work in the French metropolitan area shows the links between migration, gender, class, nationality and race hierarchies. Indeed, the segregations that affect the living and working conditions of racialized women are at the heart of the geography of work, from the international division of labor to the intimacy of bodies.

The second theme developed in this chapter (section 2.3) focused on the production of otherness in imperial and national ideologies, and in particular on the "territorial assignment" (Hancock 2008, p. 117) of minorities. From the dividing lines between "us" and "them", social racial relations are (re)constructed, in particular by mobilizing the suffering of women and sexual minorities at the international, national, city and neighborhood levels: territories assigned to otherness are thus constructed as hostile to women and sexual minorities, and other Western and white territories are said to be the sole guarantors of the rights of women and sexual minorities. These dividing lines justify inequalities and violence against racialized minorities, including women and LGBTQI+ people. Indeed, they translate into restricted and problematic access to housing and public space. Moreover, research shows that if minority people choose domestic space and working-class neighborhoods and cities as places for their professional and daily activity, it is because of the racism and sexism they experience in majority spaces, not because of a supposed "nature" or "culture".

Finally, the last theme developed in this chapter (section 2.4) was the agency of the minorities. Far from being unfazed when faced with relations of dominations, minorities deploy many strategies to negotiate and resist different forms of oppression. Central to some feminist, queer and postcolonial theories, the concept of agency allows us to conceive a diversity of actions and strategies that cannot be reduced to collective resistance in public space. Geographers have contributed to the spatialization of agency in particular through the identification of places at the margins as often being spaces of transformation, but also through the identification of different levels of agency – from the collective to the individual. In this section, we have made use of examples that cover different territories: the daily and individual strategies of Muslim women in the Paris region to counteract spatial and professional segregation, but also collective mobilizations and the blocking off of public space by the struggles of LGBTQI+ women and working-class neighborhoods and cities.

In developing these three themes, it is worth recalling that we do not claim to be exhaustive in our understanding of the interweaving of social relations. We reproduce intersectional readings influenced by feminist, queer and post-colonial theories which place the experiences of oppression at the center of the analysis. Many other geographical themes can feed into these analyses, such as the link between environment and society. Geographers have thus explored the way in which power relations and their interweaving are the product of specific political-ecological contexts, where the most vulnerable populations are excluded from access to resources and land, and often relegated to the most fragile or dangerous environments (Truelove 2011; Mollett and Faria 2013; Rocheleau and Nirmal 2015; Mollett 2017; Behzadi 2019; Sultana 2011, 2020). The study of feminist political ecology and postcolonial political ecology is beyond the scope of this chapter, but is another example of how a feminist, intersectional and postcolonial perspective can contribute to an understanding of the major issues in the geography of inequality.

2.6. References

Abirafeh, L. (2009). *Gender and International Aid in Afghanistan: The Politics and Effect of Intervention*. McFarland, Jefferson.

Abreu, M. (2017). De quelle histoire le "féminisme matérialiste" (français) est-il le nom ? *Comment s'en sortir ?*, 4, 55–79.

Abu-Lughod, L. (2013). *Do Muslim Women Need Saving?* Harvard University Press, Cambridge, MA.

Anderson, B. (1983). *Imagined Communities: Reflections on the Origin and Spread of Nationalism.* Verso, London.

Arab, C. (2009). Les Marocaines à Huelva sous "contrat en origine" : partir pour mieux revenir. *Migrations Société*, 125(5), 175–190.

Arab, C., Gouyon, M., Moujoud, N. (2018). Migrations et enjeux migratoires au prisme des sexualités et du genre. *Migrations Société*, 173(3), 15–26.

Bahramitash, R. (2006). The war on terror, feminist orientalism, and oriental feminism: Case studies of two North American bestsellers. *Critique: Critical Middle Eastern Studies*, 14(2), 223–237.

Belkacem, L., Direnberger, L., Hammou, K., Zoubir, Z. (2019). Prendre au sérieux les rapports sociaux de race. *Mouvements* [Online]. Available at: https://mouvements.info/prendre-au-serieux-les-recherches-sur-les-rapports-sociaux-de-race/.

Behzadi, N.E. (2019). Women miners' exclusion and Muslim masculinities in Tajikistan: A feminist political ecology of honor and shame. *Geoforum*, 100, 144–152.

Behzadi, N.E. and Direnberger, L. (2020). Gender and ethnicity in the Soviet Muslim peripheries: A feminist postcolonial geography of women's work in the Tajik SSR (1950–1991). *Central Asian Survey*, 39(2), 202–219.

Bentouhami, H. (2017). Phénoménologie politique du voile. *Philosophiques*, 44(2), 271–284.

Blais, H. (2009). Coloniser l'espace : territoires, identités, spatialité. *Genèses*, 74(1), 145–159.

Blidon, M. (2019). Still a long way to go: Gender and feminist geographies in France. *Gender, Place and Culture*, 26(9), 1039–1048.

Blunt, A. and McEwan, C. (eds) (2002). *Postcolonial Geographies.* Continuum, London.

Blunt, A. and Rose, G. (1994). *Writing Women and Space: Colonial and Postcolonial Geographies.* Guilford Press, New York.

Borgeaud-Garciandía, N., Araujo Guimarães, N., Hirata, H. (2020). Introduction : *care* aux Suds : quand le travail de *care* interroge les inégalités sociales. *Revue internationale des études du développement*, 242(2), 7–34.

Boubeker, A. and Hajjat, A. (eds) (2008). *Histoire politique des immigrations (post)colonials. France, 1920–2008.* Amsterdam Editions, Paris.

Butler, J. (1988). Performative acts and gender constitution: An essay in phenomenology and feminist theory. *Theatre Journal*, 40(4), 519–531.

Butler, J. (1990). *Gender Trouble: Feminism and the Subversion of Identity.* Routledge, London.

Cattan, N. and Clerval, A. (2011). Un droit à la ville ? Réseaux virtuels et centralités éphémères des lesbiennes à Paris. *Justice spatiale – Spatial justice* [Online]. Available at: http://www.jssj.org/article/un-droit-a-la-ville-reseaux-virtuels-et-centralites-ephemeres-des-lesbiennes-a-paris/.

Célestine, A. (2018). *L'encadrement politique des minorités caribéennes à Paris et New York*. Karthala, Paris.

Chaïb, S. (2008). Femmes immigrées et travail salarié. *Les cahiers du CEDREF*, 16, 209–229.

Craggs, R. (2019). Decolonising the geographical tradition. *Transaction of the Insitute of British Geographers*, 44(3), 444–446.

Crenshaw, K. (1989). Demarginalizing the intersection of race and sex: A black feminist critique of antidiscrimination doctrine, feminist theory and antiracist politics. *University of Chicago Legal Forum*, 140, 139–167.

Crenshaw, K. (1991). Mapping the margins: Intersectionality, identity politics, and violence against women of color. *Stanford Law Review*, 43, 1241–1299.

Dagistanli, S. and Grewal, K. (2012). Perverse Muslim masculinities in contemporary orientalist discourse: The vagaries of Muslim immigration in the West. In *Global Islamophobia: Muslims and Moral Panic in the West*, Morgan, G., Poynting, S. (eds). Ashgate, Burlington.

Daigle, M. and Sundberg, J. (2017). From where we stand: Unsettling geographical knowledges in the classroom. *Transactions of the Institute of British Geographers*, 42, 338–341.

Dalibert, M. (2013). Authentification et légitimation d'un problème de société par les journalistes : les violences de genre en banlieue dans la médiatisation de Ni putes ni soumises. *Études de communication*, 40 [Online]. Available at: http://journals.openedition.org/edc/5214.

Dalla Costa, M. and James, S. (1972). *The Power of Women and the Subversion of Community*. Falling Wall Press, Bristol.

Damamme, A., Hirata, H., Molinier, P. (eds) (2017). *Le travail entre public, privé et intime. Comparaisons et enjeux internationaux du "care"*. L'Harmattan, Paris.

Daulatzai, A. (2006). Acknowledging Afghanistan: Notes and queries on an occupation. *Cultural Dynamics*, 18(3), 293–311.

Davis, A. (1983). *Women, Race and Class*. Vintage Books, New York.

Delphy, C. (1998). *L'Ennemi principal*. Syllepse, Paris.

Delphy, C. (2017). La non-mixité : une nécessité politique. Domination, ségrégation et auto-émancipation [Online]. Available at: https://lmsi.net/La-non-mixite-une-necessite.

Deprest, F. (2014). La géographie, ça sert à coloniser ? Des géographes en situation coloniale. In *Histoire de l'Algérie à la période coloniale : 1830–1962*, Bouchène, B. (ed.). La Découverte, Paris.

Direnberger, L. and Schmoll, C. (2014). Ce que le genre fait à l'espace… et inversement. *Les Cahiers du CEDREF* [Online]. Available at: https://journals.openedition.org/cedref/953.

Dixon, D. (2011). Introduction: Feminist engagements with geopolitics. *Gender, Place and Culture*, 18(4), 445–453.

Dixon, D. (2015). *Feminist Geopolitics: Material States*. Routledge, London/New York.

Dixon, D. and Marston, S.A. (2011). Introduction: Feminist engagements with geopolitics. *Gender, Place and Culture*, 18(4), 445–453.

Duplan, K. (2012). Les géographies des sexualités et la géographie française peuvent-elles faire bon ménage ? *Géographie et cultures*, 83 [Online]. Available at: http://journals.openedition.org/gc/2087.

Dupont, L. and Prieur, C. (2012). Géographie et cultures : introduction [Online]. Available at: http://journals.openedition.org/gc/2020.

Dyer, S., McDowell, L., Batnitzky, A. (2008). Emotional labour/body work: The caring labours of migrants in the UKJ's National Health Service. *Geoforum*, 39(6), 2030–2038.

Eisenstein, Z. (2004). *Against Empire: Feminisms, Racism, and the West*. Zed Books, London.

El-Tayeb, F. (2012). "Gays who cannot properly be gay". Queer Muslims in the neoliberal European city. *European Journal of Women's Studies*, 19(1), 79–95.

England, K. and Lawson, V. (2005). Feminist analyses of work: Rethinking the boundaries, gendering and spatiality of work. In *Companion to Feminist Geography*, Nelson, L., Seager, J. (eds). Blackwell Publishing, Oxford.

Esson, J., Noxolo, P., Baxter, R., Daley, P., Byron, M. (2017). The 2017 chair's theme: Decolonising geographical knowledges, or reproducing coloniality. *Area*, 49(3), 384–388.

Fassin, É. (2009). La démocratie sexuelle contre elle-même : les contradictions de la politique d'"immigration subie". *Vacarme*, 48(3), 48–50.

Federici, S. (2004). *Caliban and the Witch: Women, the Body and Primitive Accumulation*. Auto Media, New York.

Ferretti, F. (2019). History and philosophy I: Decolonising the discipline, diversifying archives and historicising radicalism. *Progress in Human Geography*, 44(6), 1161–1171

Fluri, J.L. (2009). Geopolitics of gender and violence "from below". *Political Geography*, 28, 259–265.

Germain, F. and Larcher, S. (2018). *Black French Women and the Struggle for Equality, 1848–2016*. University of Nebraska Press, Lincoln.

Gimenez, M. (1998). Marxist and materialist feminism. *The Feminist Zine* [Online]. Available at: www.feministzine.com.

Gimenez, M. and Vogel, L. (2005). Marxist-feminist thought today. *Science & Society*, 69(1), 5–10.

Guénif-Souilamas, N. (2006). The other French exception: Virtuous racism and the war of the sexes in postcolonial France. *French Politics, Culture and Society*, 24(3), 23–41.

Guillaumin, C. (2016). *Sexe, race et pratique du pouvoir. L'idée de nature*. Éditions iXe, Paris.

Hanane, S. and Schaepelynck, V. (2014). Femmes en lutte 93. *Chimères*, 83(2), 82–92.

Hancock, C. (2002). Genre et géographie : les apports des géographies de langue anglaise. *Espace, populations, sociétés*, 3, 257–264.

Hancock, C. (2008). Décoloniser les représentations : esquisse d'une géographie culturelle de nos "Autres". *Annales de géographie*, 660–661(2), 116–128.

Hancock, C. (2011). Le corps féminin, enjeu géopolitique dans la France postcoloniale. *L'Espace Politique*, 13 [Online]. Available at: http://journals.openedition.org/espacepolitique/1882.

Hancock, C. and Lieber, M. (2017). Refuser le faux dilemme entre antisexisme et antiracisme. Penser la ville inclusive. *Les Annales de la recherche urbaine*, 112, 16–25.

Hancock, C. and Mobillion, V. (2019). "I want to tell them, I'm just wearing a veil, not carrying a gun!" Muslim women negotiating borders in femoniationalist Paris. *Political Geography*, 69, 1–9

Hanson, S. and Pratt, G. (1995). *Gender, Work, and Space*. Routledge, London.

Haraway, D. (1988). Situated knowledges: The science question in feminism and the privilege of partial perspective. *Feminist Studies*, 14(3), 575–599.

Hill Collins, P.H. (2000). *Black Feminist Thought: Knowledge, Consciousness, and the Politics of Empowerment*. Routledge, London.

Hill Collins, P.H. and Bilge, S. (2016). *Intersectionality*. Polity Press, Cambridge.

Hmed, C. (2009). Espace géographique et mouvements sociaux. In *Dictionnaire des mouvements sociaux*, Filleuil, O. (ed.). Presses de Sciences Po, Paris.

Hyndman, J. (2019). Unsettling feminist geopolitics: Forging feminist political geographies of violence and displacement. *Gender, Place and Culture*, 26(1), 3–29.

Ibos, C. (2016). Travail domestique/domesticité. In *Encyclopédie critique du genre : corps, sexualité, rapports sociaux*, Rennes, J. (ed.). La Découverte, Paris.

Jarry-Omarova, A. and Marteu, É. (2013). Nation/nationalisme. In *Dictionnaire. Genre et science politique. Concepts, objets, problèmes*, Achin, C. (ed.). Presses de Sciences Po, Paris.

Jaunait, A., Le Renard, A., Marteu, É. (2013). Nationalismes sexuels : reconfigurations contemporaines des sexualités et des nationalismes. *Raisons politiques*, 49(1), 5–23.

Jazeel, T. (2012). Postcolonialism: Orientalism and the geographical imagination [Online]. Available at: https://doi.org/10.1080/00167487.2012.12094331.

Jazeel, T. (2014). Subaltern geographies: Geographical knowledge and postcolonial strategy. *Singapore Journal of Tropical Geography*, 35(1), 88–103.

Jounin, N. (2009). *Chantier interdit au public : enquête parmi les travailleurs du bâtiment*. La Découverte, Paris.

Karimi, H. (2020). Des femmes entrepreneuses en réseau en France. Faire face aux discriminations multiples. *Travail, genre et sociétés*, 44(2), 107–123.

Kian, A. (2010). Mondialisation, "guerre antiterroriste", néo-orientalisme, renouveau des nationalismes et redéploiement de violence de genre. In *Violences et société. Regards sociologiques*, Ndiaye, A., Ferrand-Bechmann, D. (eds). Desclée de Brouwer, Paris.

Larcher, S. (2017). "Nos vies sont politiques !" L'afroféminisme en France ou la riposte des petites-filles de l'Empire. *Participations*, 19(3), 97–127.

Larcher, S. (2018). The end of silence: On the revival of afrofeminism in contemporary France. In *Black French Women and the Struggle for Equality, 1848–201*, Germain, F., Larcher, S. (eds). University of Nebraska Press, Lincoln.

Lawson, V. (1999). Tailoring is a profession, seamstressing is work! Resiting work and reworking gender identities among artisanal garment workers in Quito. *Environment and Planning A*, 31(2), 209–227.

de Leeuw, S. and Hunt, S. (2018). Unsettling decolonizing geographies. *Geography Compass*, 12(7), 1–14.

Lieber, M. (2016). Qui dénonce le harcèlement de rue ? Un essai de géographie morale. In *L'intersectionnalité. Enjeux théoriques et politiques*, Fassa, F., Lépinard, E., Roca i Escoda, M. (eds). La Dispute, Paris.

Longhurst, R. (2001). *Bodies: Exploring Fluid Boundaries*. Routledge, London.

Mahmood, S. (2008). Feminism, democracy, and empire. Islam and the war of terror. In *Women's Studies on the Edge*, Wallach, S.W. (ed.). Duke University Press, Durham.

Marchand, M.H. and Runyan, A.S. (2000). *Gender and Global Restructuring, Sightings, Sites and Resistances*. Routledge, London.

Marius, K. and Raibaud, Y. (eds) (2013). Genre et géographie : du questionnement à l'évidence. In *Genre et construction de la géographie*. Maison des Sciences de l'Homme d'Aquitaine, Bordeaux.

Mathieu, M. (2019). La fabrication du corps des "hôtesses de table". Comment l'uniforme produit les classes de sexe dans la restauration. *Nouvelles questions féministes*, 38(2), 16–33.

McDowell, L. (1999). Work/workplaces. In *Gender, Identity and Place, Understanding Femininist Geographies*. Blackwell, Cambridge.

McDowell, L. (2009). *Working Bodies: Interactive Service Employment and Workplace Identities*. Wiley Blackwell, London.

McDowell, L. and Court, G. (1994). Performing work: Bodily representations in merchant banks. *Environment and Planning D: Society and Space*, 12(6), 727–750.

McDowell, L. and Sharp, J.P. (eds) (2014). *A Feminist Glossary of Human Geography*. Routledge, London.

McDowell, L., Massey, D., Allen, J. (1984). A woman's place? In *Geography Matters*, Allen, J. (ed.). Cambridge University Press, Cambridge.

McDowell, L., Batnitzky, A., Dyer, S. (2007). Division, segmentation and interpellation: The embodied labors of migrant workers in a Greater London hotel. *Economic Geography*, 83(1), 1–25.

McKittrick, K. (2006). *Demonic Grounds: Black Women and the Cartographies of Struggle*. University of Minnesota Press, Minneapolis.

Mohanty, C.T. (1988). Under Western eyes: Feminist scholarship and colonial discourses. *Feminist Review*, 30, 61–88.

Mollett, S. (2017). Gender's critical edge: Feminist political ecology, postoclonial intersectionality, and the coupling of race and gender. In *Routledge Handbook of Gender and Environment*, MacGregor, S. (ed.). Routledge, London.

Mollett, S. and Faria, C. (2013). Messing with gender in feminist political ecology. *Geoforum*, 45, 116–125.

Monk, J. and Hanson, S. (1982). On not excluding half of the human in human geography. *The Profesional Geographers*, 34, 11–23.

Moujoud, N. (2008). Effets de la migration sur les femmes et sur les rapports sociaux de sexe. Au-delà des visions binaires. *Les cahiers du CEDREF*, 16, 57–79.

Moujoud, N. (2012). Métiers domestiques, voile et féminisme. *Hommes & Migrations*, 1300, 84–94.

Moujoud, N. (2018). Les sans-papiers et le service domestique en France : femmes et non-droit dans le travail. *Recherches féministes*, 31(1), 275–291.

Nagar, R., Lawson, V., McDowell, L., Hanson, S. (2002). Locating globalization: (Re)readings of the subjects and spaces of globalization. *Economic Geography*, 78(3), 257–284.

Najib, K. (2019). Géographie et intersectionnalité des actes antimusulmans en région parisienne. *Hommes & Migrations*, 1324(1), 19–26.

Najib, K. (2020). Spaces of Islamophobie and spaces of inequality in Greater Paris. *Environment and Planning C: Politics and Space* [Online]. Available at: https://doi.org/10.1177/2399654420941520.

Najib, K. and Hopkins, P. (2019). Veiled Muslim women's strategies in response to Islamophobia in Paris. *Political Geography*, 73, 103–111.

Najib, K. and Teeple Hopkins, C. (2020). Geographies of Islamophobia. *Social & Cultural Geography*, 21(4), 449–457.

Nast, H. and Pile, S. (1998). *Places through the Body*. Routledge, London.

Ndiaye, P. (2009). Les Noirs et leur perception de la discrimination raciale dans le monde du travail en France depuis les années 1960. In *Discriminations : pratiques, savoirs, politiques*. La Documentation française, Paris.

Oberhauser, A.M. (2002). Feminism and economic geography: Gendering work and working gender. In *A companion to Economic Geography*, Barnes, T.J., Sheppard, E. (eds). Blackwell Publishing, Oxford.

Pain, R. and Staeheli, L. (2014). Introduction: Intimacy-geopolitics and violence. *Area*, 46, 344–347.

Paris, M. (2020). *Nous qui versons la vie goutte à goutte. Féminismes, économie reproductive et pouvoir colonial à La Réunion*. Dalloz, Paris.

Pinna, G. (2013). Vendre du luxe au rabais : une étude de cas dans l'hôtellerie haut de gamme à Paris. *Travail et emploi*, 136, 21–34.

Pitti, L. (2008). Travailleurs de France, voilà notre nom. Les mobilisations des ouvriers étrangers dans les usines et les foyers durant les années 1970. In *Histoire politique des immigrations (post) coloniales*, Boubeker, A. and Hajjat, A. (eds). Éditions Amsterdam, Paris.

Prieur, C. (2015). Des géographies queers au-delà des genres et des sexualités ? *Espace Temps* [Online]. Available at: http://www.espacestemps.net/articles/des-geographies-queers-au-dela-des-genres-et-des-sexualites/.

Pualani Louis, R. (2007). Can you hear us now? Voices from the margin: Using indigenous methodologies in geographic research. *Geographical Research*, 45(2), 130–139.

Radcliffe, S.A. (2017). Decolonising geographical knowledges. *Transactions of the Institute of British Geographers*, 42(3), 329–333.

Rocheleau, D. and Nirmal, P. (2015). Feminist political ecologies: Grounded, networked and rooted on Earth. In *The Oxford Handbook of Transnational Feminist Movements*, Baksh, A. and Harcourt, W. (eds). Oxford University Press, Oxford.

Rose, G. (1993). *Feminism and Geography: The Limits of Geographical Knowledge*. Polity Press, Cambridge.

Said, E. (1980). *L'orientalisme, L'Orient créé par l'Occident*. Le Seuil, Paris.

Sayad, A. (1999). *La Double Absence. Des illusions de l'émigré aux souffrances de l'immigré*. Le Seuil, Paris.

Schenk, C., Gökarıksel, B.P., Behzadi, N.E. (2022). Introduction: Security, violence and mobility: The embodied and everyday politics of negotiating Muslim femininities. *Political Geography* [Online]. Available at: https://doi.org/10.1016/j.polgeo.2022.102597.

Schmoll, C. (2020). *Les Damnées de la mer*. La Découverte, Paris.

Shepard, T. (2017). *Mâle décolonisation. L'"homme arabe" et la France, de l'indépendance algérienne à la révolution iranienne*. Payot & Rivages, Paris.

Sidaway, J.D. (2000). Postcolonial geographies: An exploratory essay. *Progress in Human Geography*, 24(4), 591–612.

Simpson, R., Slutskkaya, N., Lewis, P., Hopfl, H. (2012). *Dirty Work: Concepts and Identities*. Palgrave Macmillan, Basingstoke.

Sultana, F. (2011). Suffering for water, suffering from water: Emotional geographies of resource access, control and conflict. *Geoforum*, 42(2), 163–172 [Online]. Available at: https://doi.org/10.1016/j.geoforum.2010.12.002.

Sultana, F. (2020) Political ecology 1: From margins to center. *Progress in Human Geography*, 1–10. doi:10.1177/0309132520936751.

Teeple Hopkins, C. (2015). Feminist geographies of social reproduction and race. *Women's Studies International Forum*, 48, 135–140.

Tissot, S. and Poupeau, F. (2005). La spatialisation des problèmes sociaux. *Actes de la recherche en sciences sociales*, 159(4), 4–9.

Truelove, Y. (2011). (Re-)conceptualizing water inequality in Delhi, India through a feminist political ecology framework. *Geoforum*, 42(2), 143–152 [Online]. Available at: https://doi.org/10.1016/j.geoforum.2011.01.004.

Tyler, M. (2011). Tainted love: From dirty work to abject labour in Soho's sex shops. *Human Relations*, 64(11), 1477–1500.

Vogel, L. (1983). *Marxism and the Oppression of Women: Toward a Unitary Theory*. Rutgers University Press, New Brunswick.

Wolkowitz, C. (2006). *Bodies at Work*. Sage, London.

Woon, C.Y. (2015). Postcolonialism. In *A Companion to Political Geography*, Agnee, J., Mamadouh, V., Secor, A.J., Sharp, J. (eds). John Wiley & Sons, Oxford.

Wright, M.W. (1997). Crossing the factory frontier: Gender, place and power in the Mexican Maquiladora. *Antipode*, 29(3), 278–302.

Wright, M.W. (2006). *Diposable Women and Other Myths of Global Capitalism*. Routledge, London.

Young, R.J.C. (2003). *Postcolonial Theory: A Very Short Introduction*. Oxford University Press, Oxford.

Yuval-Davis, N. (2006). Intersectionality and feminist politics. *European Journal of Women's Studies*, 13(3), 193–209.

3

Migration, Multi-situated Inequalities and the World Economy

Laurence ROULLEAU-BERGER
CNRS, Triangle, ENS de Lyon, France

According to estimates published by the United Nations, there were 272 million international migrants in 2019 compared to 51 million in 2010. Between 2010 and 2017, the global number of refugees and asylum seekers increased by about 13 million, nearly a quarter of the increase in international migrants. In 2019, one in seven international migrants was under 20 years old. According to UN sources, in 2017, there were 82 million North-South migrants and 82.3 million South-South migrants in the world, while 40 million migrants from Asian countries have left their native countries and are distributed around the world. The European Union remains an important immigration territory for various populations. Note that 2.3 million non-European migrants arrived in Europe in 2019. In 2016, 1.2 million people sought asylum in an EU country, twice as many as in 2014. In 2018, a total of 672,000 people received international protection in an EU country (refugee status, subsidiary protection or humanitarian visa).

In the context of these complex and multiplying international mobilities, we examine the relationship between migration, inequality and the world economy. In migratory circulations, migrants' social position is changed with each mobilization in the societies of departure and arrival. We approach the relationship between migration and economic inequalities from the point of view of discriminatory labor regimes and economic transnationalism "from above", "from below" and

Inequalities in Geographical Space,
coordinated by Clémentine COTTINEAU and Julie VALLÉE. © ISTE Ltd 2022.

in-between, by showing how migratory careers participate in producing "partially nationalized" social classes (Sassen 2006). We look at how the effects of collision in migratory biographies raise the question of subjectivation by informing the processes of maintaining migrants' identities.

We first outline the contours of a sociology of inequalities and migrations (section 3.1). We then deal with the conditions of migrant workers in subaltern situations in international cities, based on the ethnicization of labor markets, the globalization of care and platform capitalism (section 3.2). We show how inequalities in migratory paths accumulate, grow or are maintained in a multi-situated process, where migrants' resource repertoires are constantly recomposed, giving rise to a cosmopolitization and a social differentiation of biographies (section 3.3). We discuss the grammars of social and moral recognition that migrants must learn in each place to "take their place" with their experiences, skills and qualifications (section 3.4). Then we show how the relationship between migration, inequality and the world economy are expressed in different forms of transnationalisms[1]: transnationalism from above, transnationalism from below and transnationalism between countries *(section 3.5)*. Finally, we show how "forced migrants" can be confronted with this extreme test of inequality, namely expulsion (section 3.6).

3.1. Toward a sociology of inequalities and migrations

Mobility has continued to accelerate and traffic has intensified over the last few years. More and more migrants are moving, circulating, returning and taking different migratory routes; they are acquiring experiences and are often challenged in terms of their social, ethnic and gender identities. These international mobilities reveal what Simon (2008, 2015) called transnational spaces under tension.

Today, migrants come from all over the world. In this context of globalization, many economically developed States have become immigration countries. Indeed, the migration and displacement of populations has increased, despite the numerous restrictions imposed by States. Transnational mobilities have been reconfigured in different ways according to different migration policies (Schmoll et al. 2015; Ambrosini et al. 2020); new categories of migrants in so-called old immigration countries, such as France, and new immigration countries, such as Spain (Ambrosini 2018), have appeared. In transnational traffic, people move in a variety of ways

---

1. Transnationalism, according to Glick-Schiller et al. (1992), is the process by which migrants construct social fields that link the country of origin and the country of arrival.

within the framework of multipolar, transnational and pendular migrations, which have progressively become intertwined.

In a context of economic globalization and the internationalization of labor markets, the question of inequality, discrimination and exclusion quickly arose. This was considered very early on by Roger Waldinger (1996), who showed how migrant workers, who were mostly in excluded segments of the labor market, occupied what he called "ethnic niches". Ethnic niches were first seen as participating in the fragmentation and hierarchization of urban labor markets, and then as part of a process of de-multiplication of transnational spaces and the formation of multi-polar productive territories. Then, in the 1990s, Nina Glick-Schiller, Linda Bash and Cristina Szanton-Blanc introduced the theory of transnationalism as "the process by which migrants construct social fields that link the country of origin and their country of arrival" with the publication of *Towards a Transnational Perspective on Migration* (1992). In dialog with this theory, Portes et al. (1999) developed the concept of "globalization from below" with the emergence of transnational communities; they show that migrants develop economic activities by relying on dense, geographically extensive and supportive networks, which can give rise to transnational entrepreneurship "from below" for the least qualified, in the restaurant business, for example.

In the geo-economics of international migration, Sassen (2009) analyzes how labor migration has been built on unequal dynamics with the hyper-enrichment of labor-importing countries, the organized export – legal and illegal – of labor, and the ruling on the mobility and flexibility of high-level employees in advanced service companies. She speaks of an emerging class of transnational working poor, but also of a highly mobile transnational professional class, which integrates transnational elites to define partially denationalized classes in the context of economic globalization, where old inequalities are reinforced and new ones develop. Highly qualified migrants with international capital, that is, globalized top managers, highly qualified professions that produce immaterial and symbolic goods in legal, financial and other fields, circulate in the globalization from above (Wagner 1998). The new segmentations between these two global classes define new inequalities linked to advanced capitalisms.

Tarrius (2002, 2006) poses the question of the formation of global classes in another mode in postcolonial and post-Fordist migration; he introduces the class of "transmigrants", key figures in the diffusion of low-end products on a vast international market, who develop commercial strategies of the poor-to-poor, that is, the sale of products to populations deemed insolvent. These are, for example, Afghan migrants who come to the Black Sea to load up on electronic products manufactured in South-East Asia, passing through Dubai or Kuwait City, on their way to the ports of Bulgaria. Alongside these poor transmigrants, another category of *qualified and graduated* transmigrants appears, such as the Egyptian doctors who care for them and accompany them on *migratory territories* where nomads of globalization circulate like ants from below on the poor-to-poor markets and in the world economy (Tarrius and Missaoui 2000; Tarrius 2015). These trans-migrants may be involved in trafficking drugs and women in criminal environments. The construction of inequalities is considered here from the point of view of hierarchies between transnational economic networks, between new cosmopolitanisms internal to migrations, not entirely "communitarian" or "ethnic" but linked to cross-border sociabilities.

In addition to these approaches, it should be noted that the question of inequalities has also been addressed within the framework of a sociology of immigration and migration, influenced by structuralist or Bourdieusian thinking that focuses on the determinisms and reproduction of social inequalities (Wagner 2007; Réa and Tripier 2008; Morice and Potot 2010; Kergoat et al. 2011). The need to articulate social, class and interethnic relations has gained increasing consensus in the sociology of migration when thinking about the processes of economic and moral domination in labor markets. The intersectionality of economic inequalities in the migratory experience is weakened in numerous works around the triptych of class, gender and race, according to different theoretical modalities (Cossée et al. 2013).

Subsequently, in order to consider migrations and economic inequalities together, the sociologist has increasingly placed himself in a multi-dimensional space in order to understand how spatialities are hierarchized, as well as how these hierarchies are regularly shaken up, how individuals are more or less forced into multi-affiliations, and how transnational networks are formed above nation-states by creating social, economic and symbolic assemblages. Migrants are more and more recognized for their experiences, their mobilization, action and reflexivity skills, inscribed in a plurality of situations, spaces, societal and unequal contexts (Roulleau-Berger 2007, 2010). Migrants' perspectives on who they are and what they do are increasingly taken into account, based on the diversity of their objectives and symbolic resources and their subjectivity in migratory careers. Mobilities help to reduce or increase fragmentation and gaps in identities, between social/personal identities and identities for oneself (Goffman 1975), and between social/personal identities and "imagined" identities. The plurality of selves is permanently linked to the diversity of spaces, temporalities and situations, and we can also see how individual mobilities and work situations participate, at each spatial and temporal change, in reconfiguring selves in the permanent work of identities being made, unmade and remade. In this perspective, Schmoll (2020) has also put forward a geography of new migratory forms in the Euro-Mediterranean space, attentive to gender inequalities and migrant political subjectivities.

Finally, a sociology of migrations and inequalities is emerging today in which the problem of emotions arises with regard to the agency between space and subjectivity with a view to understanding how migratory careers are prioritized in local economies and globalized worlds of production (Bastide 2015). For example, Beatrice Zani (2019) has shown how, based on the follow-up of migratory careers of young Chinese women in China, then between China and Taiwan, and between Taiwan and China, economic geographies are constructed from social practices, aspirations, social and family ties and shared emotions in the production of digital worlds structured by online and offline networks.

These different approaches agree on the idea of the production of new inequalities, new social hierarchies, new centralities and new economic and political peripheries between which transnational, diasporic, ethnic but also intracontinental networks are woven. In this theoretical movement, the plurality and intersectionality of inequalities are not thought of in a static way, but in a dynamic way. Inequalities are defined as intersectional, but also multi-situated, spatialized and temporalized.

In this chapter, we approach the question of migrations and inequalities from a sociological perspective of mobility and moral sociology focused on local and globalized work. Indeed, in the migratory experience, individuals, especially the least qualified ones, are increasingly faced with situations of precariousness, discrimination and subalternity, which reveal multiple and intertwined inequalities. The geographical and professional mobility of migrants also reveals these multi-situated inequalities in migratory careers organized around biographical bifurcations. The rhythm of bifurcations in migrants' paths produces social differentiation and inequalities, a process that informs the moral careers of migrants, who are unequally confronted with the loss of themselves, self-shame and humiliation. Individuals then develop strategies of social and public recognition and of reclaiming themselves, which differ according to the nature and volume of their social, economic and moral resources. If local societies produce regimes of situated inequalities, these inequalities become multi-situated in the migration paths on a transnational scale where economic cosmopolitanisms are produced which, in turn, stratify and increase the power of regimes of situated inequalities, linked to hierarchical transnationalisms. We conclude by asking the question of the construction of extreme inequalities from downgrading situations , and more broadly from the expulsions experienced by migrants under duress.

3.2. International cities and migrant workers

In international cities, the processes of economic globalization produce diffraction effects on labor markets; they reveal and stimulate the formation of a diversity of work spaces, visible and invisible, singular and globalized, such as care work or digital labor, where migrant workers are particularly present. Examining the relationship between migration and economic inequalities also invites us to talk about the forms of subalternity linked to the precariat, the ethnicization of labor markets and racism at work. In Europe, for the last 15 years, with the massive arrival of new migrant workers, labor markets have been producing extreme inequalities. They are organized on the basis of the commodification of bodies and the imposition of a consent to social and economic disqualification (Burawoy 1979).

3.2.1. *Subalternity and the ethnicization of labor markets*

In the late 2000s, the occupation of foreign workers in Europe shifted from industry towards services, notably agriculture, horticulture, construction, hospitality, catering and garment manufacturing, and services account for sectors where migrant workers are highly represented (Ambrosini 2007; Réa and Tripier 2008). It is clear that migrants are massively represented in menial jobs, above all migrants from African and Maghreb countries, followed by Turkish and Portuguese migrants. In Western Europe, so-called "3D jobs" (dirty, dangerous and demeaning) are largely occupied by new, low-skilled migrant workers.

In most European cities, a dual process of employment and ethnicization of labor markets has contributed to the pulverization of labor contract conditions, due to the plurality and flexibility of transitional jobs and specific forms of work in "gray" or "black" areas, especially in ethnic niches (Roulleau-Berger 2013; Ambrosini 2018). The Mediterranean model of immigration, based on tertiarization, flexibility and informal work, still remains active in a context where new migrants are kept in irregular or precarious situations in forms of "internal relocation" (Réa 2013). The ethnicization of labor relations relies on the disqualification of migrant workers, particularly in temporary employment, or even through transnational service provision (Jounin 2009). This process clearly reflects the development of an underemployment market, at the heart of which is the figure of the migrant forced by the global labor market. It delineates the inequalities between native workers and foreign workers or workers of foreign origin, divisions that participate in the overvisibilization/stigmatization of an ethnic belonging and the invisibilization/devaluation of qualifications and professional experience acquired in the country of origin or during the migratory journey (Roulleau-Berger 2012). Over the past 30 years, the hierarchies established between the different forms of atypical work contracts – fixed-term contracts, part-time work, temporary work, seasonal work and even day work, zero-hour work, self-employment, etc. – have reinforced the processes by which migrants are overexposed, labeled and stigmatized. The lower the educational levels, the more migrants are exposed to contracts with little legitimacy whenever they have access to these contracts. Cultural context, combined with social origin, gender and generational position, plays an active role in defining forms of differentiated and unequal access to labor markets.

In international cities, migrants in subaltern situations usually work without a contract, in working conditions based on principles of indecency and of contempt for individuals confronted with situations of tyranny at work, in labor markets where they are forced into situations of high productivity, competitiveness and strong moral alienation. We can speak here of hegemonic work regimes, which are based on three types of denials of recognition (Honneth 2000): the invisibility of migrants, the depreciatory recognition of their activity and work, and the lack of recognition and social contempt for the professional experience and knowledge acquired in their country of origin and during their migratory journeys.

3.2.2. *Racism at work*

The process of access to work for migrants is based on systemic (De Rudder et al. 2000), institutional but also situational discrimination. This is reflected in downgrading, precariousness, disqualification from status and employment, and situations of racism at work, despite education, qualifications and experience comparable to or even superior to those of non-migrants; migrants are generally hired under unfavorable conditions for equal qualifications, most often on precarious contracts, while the possibilities for promotion and professional mobility remain limited and working conditions are difficult.

The process of discrimination on the part of employers can take many forms, and it is not always declared as such. Thus, migrants may experience three forms of racism in labor markets: political racism, cultural racism and institutional racism (Bataille 1997).

With political racism, migrants are openly rejected from labor markets because of their cultural background; employers display their racist positions by refusing to hire them or by asking them to change their first names, for example. Hajjat and Mohammed (2013) have shown how Islamophobia constructs stigmatizing discourse, discriminatory practices or physical aggression, which have become the weapon of a more or less visible racism. In fact, it is the migrants from the Maghreb and sub-Saharan Africa that are subjected to racism at work in scenes of contempt and insults.

Cultural racism appears when employers talk about migrants as potentially having difficulties integrating into certain work cultures. For example, the wearing of the headscarf has become a discriminating factor in access to employment for women of the Muslim faith. Cultural racism is also expressed through disguised forms of racism, innuendos and jokes, or indeed floating forms of racism, characterized by silences, unspoken words, whispers, murmurs or ignorance within work environments (Giraudo-Baujeu 2020).

Institutional racism is the product of a general system that covers the conduct of individual actors, accepting not their racist intention but the banality of their act and behavior; institutional racism can take different forms: humiliation, suspicion, a kind of internal colonialism and symbolic or even physical violence against migrants.

Migrants in a subordinate situation, who may be less gifted at school or in poverty, are discriminated against like young French people of North African origin, in particular of Algerian origin, who experience great difficulty in accessing employment; this situation cannot only be explained by a particularly low level of education, but rather by phenomena of discrimination in hiring. More qualified migrants work in conditions disrupted by forms of covert discrimination, which result in mistrust and suspicion towards them. For example, young qualified Chinese migrants and graduates of prestigious Chinese universities or the French Grandes Écoles (business schools, for example) might reach the status of senior executives in companies in France or Europe and find themselves confronted with discriminatory practices that produce, at a given moment, situations that block professional mobility opportunities (Roulleau-Berger 2013; Roulleau-Berger and Yan 2017; Yong 2020). These qualified migrants come up against a glass ceiling, and hierarchical career progression is prevented by invisible barriers – the barriers of latent and very active racism which expresses the inhumanity of ethnic inequalities.

3.2.3. *The globalization of care*

In addition, international migration has become more feminized, and women's work has been organized into three urban markets in particular: domestic work, care work and sex work. Today, most women from poor countries are forced to do domestic work, relegated to demeaning jobs where they often work without being declared. These unequal situations cannot be dissociated from the process of globalization. The disqualifications and humiliations suffered by migrant women are particularly clear with the expansion of the global market for domesticity. Care work shows how gender, ethnicity and global social stratification can be combined in a "negative" way, distributing women over transnational spaces by giving them access to invisible forms of work. Care work shows how economies are dematerialized and how migrant women play a central role in this process where the exploitation of material resources is coupled with the exploitation of the *emotions of care workers* (Ehrenreich and Hoschschild 2004; Mozère 2004). In international cities, care work accounts for forms of inequality that result from the combination of processes of economic globalization, ethnicization of labor markets and the subalternization of the labor market. It unfolds in the invisibility of work, where service relationships and bonds of intimacy merge and where social identities constructed in other spaces are blurred. While domesticity can evolve into sex work, Lieber and Lévy (2009) have shown, for example, that in European cities, faced with the closure of European labor markets and highly unequal situations, Chinese women, both young and old, came to perceive their bodies and their sexuality as migratory resources within the framework of economic-sexual arrangements in different ways. Indeed, the international trafficking of women for the sex industry has increased significantly over the past decade, both within and outside Asia and the former Soviet Union.

3.2.4. *Migration and platform capitalism*

In Asian megacities and European cities, more and more young, low-skilled migrants are working on digital platforms for e-commerce, express delivery, group buying, food delivery and cab services, which have grown rapidly in recent years. Young migrants, both male and female, are joining microwork platforms without the employment status associated with professional activity and become "click slaves" (Casilli 2019), performing unskilled tasks at home for poverty wages.

Forms of piecework are re-emerging through micro-employment platforms and primarily involve migrant workers. The crowdsourcing of micro-tasks was launched by the American web giant Amazon and is now practiced by the Chinese giant Alibaba Group. Underpaid workers are now drawing attention to their struggles: their time is exploited, the time needed to complete the task is underestimated, unpaid tasks are numerous and the minimum wage is not respected (Barraud De Lagerie and Sigalo Santos 2018).

In European cities such as France, the activity of migrant workers on platforms and in uberization is largely participating in the expansion of platform capitalism. Zani (2020) has shown that between China and Taiwan, young low-skilled Chinese migrants, in transnational migration, bring into existence a material and emotional kind of "small capitalism" through e-commerce.

In the context of increasing international migration, hyper-capitalization and rising inequalities, we see a diversification of forms of work according to their degree of commodification, legitimacy and visibility. Forms of work are multiplying and hierarchizing differently according to the cultural, economic and political histories of European, Asian, African, Eastern, Middle Eastern and Latin American cities. They are integrated into market and non-market, monetary and non-monetary, abundance and "survival", competitive and underground economies. This plurality of economies denotes spaces of competition and legitimization that make labor markets appear increasingly multipolar, and political powers and modes of legitimization increasingly polycentric.

3.3. Multi-situated inequalities and biographical bifurcations

The experiences of migrants in different workspaces produce biographies punctuated by bifurcations linked to changes of place. Migrants move from place to place at each stage in society, spaces and places that are stratified differently according to the political, social and economic histories of the country they are in. In the passage from one context to another, more or less strong gaps are built between social positions that vary according to societal contexts and migrants' routes. Inequalities either accumulate, or they are weakened by the effect of differentiation between weak positions in one societal context and strong positions in another, or they are maintained.

3.3.1. Migration and multi-situated inequalities

Today, in the context of globalization, the migrant passes from one societal regime to another several times. The figure of the migrant is constructed in two or more contexts – of departure, arrival and transit – all of which produce different inequalities. At each stage of migration, individuals place themselves or are placed in a social space governed by orders of recognition constructed differently according to societal contexts. In migratory movements, the effects of collision produce violence, domination and inequalities that are constructed through differentiated access to social, economic and symbolic resources, as well as to knowledge, abilities and skills.

However, depending on the economic, cultural or political differences between the different societal contexts, inequalities can increase or decrease during the migration process. For example, when the contexts of departure are less economically developed than the contexts of arrival, migrants from the middle or working classes are more likely to follow paths of upward social mobility in the societies of arrival, and the inequalities experienced in the society of departure are then likely to diminish; but when migrants occupied a "high" social position in the society of departure, they often find themselves in situations of social decline in the society of arrival. The amplification or reduction of social inequalities appears to be a multidimensional, discontinuous, reversible process, in the sense that each migratory stage imposes a re-composition of the repertoire of economic, social, and ethnic resources of migrants, whose social position varies according to the contexts and the routes followed. We have spoken of *multi-situated inequalities* in this regard (Roulleau-Berger 2010).

3.3.2. Inequalities and biographical bifurcations

At each stage of migration, individual resource repertoires are reordered and bring into play the effects of biographical discontinuity. The wider the repertoire of resources, the more ordered they are, and the more individuals can manage the effects of biographical discontinuity. Multi-situated inequalities, due to migrants' repeated mobilities, result in discontinuous and hierarchical access to labor markets in different societal contexts. Migrants mobilize repertoires of social, educational, economic, symbolic and even religious resources, mobilized through sequences of relatively predictable actions.

Our research required us to use the notions of bifurcation (Grossetti 2004), event, transition and rupture to understand how multi-situated inequalities are constructed (Roulleau-Berger 2010). The biographical bifurcations of migrants are formed when professional and geographical mobilities come together, and their multiplication varies according to educational qualifications, social and economic resources, and employment opportunities. In the diversity of low-skilled migrants' careers, identity resources are mobilized in a discontinuous mode, and mobilities produce both resources and constraints; economic, political and societal contexts have different effects on the processes of accessing increasingly differentiated and hierarchical labor markets. At each stage, the repertoires of individual resources are rearranged, and status, place and social identity are redefined on the basis of individual and collective capacities for action. Migrants mobilize their resources in these changing biographical sequences, where individuals move from one space to another, from one economic regime to another.

The frequency of bifurcations in migrants' lives constitutes a principle of differentiation and inequality that accounts for the discontinuity of work experiences; a rapid frequency means there is discontinuity between experiences in very different jobs. A short obligatory presence in a job, whether formal or informal, does not leave time to find a place for oneself and to capitalize on new social and symbolic resources; migrants are then forced into horizontal mobilities. Close bifurcations arise from professional discontinuities and spatial discontinuities, producing migratory careers that take place in spaces of low economic legitimacy, and may force migrants to return to their region of origin.

These bifurcations also express the capacities for action and reflexivity of these mid-level managers, who leave a job when they can no longer stand it and look for another. The less qualified tend to move along horizontal network lines, while those with more personal and social resources tend to move along vertical network lines. And the amplification or reduction of social, ethnic and gender inequalities imposes a recomposition of the repertoire of personal resources at each migratory stage.

In migration careers, there is also the question of the intentionality of individuals, often translated into the notion of a migration project. Each time migrants move, a new biographical crossroads appears, open to a wide spectrum of possible choices, giving rise to uncertainties. Individuals construct their migration careers from a multiplicity of roles and affiliations linked to heterogeneous socialization spaces. Beck (2006) spoke of the cosmopolitization of biographies to express how globalization affects the ways in which migrants' biographies are constructed, and we have spoken of *individuation that is both situated and globalized* to define migrants' plural identities, which are both situated and global (Roulleau-Berger 2007).

3.4. Moral careers and the struggle for recognition

If biographical bifurcations punctuate migrants' careers in their objective dimension, their moral dimension also constantly informs the way in which mobilities follow one another. Migrants leave societies where, in most cases, they had a place that made them appear "small" or "big" (Tarrius and Missaoui 2000). In each migratory experience, in each biographical moment, migrants never achieve the same recognition; they are confronted with different norms and must place themselves in a relationship of adherence to these norms in order to achieve a position in the society of arrival. The least qualified migrants become increasingly "small" in short networks and are often confronted with the experience of losing know-how, skills and qualifications. They most often go through a succession of spaces of low legitimacy, where identities ascribed by others produce a negative devaluation of what they do or think they do.

In the cosmopolitanization of these biographies, the question of ownership and loss of self becomes crucial. The more migrants circulate between economic and social spaces that are contrasted by their degree of legitimacy, the more they are confronted with different normative orders; they are then sometimes recognized, sometimes not, sometimes misunderstood. In the construction of multi-situated inequalities, identity switches between recognition and social contempt, between mistrust and confidence in the "other", between self-esteem and shame.

It is around social and moral goods, confidence in the "other" and in oneself, social respect and self-respect, social esteem and self-esteem, that social and ethnic competition and inequality are reorganized in a blurred manner. This phenomenon then actively gives rise to risks of social exclusion by producing phenomena of alteration of the self. Confronted with identity reshuffles, readjustments and conflicts, migrants find it increasingly difficult to adjust their different selves, to keep face. They oscillate between social esteem and contempt, between self-esteem and self-shame, depending on the roles they play in different social and economic spaces (Roulleau-Berger 1999). Self-esteem and shame appear to be reversible and dynamic aspects of identity. But the phenomena of repeating and intensifying situations of disqualification and humiliation can make these feelings of shame irreversible.

The question of ownership and loss of self in the migratory experience is thus regularly raised. The higher the degree of legitimacy of the spaces crossed during the migratory experiences, the more the forms of social recognition accumulate to give rise to public recognition. The more the migrants cross spaces of socialization where the identities attributed by others produce positive recognition, the more we can speak of a reduction in the gaps between different orders of recognition and the opening of spaces where subjects capable of being actors and producing experiences are built.

Holding up, keeping going, is a major moral issue for migrants (Tcholakova 2016), which can be partially ensured by digital economies. These economies ensure that migrants, in tension between several spaces and several temporalities, are not cut off from their families, and thus remain connected, to use the words of Diminescu (2014). Indeed, information and communication technologies (ICTs) are now part of the daily life of individuals on the move. They represent a means of producing new opportunities for exchange and communication with friends and family back home. Smartphones, online applications and digital platforms ensure the simultaneous maintenance of links with the society of origin and the production of transnational links. From now on, migrants are no longer confronted with a "double absence" (Sayad 1999), but rather inscribed in a "connected presence" composed of different forms of potential and actualized presences (Diminescu 2019). The maintenance of self through emotions and feelings is thus partially ensured by digital resources, which come to combine with social, economic and moral resources.

Ownership, maintenance and loss of self show how regimes of otherness (Abélès 2008) are complex and multiplying, producing forms of unequally legitimized recognition. We speak of *regimes of weak otherness* when migrants with few resources and little protection from collective systems are the object of social, economic and ethnic inequalities in social worlds with little legitimacy, which distribute little social and public recognition and little social esteem. We speak of *regimes of strong otherness* when migrants who are well equipped with resources and protected by collective systems are engaged in processes of social, economic and cultural affiliation in legitimized institutions that distribute social and public recognition and social esteem. We speak of *regimes of partially autonomous otherness* when migrants, poorly equipped in terms of resources and designated as having weakly recognized social competences, develop capacities of collective and individual mobilization, social creativity and even resistance (Roulleau-Berger 2014).

3.5. The plurality and hierarchy of transnationalisms

If the relationship between migration and economic inequalities can be understood from the condition of subaltern and the social inequalities, ethnic discriminations and racism at work, they also appear very clearly in a diversity of economic transnationalisms and hierarchies between them. We make the following distinction between:

– transnationalism from above, with the formation of economic elites or transnational upper classes;

– transnationalism and bazaar economies;

– transnationalism via international trade.

3.5.1. *Transnationalism "from above" and cosmopolitan spirit*

Since the end of the 1980s, world trade, foreign investments and the circulation of capital have accelerated, and the dynamics of migration have continued to multiply and diversify. The migration of economic, scientific and technical elites expresses the forms of renewal of these mobilities. Globalization "from above" shows how a fraction of today's new cosmopolitan bourgeoisie is being formed, partly residing in Europe (Wagner and Gérard 2015) and made up of highly qualified, highly skilled transmigrants from continental China, Central and Eastern Europe, the Maghreb and the Middle East. A new cosmopolitan bourgeoisie is thus emerging, engaged in transnational mobilities that build new transnational productive territories and contribute to the development of multipolar economies.

In European cities, young qualified Chinese executives have arrived to work in import-export companies, in the banking sector, in engineering offices, in international trade, in food processing companies, in household appliances, etc. These young, qualified Chinese migrants produce globalized work in China and Europe. They have all developed strong geographical and professional mobility by accumulating social and spatial capital. They also have the idea of wanting international lives in common, displaying "a cosmopolitan spirit" (Ciccelli 2012). In the fashion, cosmetics, luxury goods, international tourism and art sectors, highly skilled migrants from the Maghreb, Central Europe, Eastern Europe and China produce globalized work in transnational mobilities whereby new arrangements are formed in global market sectors, by combining local and international dimensions from these plural arrangements in the development of material and immaterial labor economies, for example, in the computer or multimedia sectors. Migratory skills here rely on high international social capital and strong spatial capital (Roulleau-Berger and Yan 2017). Global labor can also be expressed through new commercial centralities, as with middle-class Japanese migrants who work in gastronomy, the art market, etc. (Dubucs 2014).

These migrants actively participate in the definition of multi-situated, productive territories between different international cities as places where goods, products and values circulate and accumulate. Transnational careers are organized in the layering of differentiated economies and cultures, highlighting new forms of international capital accumulation. Interests and identities are constantly being redefined in these migratory circulations which are structured around access to social prestige.

3.5.2. *Transnationalism "from below" and bazaar economies*

Ethnic and multi-ethnic neighborhoods exist in every international city and are always linked to other ethnic spaces in other international cities. For residents, these neighborhoods may appear as urban enclaves, while for migrants, they are a place of economic production and international exchange. Within these transnational spaces, transnational *bazaar economies* (Geertz 1979) emerge. Locality, trade and ethnicity construct assemblies between multipolar economies. For example, in the bazaars of La Guillotière in Lyon (Battegay 2003), Via Padova in Milan, Château-Rouge in Paris, and Belsunce in Marseille, African, North African, Indian and Chinese traders and entrepreneurs, among others, sell clothes, belts, scarves, bags, bracelets, calculators, watches, toys, mobiles, etc., sourcing from global markets in China. When we speak of ethnic enclaves in France, we think of Chinese migrants, but also of migrants of North African or African origin hired by North African or African employers. On the other hand, migrants from Central and Eastern Europe are less visible in ethnic enclaves. The least qualified migrants are more likely to be found in the restaurant, food, small-scale distribution and garment sectors. Places of origin and situations of linguistic security or insecurity play a role in the distribution and allocation of places in ethnic enclaves. For low-skilled migrants in situations of linguistic insecurity, whatever the societal context, the ethnic enclave appears as a first step in the process of economic insertion. These ethnic enclaves arise from transnational networks that are obviously based on highly structured forms of economic organization, where certain economic, ethnic and social dominations can be exercised through assignments to socially devalued places, and the imposition of horizontal mobilities on disqualified and disqualifying market segments. With the intensification of international migration, traditional ethnic enclaves are becoming saturated and urban enclaves are becoming more and more multi-ethnic.

Ethnic enclaves contain ethnic entrepreneurship in the catering, mainstream clothing and hairdressing sectors, among others. More qualified migrants, for example young Chinese migrants, create travel agencies, computer companies and luxury clothing brands, which also contribute to the creation of an intermediate economic transnationalism. We can see how spatial movements are embedded in social relations specific to the society of departure and to the societies crossed, and how migrants rely on resources acquired or inherited in their society of origin, by manipulating spatial capital that will allow them to integrate into transnational networks. The conditions for successful forms of entrepreneurship depend on situations of strong or weak solidarity, which do not always appear to guarantee economic success; situations of limited solidarity provide competitive advantages because of the trusting relationships within the group, while limiting the obligations of solidarity (Steiner 1999).

3.5.3. *Intermediate transnationalism and international trade*

Finally, it is worth mentioning the forms of intermediary transnationalism that are developing in international marketplaces, such as Yiwu in China, a global city in the province of Zhejiang, which is one of the largest wholesale markets in the world, located at the origin of the "New Silk Roads", supplying much of the global market with small commodities. Yiwu, a multi-million-dollar city, hosts 4,300,000 m^2 of markets, with over 400,000 types of products offered by over 100,000 suppliers.

Yiwu was a small city in 1970; gradually, Chinese traders and entrepreneurs developed internal economic networks in China with other local markets. The city subsequently attracted more and more entrepreneurs and traders from different Arab countries, India, Pakistan, Syria, Turkey, Egypt, Yemen, different African and Maghreb countries, Central and Eastern Europe, etc. Thus, a multi-ethnic urban co-presence was produced, organized around the manufacture of an economic cosmopolitanism, partly Muslim, and both global and local. Yiwu is thus as a *non-Western global city*.

Yiwu appears to be a privileged place of economic globalization, relatively discreet (Choplin and Pliez 2018), implying a global division of labor, spatial reorganization of production, planetary industrial restructuring, development of digital economies and informalization of labor. Economic life in Yiwu demonstrates that we are witnessing a reorientation of migratory movements, notably between China, the Middle East, India, Pakistan, Iraq, Syria, Africa, and Central and Eastern Europe, and a multiplication of migratory circulations, which actively contribute to the displacement and redefinition of the borders of new transnational productive territories. In Yiwu, local and transnational markets are being developed from the establishment of agreements and economic exchanges based on international relations between Chinese merchants and entrepreneurs and others from other countries mentioned above. Yiwu is linked to other Chinese and international cities by social, economic and religious networks. These "non-Western" global markets are fed by local economic networks, for example small-scale global production sites located in the surrounding villages and towns, connected to transnational spaces.

How are these non-hegemonic cosmopolitanisms constructed? Economies of hospitality and trust, produced by Chinese and international entrepreneurs and traders, are arranged in transnational spaces, codified by shared conventions and norms. These cosmopolitanisms link Chinese cities such as Keqiao, Qingdao, Yongan, Shenzhen and Ningbo, and create links between African, Indian, Middle Eastern, Central European and Eastern European cities. The migratory paths of transnational entrepreneurs and traders allow us to see the routes of these non-Western economic networks, both material and digital, where economic, social, religious and moral resources circulate, which are constantly being mobilized, transformed and increased with each change of place and country.

In Yiwu, as in other non-Western cities, Chinese Muslim migrants and other Muslim communities (Indian, Pakistani, Yemeni, Jordanian, African) produce *circulatory territories* (Tarrius and Missaoui 2000) that interact with each other, but also with Western spaces. These migrations of Muslim traders and entrepreneurs from China, India, Africa and the Middle East reveal forms of economic mobilization that counter the inequalities imposed by authoritarian capitalisms.

3.6. Forced migration, downgrading and expulsions

Karen Akoka, Olivier Clochard and Albena Tcholakova, in a 2017 issue of the *Revue européenne des migrations internationales*, entitled *Reconnu·e·s réfugié·e·s et après ?* (Granted refugee status – but what next?), have shown that since 1990, refugee studies and forced migration studies have emerged as new fields of social science research, developing alongside the field of international migration. Indeed, more and more people are fleeing wars, persecution and ethnic and religious violence across the world to seek asylum in "peaceful" countries, especially within the European Union. These new migrants will primarily be asylum seekers, and some of them will be able to obtain refugee status.

If social inequalities seem to disappear at certain moments in the migratory ordeal, they reappear very quickly during the waiting period for migrants in fear, who must take up a position, seize opportunities to mobilize inherited resources and convert the social and professional experience acquired before "arriving". The careers of migrants under constraint are constructed in the exacerbated intersectionality of social relations related to the social position of origin, gender and ethnicity. Social mobilities can only be understood from the different experiences and situations of employment and work in different contexts.

The experience of downgrading is at the heart of the trajectories of forced migrants, especially the most qualified. The higher the position of the individuals in their country of departure – or if they had developed upward social mobility in their country of origin – the more they will experience professional de-qualification, and the stronger their feeling of disqualification. The ordeal of social downgrading is central to the pathways of migrants under threat who experience social, status and salary downgrades as though forced migration implied owing a debt to the societies of arrival (Roulleau-Berger 2017). It always involves losses of social, economic and moral resources. The conception of the self is profoundly altered when individuals have been abused, mistreated, tortured in their home countries and during the migratory journey. While migrants are often downgraded upon arrival in an immigration country, some manage to repurpose their resources in the medium to long term (Bidet 2018).

Asylum seekers and refugees are forced into a model of resignation, given that they are unable to legitimize the qualifications and professional experience gained in their home country and during their migratory journey. The imposition of disqualifying forms of work reveals violent forms of economic domination based on ethnic differentiation and distinction. The majority is forced to mourn their past and future aspirations. Finally, the violence of symbolic dominations is expressed in some cases by the imposition of situations of inactivity, where the know-how and skills acquired in the contexts of origin and on the migration routes are erased. The maintenance of the capital of experience in migratory routes appears rather as an exception. The ordeal of social decline imposes the reinvention of oneself, being confronted with the obligation to rewrite one's own history in a society that is foreign to oneself.

While the diversity of the biographies of forced migrants from the upper or middle classes was built on professional experiences consistent with their initial training, the biographies of migrants from the working or farming classes were instead organized in forms of polyactivity or pluriactivity, which create situations of precarity and resignation to unpredictability. Most migrants under duress have first had to develop, in spite of themselves, adaptive capacities in their societies of origin where they have experienced dramas and traumas. They have then had to develop resistance skills and survival strategies in threatening situations. In contexts of great violence, practical skills have been produced in emergency situations; they will be partially transferred and activated in other emergency situations in the societies of arrival.

On the roads of forced migration, men and women are constantly hunted down by the police of different countries, experience prison and sometimes torture, especially in Libyan prisons and life in various camps. Violence, expulsions and indecency are all part of the journey of these migrants. States, whether it be through border controls, migration management, route orientation, or even expulsions and deportations, deploy via their police forces forms of exacerbated brutality in the treatment of migrants (Lardeux 2015; Agier et al. 2018). Asylum seekers have no right to singularity or justice for who they are, identified as "illegitimate" (Sayad 1999), condemned to live in fear and shame. Indeed, asylum seekers and refugees, excluded from civil rights and the "legal" labor market, find themselves caught between a denial of existence and an attempt to gain status.

Rejected asylum seekers become "expelled from the world": the expulsion process exacerbates social, economic, ethnic and gender inequalities to an extreme degree. Although inequalities develop in this process of expulsion from the world society, migrants can be middle or upper class, peasant or working class. These migrants are forced into a denial of existence, into "wasted lives" made up of situations of great moral and material insecurity, finding themselves lost and cut off from their families, wives, husbands and children. Those expelled from the world find their place nowhere. Forced to remain silent while enduring irregularities, threats of deportation to various countries, living in fear of being hunted down and described as undesirable, these migrants write the narrative of a global society of expelled people, condemned to "wasted lives" (Bauman 2006).

3.7. Conclusion

We have shown how thinking about the complexity and plasticity of the relationships between migrations and inequalities in local and global contexts invites the sociologist to adopt a constructivist reading of geographical mobilities in order to grasp both the structures in process – the relationships of domination, competition and subordination in the migratory space – the social interactions of migrants in geographical spaces, their skills of action and mobilization, and their subjectivities. The staging of the plurality of local and transnational spaces inhabited by migrants, located on different scales and hierarchized between them, has highlighted the relationships of exchange, conflict, complicity and competition between them. This relationship between migration and inequalities makes it possible to understand how differentiated migratory spaces fit together to produce unequal cosmopolitanisms. This approach invites us more broadly to hear the voices of all migrants around the world, and to recognize their struggles for dignity and respect; it is based, in fact, on a methodological cosmopolitanism to move toward a non-hegemonic sociology, which opens up new perspectives on migration and inequalities based on a non-Western-centric approach. In conclusion, the scientific challenge involved in developing a theory of inequalities and migrations today also requires the international recognition of non-Western knowledge to advance with a view to producing new knowledge in the field of the sociology of inequalities, in line with a post-Western sociology (Roulleau-Berger 2016; Xie and Roulleau-Berger 2017; Roulleau-Berger and Peilin 2018).

3.8. References

Abélès, M. (2008). *Anthropologie de la globalisation*. Payot, Paris.

Agier, M., Bouaga, Y., Galisson, M., Hnappe, C., Pette, M., Wanesson, P. (2018). *La Jungle de Calais*. Presses Universitaires de France, Paris.

Akoka, K., Clochard, O., Tcholakova, A. (2017). Editorial – la condition de réfugié : expériences subjectives et mobilisations collectives. *Revue européenne des migrations internationales*, 4(33), 7–21.

Ambrosini, M. (2007). Employment and working conditions of migrant workers. Report, European Foundation for the Improvement of Living and Working Conditions, Dublin.

Ambrosini, M. (2018). *Irregular Immigration in Southern Europe – Actors, Dynamics and Governance*. Palgrave MacMillan, London.

Ambrosini, M., Cinalli, M., Jacobson, D. (eds) (2020). *Migration, Borders and Citizenship*. Palgrave MacMillan, London.

Barraud De Lagerie, P., Sigalo Santos, L. (2018). Et pour quelques euros de plus. Le crowdsourcing de micro-tâches et la marchandisation du temps. *Réseaux*, 36(212), 51–84.

Bastide, L. (2015). *Habiter le transnational. Espace, travail et migration entre Java, Kuala Lumpur et Singapour*. ENS Editions, Lyon.

Bataille, P. (1997). *Le Racisme au travail*. La Découverte, Paris.

Battegay, A. (2003). Les recompositions d'une centralité commerçante immigrée : la Place du Pont à Lyon. *Revue européenne des migrations internationales*, 19(2), 9–22.

Bauman, Z. (2006). *Vies perdues : la modernité et ses exclus*. Payot, Paris.

Beck, U. (2006). *Qu'est-ce que le cosmopolitisme ?* Aubier, Paris.

Bidet, J. (2018). Migrations et mobilités sociales en contexte transnational. *Actes de la Recherche en Sciences Sociales, Capital social et migration*, 228(1), 47–61.

Burawoy, M. (1979). *Manufacturing Consent: Changes in the Labor Process under Monopoly Capitalism*. University of Chicago Press, Chicago.

Casilli, A. (2019). *En attendant les robots*. Le Seuil, Paris.

Choplin, A. and Pliez, O. (2018). *La mondialisation des pauvres*. Le Seuil, Paris.

Ciccelli, V. (2012). *L'esprit cosmopolite*. Presses de Sciences Po, Paris.

Cossée, C., Miranda, A., Ouali, N., Séhili, D. (eds) (2013). *Le genre au cœur des migrations*. Petra, Paris.

De Rudder, V., Poiret, C., Vourc'h, F. (2000). *L'Inégalité raciste. L'universalité républicaine à l'épreuve*. Presses Universitaires de France, Paris.

Diminescu, D. (2014). Traces of dispersion: Online media and diasporic identities. *Journal of Migration and Culture*, 5(1), 23–39.

Diminescu, D. (2019). Les risques et les opportunités de la migration connectée : entretien avec Dana Diminescu. *Socio-anthropologie*, 40, 203–213 [Online]. Available at: https://doi.org/10.4000/socio-anthropologie.6330.

Dubucs, H. (2014). Les Japonais à Paris. Entre invisibilité et hypervisibilité commerciale. *Hommes&Migrations*, 1308, 46–52.

Ehrenreich, B. and Hochschild, A.R. (2004). *Global Woman: Nannies, Maids and Sex Workers in the New Economy*. Owl Books, New York.

Geertz, C. (1979). *Meaning and Order in Moroccan Society. Three Essays in Cultural Analysis*. Cambridge University Press, Cambridge.

Giraudo-Baujeu, G. (2020). Messes-basses et "silences qui parlent" ou comment "entendre" le racisme flottant. *Socio-anthropologie*, 41, 147–161.

Glick Schiller, N., Basch, N., Blanc-Szanton, C. (1992). Transnationalism: A new analytic framework for understanding migration. In *Towards a Transnational Perspective on Migration: Race, Class, Ethnicity, and Nationalism Reconsidered*, Glick-Schiller, N., Basch, N., Blan-Szanton, C. (eds). The New York Academy of Science, New York.

Goffman, E. (1975). *Stigmates*. Éditions de Minuit, Paris.

Grossetti, M. (2004). *Sociologie de l'imprévisible*. Presses Universitaires de France, Paris.

Hajjat, A. and Mohammed, M. (2013). *Islamophobie : comment les élites françaises fabriquent le "problème musulman"*. La Découverte, Paris.

Honneth, A. (2000). *La lutte pour la reconnaissance*. Éditions du Cerf, Paris.

Jounin, N. (2009). *Chantier interdit au public : enquête parmi les travailleurs du bâtiment*. La Découverte, Paris.

Kergoat, D., Miranda, A., Ouali, N. (eds) (2011). Migrantes et mobilisées. *Cahiers du genre*, 51.

Lardeux, L. (2015). *Retours d'exil*. Éditions de l'EHESS, Paris.

Lieber, M. and Lévy, F. (2009). La sexualité comme ressource migratoire. Les Chinoises du Nord à Paris. *Revue française de sociologie*, 4(50), 719–746.

Morice, A. and Potot, S. (2010). *De l'ouvrier immigré au travailleur sans papiers. Les étrangers dans la modernisation du salariat*. Khartala, Paris.

Mozère, L. (2004) Travail informel et projet de vie. Les domestiques philippines à Paris. In *Economies choisies*, Barre, N., Latouche, S. (eds). Éditions de la MSH, Paris.

Portes, A., Guarnizo, L.E., Landolt, P. (1999). The study of transnationalism: Pitfalls and promise of an emergent research field. *Ethnic and Racial Studies*, 22(2), 218–237.

Réa, A. (2013). Les nouvelles figures du travailleur immigré : fragmentation des statuts d'emploi et européanisation des migrations. *Revue européenne des migrations internationales*, 29, 15–35.

Réa, A. and Tripier, M. (2008). *Sociologie de l'immigration*. La Découverte, Paris.

Roulleau-Berger, L. (1999). *Le travail en friche. Les mondes de la petite production urbaine*. Éditions de l'Aube, La Tour d'Aigues.

Roulleau-Berger, L. (ed.) (2007). *Nouvelles migrations chinoises et travail en europe*. Presses Universitaires du Mirail, Toulouse.

Roulleau-Berger, L. (2010). *Migrer au féminin*. Presses Universitaires de France, Paris.

Roulleau-Berger, L. (2012). Circulations, travail au féminin, inégalités multisituées et individuation. In *Le genre au cœur des migrations*, Cossée, C., Miranda, A., Ouali, N., Sehili, D. (eds). Petra, Paris.

Roulleau-Berger, L. (2013). Chinese migrations, inequalities and transnational spaces in Routledge. In *China's Internal and International Migration*, Li, P., Roulleau-Berger, L. (eds). Routledge, London/New York.

Roulleau-Berger, L. (2014). Plural inequalities, vulnerabilities and urban careers in Chinese cities. In *Globalization and New Intra-Urban Dynamics in Asian Cities*, Aveline-Dubach, N., Jou, S.-C., Hsiao, H.-H.M. (eds). NTU Press, Taipei.

Roulleau-Berger, L. (2016) *Post-Western Revolution in Sociology. From China to Europe*. Brill, Leiden/Boston.

Roulleau-Berger, L. (2017). In commemoration of the legacy of Ulrich Beck: Theory of migration and methodological cosmopolitanism. *Development and Society* [Online]. Available at: https://www.questia.com/library/journal/1P4-1968400127/in-commemoration-of-the-legacy-of-ulrich-beck-theory.

Roulleau-Berger, L. and Peilin, L. (2018). *Post-Western Sociology – From China to Europe*. Routledge, London/New York.

Roulleau-Berger, L. and Yan, J. (2017). *Travail et migration. Jeunesses chinoises à Shanghai et Paris*. Éditions de L'Aube, La Tour d'Aigues.

Sassen, S. (2006). *Territory, Authority Rights: From Medieval to Global Assemblages*. Princeton University Press, Princeton.

Sassen, S. (2009). *La globalisation. Une sociologie*. Gallimard, Paris.

Sayad, A. (1999). *La Double Absence. Des illusions de l'émigré aux souffrances de l'immigré*. Le Seuil, Paris.

Schmoll, C. (2020). *Les Damnées de la mer*. La Découverte, Paris.

Schmoll, C., Thiollet, H., Withol de Wenden, C. (eds) (2015). *Migrations en Méditerranée. Permanences et mutations à l'heure des révolutions et des crises*. CNRS Éditions, Paris.

Simon, G. (2008). *La planète migratoire dans la mondialisation*. Belin, Paris.

Simon, G. (ed.) (2015). *Dictionnaire des migrations internationales. Approche géopolitique*. Armand Colin, Paris.

Steiner, P. (1999). *La sociologie économique*. La Découverte, Paris.

Tarrius, A. (2002). *La mondialisation par le bas*. Balland, Paris.

Tarrius, A. (2015). *La mondialisation criminelle*. Éditions de L'Aube, La Tour d'Aigues.

Tarrius, A. and Missaoui, L. (2000). *Les nouveaux cosmopolitismes. Mobilités, identités, territoires*. Éditions de l'Aube, La Tour D'Aigues

Tarrius, A. and Missaoui, L. (2006). Villes et migrants, du lieu-monde au lieu-passage. *REMI*, 22(2), 43–65.

Tcholakova, A. (2016). Le remaniement identitaire entre reconnaissance et maintien de la cohérence biographique. L'exemple des réfugié.e.s en France. *Sociologie*, 7(1), 9–76

Wagner, A.-C. (1998). *Les nouvelles élites de la mondialisation. Une immigration dorée en France*. Presses Universitaires de France, Paris.

Wagner, A.-C. (2007). *Les classes sociales dans la mondialisation*. La Découverte, Paris.

Wagner, A.-C. and Gérard, E. (2015). Elites et savoirs. *Cahiers de la recherche sur l'éducation et les savoirs*, July 13.

Waldinger, R. (1996). Newcomers in the workplace: Immigrants and the restructuring of the US Economy. *Journal of American Ethnic History*, 15(4), 67–69.

Xie, L. and Roulleau-Berger, L. (eds) (2017). *The Fabric of Sociological Knowledge: The Exploration of Post-Western, Sociology*. Beijing University Press, Beijing.

Yong, L. (2020). The identity crisis of Chinese graduates in France. In *Chinese Immigrants in Europe: Image, Identity and Social Participation*, Liu, Y., Wang, S. (eds). De Gruyter, Berlin/Boston.

Zani, B. (2019). In-between: Re-migration, emotional circulations and new cosmopolitan biographies. *Asian Pacific Viewpoint*. doi:10.1111/apv.12254.

Zani, B. (2020). We chat, we sell, we feel: Chinese migrant women's emotional petit capitalism, special issue migration, digital media and emotion. *International Journal of Cultural Studies*, 23(5), 803–820.

4

The Geographical Dimension of Inequalities in Access to Employment

Philippe ASKENAZY[1] and Verónica ESCUDERO[2,3]
[1] Centre Maurice Halbwachs, CNRS, ENS, Paris, France
[2] International Labour Organization, Geneva, Switzerland
[3] Center for Effective Global Action, UC Berkeley, USA

4.1. Introduction

Most countries have significant and persistent spatial disparities in access to employment. These disparities concern all dimensions of access to employment: whether or not one is working; the nature and amount of earnings received; whether one has a job that corresponds to one's aspirations; and the type of job (full-time, part-time, self-employed, etc.). The dispersion of unemployment rates at different territorial levels provides an entry point for this chapter, which explores the significance of geographical processes (essentially internal to a country) in inter-individual inequalities by covering all dimensions of access to employment.

The magnitude of the differences in unemployment, wages or income[1] within countries is as great as between countries at the same level of development whether

---

1. Wages are a form of remuneration for work in a given salaried job, paid on an hourly, monthly or even piecework basis. The definition of employment income is broader, including all earnings from work over a given period of time (usually a year), including wages for different jobs and earnings for self-employed activities. In addition, labor income also includes transfers that are directly related to being in the labor force, such as unemployment

the analysis is conducted at a regional level (NUTS 1 and 2 within the European Union, for example) or more locally.

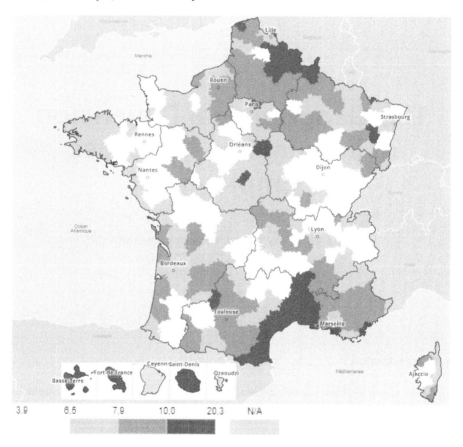

Figure 4.1. *Average annual unemployment rate by employment zone in metropolitan France and overseas departments, 2021 (sources: IGN and Insee localized unemployment rate; extracted from the INSEE local statistics website: statistiques-locales.insee.fr). For a color version of this figure, see www.iste.co.uk/cottineau/ inequalities.zip*

---

insurance benefits. Finally, income in the broadest sense includes other sources of financial transfers: investment earnings, pensions, donations, etc. Wages and income can be expressed as gross or net of social contributions and/or taxes.

In France, for example, there are large disparities between the unemployment rates of different employment areas (Figure 4.1), with a wide spectrum in metropolitan France ranging from Les Herbiers in the Vendée to Agde-Pézenas in the Hérault (with 3.9% and 15.2% rates of unemployment in 2021, respectively), exceeding 16% across the overseas departments of Guadeloupe and La Réunion.

	Regions with the highest unemployment rate	2019	Regions with the lowest unemployment rate	2019
Belgium	Brussels-Capital	12.6	Antwerp Province	3.6
	Prov. Hainaut Province	8.6	Oost-Vlaanderen Province	2.9
	Namur Province	7.0	West-Vlaanderen Province	2.5
Spain	Autonomous City of Melilla	27.0	Aragón	10.0
	Autonomous City of Ceuta	25.8	País Vasco	9.2
	Extremadura	21.5	Comunidad Foral de Navarra	8.2
Hungary	Észak-Alföld	6.3	Pest	2.4
	Dél-Dunántúl	4.8	Közép-Dunántúl	2.0
	Észak-Magyarország	4.5	Nyugat-Dunántúl	1.8
Italy	Calabria	21.0	Emilia-Romagna	5.5
	Campania	20.0	Provincia Auton. Di Trento	5.0
	Sicilia	20.0	Provincia Autonoma di Bolzano/Bozen	2.9
Poland	Lubelskie	5.4	Slaskie	2.4
	Podkarpackie	5.1	Lubuskie	2.0
	Mazowiecki regionalny	4.6	Warszawski stoleczny	2.0
Slovakia	Východné Slovensko	9.1	Západné Slovensko	4.0
	Stredné Slovensko	6.1	Bratislavský kraj	2.3

Table 4.1. *Regions (NUTS 1) with the highest and lowest ILO unemployment rates (in %) within selected European countries, 2019 (source: Eurostat)*

Regional differences are significant in nearly all of the countries of the European Union, sometimes even more pronounced than in France (Table 5.1). Over the last three decades, northern Italy has experienced an unemployment rate that is three or four times lower than that of southern Italy (Kline and Moretti, 2013). Similar results can be seen for the United States. The unemployment rate in Flint (Michigan) was nearly six times higher than that of the city of Iowa (Iowa) (*ibid.*).

These geographic differences persist over several decades (Blanchard and Katz 1992; Moretti 2011) and across generations (Chetty et al. 2014). Moreover, they do not simply reflect differences in the average characteristics of residents. The degree of variability remains when rates are adjusted for education, age, gender or ethnicity. Beginning with an analysis of the sources of this variability in terms of unemployment allows us, in this chapter, to progressively explore the multiple geographic channels that affect the various social gradients in access to employment.

Different models have been used over the years to study spatial differences in unemployment from an economic perspective. Regardless of their assumptions, all models conclude that unemployment differentials depend on labor supply factors (such as changes affecting the labor force, labor force participation, commuting patterns, migration and other preferences of workers, etc.); labor demand factors (such as job vacancies and amenities that affect the production function of firms); and wage setting (including wage levels, how well job seekers are matched to existing vacancies, etc.) (Elhorst 2003). However, not all models take into account all aspects that can be classified into these three broad categories of factors. In fact, space characteristics, such as housing conditions, property values, infrastructure, including transportation, public services and the perception of disamenities such as insecurity, pollution, etc., are often not incorporated, although they may determine variations in labor supply and demand, and more often than not both simultaneously. For example, the value of land will affect both. On the one hand, it can limit or increase the costs of firms attracting more or fewer jobs. On the other hand, it will allow or prevent households from residing near workplaces. For this reason, we have chosen to present simple models of migration and amenities as a starting point for this discussion, as they allow us to explore the role of geography in creating inequalities in access to employment.

However, these models are based on a strong assumption of costless and frictionless labor mobility, which is not the case either for movements within a country (economic, social, family and emotional costs of moving) or internationally (language barriers, legal barriers, etc.). Thus, explaining the persistence of large spatial disparities in labor market access within countries requires us to go beyond existing models. This investigation will reveal how geographic mechanisms can generate, amplify or moderate inequalities in gender, age, education or ethnicity in access to (decent) jobs. Many channels emerge. In this chapter, we develop those that seem to us to be the most illustrative. They can be divided into three groups, each of which addresses a hypothesis of migration or amenity models: residential immobility and spatial mismatch (section 4.3); how models and their assumptions need to be adapted when looking at employed couples rather than the individual (section 4.4); and the lack of free access to the labor market and the question of networks (section 4.5).

Finally, the last section of the chapter deals with digital space (section 4.6) to explore whether some of the changes brought about or facilitated by digital technologies might erase the geographical dimension of access to employment, and their consequences in terms of (un)equal access to employment.

4.2. Compensatory differences between territories

The economic literature pays particular attention to the role of interregional labor migration as a mechanism for balancing the performance of regional labor markets (Pissarides and McMaster 1990; Molho 2001; Layard et al. 2009). This section presents two generic models taken from this literature, followed by the findings of empirical studies testing their relevance.

4.2.1. *From the immigration model to the amenities model*

One strand of this work identifies interregional migration as the key aspect of reconciling spatial and regional differences in labor market and economic opportunities (Hunt 1993). Migration models assume that the decision to move residentially is determined by the costs and benefits of moving from one area to another (Groenewold 1997; Molho 2001). Unemployment and wages are key variables in this decision, as workers are expected to migrate to balance these two factors (among others). Indeed, according to traditional economic theory, areas of high unemployment experience a decline in relative wages, which in turn causes individuals to migrate to other areas. At the same time, the decline in relative wages also leads to an increase in the relative demand for labor, and emigration leads to a decrease in the relative supply of labor. In the second stage, unemployment therefore falls in these areas, and relative wages rise, causing workers to move to these areas from other locations. The repetition of this process tends toward an equilibrium.

However, in Hunt (1993), Molho (2001) and Pissarides and McMaster (1990), the migration process is assumed to be slow, and thus while an equilibrium can be reached, it will only be long term through compensating differentials in local unemployment and wage. In this simple theoretical version, net migration is assumed to be zero. An extension of the model relaxes this assumption, allowing market conditions other than unemployment and wages (job vacancies and amenity differences, such as housing prices and public services) to play a role (Groenewold 1997). But the basic assumption of these approaches is that a regional imbalance in unemployment and wages is only slowly resolved by interregional migration flows, among other factors.

In contrast, a second strand of the literature assumes that local economic and labor markets, as well as the migration process, are efficient. Thus, any differences in individuals' preferences for wages, unemployment and other economic opportunities are quickly mediated by migration, which quickly restores equilibrium differentials between localities. This is the basis of the commodities or amenities model, which supports a spatial equilibrium view of unemployment (Elhorst 2003). According to this model, relocation is driven by the availability, consumption and relative prices of amenities, and the perception of disamenities in residential areas. Thus, in this model, the accessibility (or lack of accessibility) of amenities is the factor that compensates for spatial differences in unemployment. Utility differentials (i.e. people's preferences for certain amenities) are not emphasized in these models, as they will be automatically compensated for by residential mobility. What matters are changes in the demand for and supply of amenities (and their upstream determinants, such as increases in real incomes), because they will lead to a momentary disequilibrium.

4.2.2. Empirical findings

The empirical findings do not support some of the assumptions of the migration and amenities models, nor their key theoretical prediction that intra-regional differences in unemployment will reach equilibrium (albeit in the long run).

First, empirical analyses have struggled to demonstrate that people move primarily to take advantage of better amenities, and that geographic differences in employment opportunities can be quickly arbitrated by migration. In fact, other factors play an important role, such as changes in local real wages and household rent (Blanchard and Katz 1992; Diamond 2016); mobility costs, which are disproportionately higher for more vulnerable groups (Bound and Holzer 2000; Moretti 2011); changes in local labor demand, such as shifts in the sectoral composition of firms (Blanchard and Katz 1992; Moretti 2011); and so on. Moreover, rather than reducing interregional inequalities, the migration of people to areas with better jobs and better amenities can lead to the labor market segmentation, spatial segregation of workers according to their level of income or qualifications, and greater economic inequality. This is what Diamond (2016) found when she studied the geographic sorting of young people in the United States from 1980 to 2000. She found that the most educated job seekers settled in areas with better jobs and amenities, while the least educated job seekers moved to areas with worse jobs and amenities.

Second, various studies have shown that labor markets remain fairly local. Indeed, even when people want to move, they prefer not to move far away. For example, Manning and Petrongolo (2017), in their study of local labor markets in England and Wales, found that job seekers are less interested in jobs the further away they are. In addition, many people who would like to move are unable to do so because they cannot always find jobs in other locations (Gobillon et al. 2007).

Finally, even in countries where interregional migration is a widespread phenomenon, such as the United States, it is insufficient to balance regional labor markets in the long run. For example, in 2009, the average hourly wage of a worker in Stamford, Connecticut, was twice that of another worker with the same education, age, gender and race in Jacksonville, North Carolina (Kline and Moretti 2013). The difference was even greater for job opportunities.

All in all, the empirical results show that the simplifying assumptions of existing theoretical models do not allow these models to accurately represent the complex realities of individuals and households with respect to the geographical dimension of inequalities in access to employment. It is therefore necessary to introduce new, more realistic mechanisms into the analysis. This is what we do throughout the rest of the chapter, where we discuss immobility and spatial mismatch (section 4.3); how models and their assumptions change when we no longer look at the worker as a single person but as a member of a household (section 4.4); the absence of free access to the labor market and the question of networks (section 4.5); and finally the digital space (section 4.6).

4.3. Immobility and spatial mismatch

When jobs are far away from the people seeking them, there is a spatial mismatch. In particular, this common phenomenon affects low-income households around the world. In some countries, such as the United States, particularly in former large industrial cities, this mismatch is fueled by the concentration of jobs in the suburbs and the concentration of affordable housing in the inner cities. Other geographic areas suffer from a reverse pattern of this spatial mismatch. For example, in many contemporary cities, particularly in Europe (Berlin, Paris, London, Milan, etc.), high-income jobs and the most expensive housing are concentrated in the city centers, pushing more affordable housing to the suburbs, where the jobs to which these populations are entitled are rarely located. This pattern creates a displacement problem, especially for vulnerable workers, including people with disabilities, who cannot take advantage of distant employment opportunities, especially in the absence of reliable public transportation.

4.3.1. *Residential sorting and access to employment*

The spatial mismatch hypothesis was pioneered by Kain (1965). Using data for Detroit and Chicago in 1952 and 1956, he concluded that African Americans were concentrated in inner-city housing, suffering from significant residential immobility (linked to racial discrimination – which we will return to in the next subsection). This, combined with the suburbanization[2] of jobs, has reduced the employment opportunities for this group.

The phenomenon of spatial mismatch has been the subject of much empirical research, generally confirming its initial predictions. In the United States, most studies have focused on the effects of spatial mismatch on the labor market outcomes of Black workers. Parks (2004), for example, finds that improved geographical accessibility[3] to jobs is associated with lower unemployment rates among Black workers. Weinberg (2004) finds that Black residential centralization can explain a large portion of the employment differential (48–62%) between Black and White workers. Hu (2019) extends this analysis to other racial/ethnic groups. Using longitudinal and census demographic data, combined with travel time matrices, his studies focus on Hispanic and Asian populations in the Los Angeles area. He finds that when Hispanic people with low or moderate education have low job accessibility, the result is a lower probability of employment than White people. In the case of Asian job seekers, the spatial mismatch hypothesis is confirmed, even when they are highly educated.

Meanwhile, in Europe, Gobillon et al. (2011) assess whether differences in unemployment duration in Île-de-France (Greater Paris Area) reflect residential sorting. The authors use duration models based on an administrative dataset containing spells of unemployment, workers' characteristics and their place of residence between 1996 and 2003. The study finds that local indicators, composed mainly of measures of residential segregation, capture 70% of labor market disparities. These findings are supported by Korsu and Wenglenski (2014), who explain that being located far from employment in the Paris Region tends to complicate individuals' access to employment. Finally, Åslund et al. (2010) study this issue for refugees in Sweden. The authors draw on a government policy that randomly assigns refugees to neighborhoods with different degrees of accessibility, combined with rich individual-level data for 1990–1991 and 1999. The study finds that neighborhoods with twice as many jobs

---

2. "North-American" suburbanization differs from European suburbanization (Hervouët 2001). Suburban areas are positioned between peri-urban and urban areas. Suburbanization is the movement of a population from the center to the suburbs.
3. Accessibility in these studies is generally measured using an index capturing the distance between residences and potential workplaces (Gobillon et al. 2007).

have a 2.9 percentage point higher probability of refugee employment on average. In addition, sorting individuals into areas with low job availability permanently worsens their labor market outcomes 10 years later.

While these studies confirm the effect of spatial labor market mismatch on the employment of vulnerable workers, other studies have focused on the mechanics of this effect. Indeed, spatial mismatches are driven by the barriers faced by workers, primarily the most vulnerable, to commute or relocate to geographic areas where jobs exist. These barriers are discussed in the following sections.

4.3.2. Gradients in residential immobility

Some studies in geography and sociology see residential immobility and even segregation as a voluntary choice demonstrating an attachment to one's land or neighborhood, to one's roots and community (Cooke 2011), which may even have benefits (Peach 1996). However, many studies explore the mechanisms (social and economic, but also legal[4]) of involuntary residential immobility and its links with access to employment and the labor market.

Social housing recipients face a double challenge (Hu 2019), namely the spatial concentration of supply and waiting lists that make it difficult to obtain housing in a distant locality where the worker would have obtained a promise of employment. Mobility must therefore precede the search for employment. Even in France, where municipalities are required to maintain a quota of low-cost housing, it is concentrated in large cities in certain neighborhoods (see Chapter 7).

At the same time, access to rental housing in the private sector is hampered by the unequal financial capacity of individuals. In growing employment areas in particular, landlords can charge higher prices and be selective by requiring a job, a promise of stable employment or a deposit. Young people are particularly exposed to these requirements. This creates a very strong gradient and a social reproduction of inequalities in terms of opportunities: a young person whose parents have wealth and/or a comfortable income will be able to leave the family home to move and get closer to a job market where their skills will be most valued, unlike a young person with the same skills whose lack of family support will prevent them from moving.

In addition, some private landlords discriminate against certain populations, even though this is illegal in many countries. Kain's (1965) original hypothesis of racial

---

4. For example, Schleicher (2017) offers an impressive list of legal devices that "trap" US households especially in cities in decline.

discrimination in the housing market limiting residential choice for African Americans has since been largely validated. Online rental offers have provided a field for numerous experimental analyses in different countries. They systematically point toward clear statistical discrimination, as well as a discrimination of preference against ethnic minorities (except in neighborhoods and localities where they are already concentrated), thus compounding spatial segregation and trapping these minorities in low employment opportunities (e.g. Bosch et al. 2010, on Spain).

Homeowners are a priori exempt from these constraints. Nevertheless, especially for those on the lowest incomes, ownership can become a straitjacket (Askenazy 2021). Transfer costs include a fixed share, and the transfer of credit from one dwelling to another can also be costly. Above all, homeownership involves being overexposed to local economic downturns. If, for example, an employment area suffers the closure of a large factory, not only will employment opportunities plummet but housing values will also decline, making it impossible for a homeowner to sell and acquire a home in an up and coming area. Thus, homeowners may have less residential mobility than renters. Hassan et al. (1996), for example, illustrated this in the case of Australia. Such vicious cycles particularly affect certain categories or minorities, such as low-wage workers in Australia or Black and Latino populations in the United States (Hall et al. 2018). At a more macrolevel, these mechanisms participate in a divergence of employment or unemployment rates between employment areas following economic recessions or restructuring (e.g. with reference to France, Askenazy 2018).

Social barriers appear across the board, whether someone is an owner or a tenant. For example, local friendship and family networks offer daily support that allows for reconciling family and professional life, and accessing jobs with staggered hours or on weekends, especially when childcare services are limited. Mobility can break these social barriers down. Here too, a social gradient appears whereby young, single mothers with children, and in the case of the United States, Black mothers, are the most dependent on maintaining such networks for their participation in the labor market (Parish et al. 1991).

All in all, mobility is limited by numerous fixed costs and barriers that ultimately reinforce the social and ethnic gradient in access to employment.

4.3.3. *Commuting patterns*

The empirical literature supports the intuition that extending commutes increases employment opportunities and, in part, resolves spatial mismatch (Bastiaanssen et al. 2020). While spatial mismatch theoretically allows one to escape from a monopsonic local labor market (see Box 4.1), and thus experience an increase in job quality (and in wages, first and foremost), its positive effects are not so clear in practice, at least for certain groups of workers.

> A monopsony is a market situation that is symmetrical to that of a monopoly: demand is essentially the result of one player. In the labor market, a monopsony is an employer who does a large share of the hiring, and an oligopsony is a limited group of employers who concentrate most of the jobs or hires. A degree of concentration or monopsony in a labor market can be calculated: for example, the Herfindahl-Hirschmann index is calculated by squaring the employment (or hiring) share of firms recruiting in a given market.
>
> In practice, a monopsony is assessed for a segment of the labor market and is often location-based. For example, in a given catchment area, a large factory may concentrate most of the industrial jobs; a supermarket may be the only source of part-time jobs for low-skilled women in the area. Monopsonic situations are frequent but often hidden; for example, in the city of Paris, the Casino distribution group concentrates nearly half of the jobs in the food retail sector through a multiplicity of different brands (Monop', Franprix, Naturalia, Leader Price, etc.).
>
> The monopsony has market power that allows it to capture workers' rents and, in particular, to crush wages (below the theoretical level of the competitive model). The level of employment is itself sub-optimal. The prevalence of a monopsony is thus one of the main theoretical and empirical explanations for the absence of a negative impact on employment of the introduction of a minimum wage or of a significant increase to it, a phenomenon observed in particular since 1999 in the United Kingdom and since 2015 in Germany (Gautié 2020).

Box 4.1. *Monopsony: a key concept in labor economics*

A journey by private car involves significant fixed costs (purchase and maintenance of the vehicle, parking space, etc.) and variable costs (fuel, possible tolls) to be weighed against the opportunities to which this journey gives access. This trade-off therefore tends to reinforce inequalities in access to employment between professional categories. In fact, we observe much longer journey times for executives than for employees. This also implies a generational bias, with young people (Brandtner et al. 2019), as well as poorer households (Jouffe et al. 2019) less likely to have their own vehicle.

From this perspective, public transport infrastructure plays a key role in reducing inequalities in access to employment. This argument has long been discussed statistically, as the presence of infrastructure is partly endogenous to the distribution of housing and jobs: for example, the construction of a subway line may be decided because there are ex ante flows of workers from their place of residence to their place of work. Recent work has moved beyond the critique of the endogeneity of infrastructure as a response to pre-existing routes. They reference natural experiments, such as a disaster that cuts off transportation lines for an extended period (e.g. Tyndall 2017, based on Hurricane Sandy in New York City), and support the influence of infrastructure on inequality. Young people are the primary beneficiaries of public transportation in terms of access to employment (Brandtner et al. 2019).

In addition to its direct effects, the improvement of individual and collective transport infrastructures involves positive and negative externalities. Its impact in terms of inequalities in access to employment is thus ambiguous. Better infrastructure enhances the attractiveness of the area that benefits from it, not only for workers but also for employers and consumers. Numerous studies confirm that it accentuates the agglomeration of activities (e.g., Ghani et al. 2016, with reference to India); this agglomeration therefore offers increased employment opportunities to all the residents who are beneficiaries. Yet, conversely, it tends to reinforce the geographic segmentation of a space with – to use the terms of Krugman's (1991) initial model – cores where jobs are concentrated and peripheral territories where residents suffer from a deficit of employment opportunities.

Moreover, promoting longer commutes affects the quality of employment, the environment, and the lives of individuals. Indeed, the length and nature of these trips are a working condition. Commuting can be a factor of increased fatigue and stress, especially for the longest journeys, and automatically increases risks (accidents in private vehicles, picking up an infection on public transport). Above all, commuting time replaces health activities, such as meal preparation, time spent with family for meals or physical activities (Christian 2012). Overall, travel time tends to worsen individuals' health indicators, and even more so their perceptions of their health (e.g. Hansson et al. 2011, with reference to Sweden). The improvement of infrastructure thus has ambiguous effects for the inhabitants of the areas concerned: it generates new journeys and encourages longer commutes, but it reduces the time spent in transport for a given distance, and by agglomeration makes it possible to offer similar employment opportunities for shorter trips in terms of distance and time.

In sum, a number of barriers impede the ability of workers, especially the most vulnerable, to commute to or relocate to geographic areas where jobs are available. In addition, the dynamism of firms' locations in geographic areas can also determine spatial mismatch. Theoretical models suggest that employment centers emerge when built-in areas become large enough to allow for greater demand, which depends on economies of scale and transportation costs (Krugman 1991). Empirical analyses show that this geographically concentrated production is indeed a factor in regional unemployment differentials (Elhorst 2003). Polycentrism, or the decentralization of certain economic sectors, is also a dynamic phenomenon, given the constant rise and fall of industries and firms, and the changing organization of metropolises. In these circumstances, the availability and affordability of transport and housing become all the more important, because, in practice, reassignment and commuting are the only mechanisms for absorbing sudden changes in labor demand in terms of skills and locations.

Lastly, it will be interesting to monitor the long-term impact of the Covid-19 health crisis on commuting, both in terms of inequality in access to employment and health. In addition to telecommuting, which will be discussed in section 4.6, the crisis may have increased distrust of public transport; it has also accelerated the construction of bicycle infrastructure in many cities, which combines mobility and physical activity for distances of a few kilometers.

4.4. The importance of couples' geographic trade-offs in individuals' access to employment

So far, we have considered isolated individuals or households[5] without distinguishing between their members. However, while some choices may remain individual, some are fundamentally shared within a household. The space in which the household establishes its main residence is one of the most structurally significant, since it is one of the determinants of its members' labor markets. Looking within a household reveals new mechanisms linking space and inequalities in access to employment. As in most existing work, we restrict ourselves here to heterosexual, dual-earner couples living in the same dwelling, with or without children (see Figure 4.2) – the main configuration of non-retired households in many advanced, emerging and developing countries.

---

5. According to the Eurostat definition, a household consists of a person living alone or a group of persons not necessarily related to each other, residing at the same address, sharing at least one meal a day, or sharing a living room.

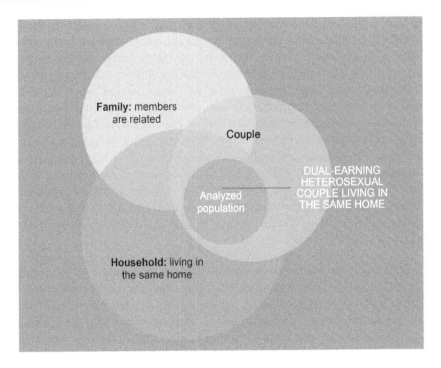

Figure 4.2. *Between couple, family and household, the position of dual-earning heterosexual couples living in the same home. For a color version of this figure, see www.iste.co.uk/cottineau/inequalities.zip*

4.4.1. *A theoretically gendered space*

A bulk of work in family economics has broken down unitarian views of the household (Donni and Ponthieux 2011). Unlike, for example, Becker's (1974) approach, family choices are not made by an altruistic head of household who seeks to maximize total household income. They are the result of negotiations between two adults.

Frank (1978) combines this household approach with job search theory to rationalize the differential in job access and earnings between men and women in couples. Women are more likely than men to be unemployed or in positions below their education level because of the priority given to the man's career in deciding where the family will live. Women are then locked into a local labor market that is suboptimal for them, which reinforces income inequalities between men and women. This theory is consistent with the observation that women are overqualified for the jobs they hold. In the labor market, the geographical dimension thus reflects the inequality of relative bargaining power within the household.

The integration of gendered responsibilities amplifies the bias against women in access to employment, by reducing the radius of the labor market on which women operate. Indeed, theoretical studies show that, even when households change residence, it is women who minimize commuting (Clark et al. 2003). Thus, the assumption that women are responsible for the household (childcare, housework), which is largely confirmed by empirical measures, theoretically reduces the time available for women to "commute". The birth of a child results in an atrophy of the labor market accessible to mothers, especially since it is not necessarily accompanied by a change in place of residence. The break-up of a couple does not necessarily break the residential dependence because, very often, the mother retains custody of the children, and sometimes also the associated family dwelling (40% of women with sole custody of the children retain it after a divorce in France (Bonnet et al. 2015)). If she is forced to move out, the proximity to the children's schooling becomes the priority, even if it means moving to a much smaller dwelling.

It should be noted that the literature based on a job search approach automatically makes the male/female differential the result of a supply effect, as concluded by Le Barbanchon et al. (2020). However, it cannot be ruled out that, for example, local monopsonic firms take advantage of the spatial limitation of women to impose a lower quality of employment (working conditions and wages) on them[6].

In these theoretical frameworks, the larger, denser and more diverse the labor market, and the more rapid transportation options are developed, the more opportunities women have. Thus, the less they should suffer from being disadvantaged in comparison to men.

4.4.2. Indicators of a restricted labor market for women

A large body of literature has empirically explored these theoretical mechanisms and tends to validate them overall. Within the OECD, for example, it has been observed that women's commuting times or distances to work are sometimes significantly shorter than men's commuting times or distances to work. Unemployed women also tend to look for work within a smaller radius than men. Small differences can have significant impacts. For example, using French administrative

---

6. An empirical study of firms' profits would make it possible to differentiate between the supply and demand effects. Profits should be reduced by a less efficient matching in the first case and increased in the second. To our knowledge, there is no such work.

data, Le Barbanchon et al. (2020) find that unemployed women are less "willing" to commute, generating a "voluntary" wage loss of about 10% of the male/female differential in their job search model. However, according to the European Working Conditions Surveys, the difference in commuting time between employed women and men in France is smaller, compared with some countries, such as Germany, the United Kingdom, Ireland and Austria (Table 4.2). It should be noted that the comparison of gender differences must be assessed in countries with a similar level of female participation. The apparent near-equality in commuting time in Italy and Poland is explained by a much lower female employment rate.

In particular, a body of work suggests that parenthood affects women's commuting distances but has no effect on men's commutes (e.g. McQuaid and Chen (2012) with regard to the UK, or Lee and McDonald (2003) with regard to South Korea). It suggests that commuting time has a more severe impact on women's decision to leave their jobs, while hourly wages have a more significant impact for men. This explains why women accept more precarious jobs in exchange for a shorter commute (Nafilyan 2019). However, the risk of being overqualified decreases with commuting distance for both men and women (Büchel and Battu 2003). The very rich article by Skora et al. (2020) explores the complete chain of events leading to a wage decrease for mothers. The authors exploit the German Socioeconomic Panel (GSOEP) from 2001 to 2017. Their results show that the transition to first-time parenthood is associated with a partial withdrawal from the labor force. For women remaining in employment, transition to motherhood is associated with a one-third decrease in the distance of their commute, while the transition to fatherhood has no effect. Moreover, the more mothers reduce their commuting distances after the transition to parenthood, the more they suffer a wage penalty. The authors suggest that wage penalties for mothers who change jobs to secure one closer to their place of residence are subject to not only a mismatch in their skills profile but also a potential loss of firm-specific human capital, as the change involves moving to jobs in firms with lower wages. In total, one quarter of the wage discount of German mothers could be explained by the shrinking of their labor market.

The nature of the local housing market also seems to play a role. Thus, if we look at Germany, Nisic (2017) shows that the gender wage differential for a given level of education is much less pronounced in large cities. It should be noted that while there is a concentration of couples in which both members have a high level of education in large urban areas[7], this does not mean that this choice of abode

---

7. The concentration of graduate couples is higher in these areas because of the concentration of single graduates.

corresponds to a search for balance between the careers of the two partners: a study by Compton and Pollak (2007) based on the American Panel Study of Income Dynamics suggests that, even in these couples, the man's career tends to sway the choice of location.

	Men (M)	Women (W)	Difference (M-W)	Female employment rate (15–65 years-of-age)
Belgium	51.1	45.0	6.1	58.0
Czech Republic	37.5	33.7	3.8	62.4
Denmark	48.2	48.4	– 0.2	68.7
Germany	48.7	41.7	7.0	69.9
Ireland	52.5	44.4	8.1	59.3
Greece	33.1	31.9	1.2	42.5
Spain	37.1	36.4	0.7	52.7
France	46.7	43.0	3.7	60.6
Croatia	37.5	38.4	– 0.9	51.6
Italy	28.6	27.3	1.3	47.2
Latvia	52.9	45.4	7.5	66.4
Netherlands	46.9	43.1	3.8	69.2
Austria	45.7	34.1	11.6	67.1
Poland	35.3	36	– 0.7	56.6
Portugal	25.7	25.1	0.6	61.1
Romania	41.8	38.7	3.1	53.2
Slovenia	42.3	37.5	4.8	61.0
Sweden	53.2	46.6	6.6	74.0
United Kingdom	57.9	46.4	11.5	67.9

Table 4.2. *Average time spent commuting between work and home (in minutes) by gender, 2015. Selected European countries (source: Eurofound [QOE_EWCS_3C3] and Eurostat (employment rates))*

Why, then, do some countries with high female employment rates, such as Denmark (see Table 4.2), show more equality between men's and women's commuting times? Does this equality translate into reduced disparities in working conditions? Although the empirical literature is sparse, existing studies shed some light on this question. If women accept less advantageous working conditions in exchange for greater flexibility and shorter commutes, then reducing gender inequalities in the labor market would require us to address the reasons why women prefer more flexible jobs. One such reason is the desire to balance work and family life, as women take on the majority of child-related tasks, as well as those related to elderly parents and relatives (Gimenez-Nadal and Molina 2016; Nafilyan 2019). Providing affordable childcare, encouraging flexible work practices and promoting more egalitarian gender norms (as in Denmark) could be good ways to eliminate inequalities in working conditions between the sexes.

4.5. Labor market networks and access to employment

Free entry into the labor market is marked by information asymmetries for both employers and workers. Despite the signals provided by the diploma, the orientation and filtering work of public employment services, and the service of digital platforms of vacancies and applicants' profiles, employers have only imperfect information on the quality of a candidate for employment. Conversely, a candidate has only partial public information on the working and salary conditions of an open job. A very large body of work views the use of personal contacts (or social networks) as a means of recruitment that allows agents to limit these asymmetries (Ioannides and Loury 2004). A person already employed in a company is able to give precise indications about the nature of the job, the employer's requirements or what it is like to work there. Conversely, the employer can extract information about a candidate from their referee, which also reduces the employee's "moral hazard"[8]. The interest in networks in the labor market is justified in practice: in many countries, the use of personal contacts is a major way, if not *the* main way, of hiring new entrants[9] (for Europe, see Pellizzari (2010)). A social network is based on multiple dimensions, including ethnicity, religion and alma mater[10]. We focus here on its geographical dimension, and more specifically on its residential dimension.

---

8. In labor economics, a moral hazard arises from information asymmetries between the employer and the employee. The employee exploits the inability of the other party to observe their behavior perfectly, to reduce effort, thus failing to adhere to the terms of the labor contract.
9. The irruption of digital job platforms rather seems to have reinforced the importance of social networks in the labor market (Kuhn and Mansour 2014).
10. As suggested by the "strength of weak ties" theory developed by the American sociologist Mark Granovetter in 1973, which has taken on new life with social networks, a job seeker is more likely to find a job by sharing their search with members of their extended social circles (i.e. their weak ties) than by asking their close network (family, friends, etc.).

4.5.1. *The empirical relevance of residential networks*

If recruitment to a university position, whether permanent or not, after a doctorate can be attributed to a network of professional contacts without, a priori, a particular residential dimension, this configuration represents the exception rather than the rule. A series of studies have highlighted the role of residential networks in the labor market[11].

For example, Hellerstein et al. (2011), using establishment-level matched employer–employee panel data covering most of the United States, explore an immediate residential effect. Although they do not have a direct indicator of neighborhood contacts, the authors show that there is an overrepresentation in U.S. establishments of employees who reside in the same census tract (a scaled-down level of about 1,500 people). The residential effect is more significant for low-skilled, Black and Hispanic workers, the latter being overrepresented in the informal economy. The residential network also affects the quality of the job. Again, in the United States, the more employees from the same place of residence work in the same establishment, the higher their wages are and the less frequently they resign or are fired (Hellerstein et al. 2014).

More recently, Jahn and Neugart (2020) investigated whether residential networks helped workers to find a job after being laid off due to a plant closure in Germany. Combining rich spatial information with administrative data, they find that a 10-percentage point higher neighborhood employment rate causally increases the probability of finding a job by about 2 percentage points. Laid-off workers not only benefit from residential networks in terms of higher earnings and longer job stability, but also have a greater chance of finding a job in the plant that already employs a neighbor.

4.5.2. *Networks that generate spatial inequalities?*

The development of matched employer–employee databases, and even more so data from online social networks or mobile telephony, should make it possible to observe real networks of residential acquaintances, and provide new empirical evidence of their impact on the labor market (Topa 2019).

---

11. The longitudinal dimension of the data used in these studies makes it possible to address reverse causality if the choice of housing not only influences, but is influenced by the professional network. For example, a work colleague can provide information on the existence of a sale or rental opportunity, and on the amenities and the neighborhood.

These new data will also allow us to further explore the impact of residential networks on residential inequalities in access to employment. The theoretical approaches of Topa (2001) and Calvó-Armengol and Jackson (2004) emphasize the externalities of residential networks: if your neighbors are unemployed or work in firms with few job opportunities, your chances of getting a (good) job are diminished, and vice versa. Equally, your own access to employment influences the chances of your neighbors. These externalities then generate residential polarization, with blocks of neighbors having few job opportunities and high unemployment, and others having privileged access to employment. Empirical analyses do seem to validate a large-scale spatial correlation of employed persons (e.g. Conley and Topa 2007).

The importance of local recruitment networks for the lower skilled may also affect their mobility opportunities. This is also true for workers in precarious segments of the labor market. Thus, in France, more than 80% of hires are for short-term jobs, and two-thirds are in fact rehires (recruitment of a former employee); in this way, precarious workers have reputational capital via their network of former employers, which they would squander if they moved to other segments or areas offering better quality jobs.

4.6. Digital space: the abolition of geographical constraints?

Like any technological revolution, the digital one reshapes with each wave the nature and location of economic activities, as well as the organization of territories, especially the city. Beyond this power to transform the demand for labor and the geography of jobs, certain changes brought about or facilitated by digital technology may erase the geographical dimension of access to employment. Digital technology could then abolish certain inegalitarian mechanisms that we have described previously. We explore three of these global changes here: recruitment platforms, teleworking and digital microwork. The first is capable of opening up a labor market without physical limits, while the other two are capable of breaking down the location-based nature of employment. Two questions arise: do they really erase the geographical dimension? And what are their consequences in terms of (un)equal access to employment?

First, it is important to note that to seize the potential opportunities associated with these changes, one would first need access to the digital spaces. Even in the most advanced countries, there are still areas in rural regions without access to mobile telephones, mobile Internet or high-speed Internet (Figure 4.3). Indeed, the rollout of wireline networks outside dense cities remains limited and territorial divides will deepen at least in the medium term[12]. These divides will interact with individual barriers to access to technologies because of the fixed costs they involve and the minimum skills, including literacy, required for their use. Beyond this mechanical inequality, each change has its own dynamics that we will analyze.

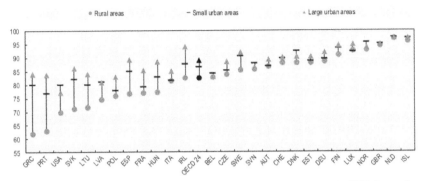

Scope: Proportion of households living in a home with broadband internet access in 2018. Data refer to 2017 for the United States and Switzerland.

Figure 4.3. *The broadband access gap between urban and rural areas in OECD countries in 2018 (source: OECD ICT Access and Usage by Households and Individuals (database)[13]). For a color version of this figure, see www.iste.co.uk/cottineau/inequalities.zip*

4.6.1. *The emergence of online job portals and professional networking platforms*

The development of the Internet has changed the way people search for jobs, making it easier to search for jobs from a distance within a country. In particular, over the past two decades, corporate online job portals (e.g. careers.accor.com, for the worldwide postings of the Accor hotel group) as well as cross-company (e.g. CareerBuilder) and professional networking platforms (e.g. LinkedIn) have emerged as important players for both employers and salaried job seekers. However, existing economic literature struggles to demonstrate that these tools have improved job search efficiency, especially for remote jobs. One of the main difficulties is capturing causal effects. Indeed, available sources of exogenous variation in Internet

---

12. The deployment of satellite constellations to cover the entire surface of the Earth is under way. While the first commercial proposals should emerge in North America as early as 2021, it is expected that this kind of infrastructure could take until the end of the decade to mature. The cost of access is also unknown.

13. Available at: https://stats.oecd.org/Index.aspx?DataSetCode=ICT_HH2.

use are scarce, meaning that at an individual level, identification is difficult due to the natural self-selection of people in specific methods (Kroft and Pope 2014).

Nevertheless, some studies tend to confirm the positive effects of online search and recruitment on the labor market with the growing maturity of tools and uses. For example, in the United States, Kuhn and Mansour (2014) study job search patterns using the National Longitudinal Survey of Youth (NLSY97) for the period 2005 to 2008. Unlike the weak results of Kuhn and Skuterud (2004), covering an earlier period (1998 to 2001), the authors found that unemployed individuals who search for a job online are rehired 25% faster than comparable individuals who search for a job by other means. Examining online job search and match quality in Germany, using individual data from the German Socioeconomic Panel (SOEP), Mang (2012) also observes that job seekers who search online are more satisfied with the job found than their counterparts who searched for a job through other channels (e.g. newspapers, friends, employment agencies, etc.).

The benefits of online job portals can be expected to multiply and extend to more job seekers as Internet access becomes more widespread – Internet penetration is now approaching 90% in advanced countries[14] – and as job vacancies continue to migrate to the Internet. This raises the question of whether existing inequalities in the labor market will be reduced or exacerbated by these portals and platforms. Two opposing mechanisms seem to be at work.

On the one hand, online job searches can open up new avenues for some workers who lack professional or personal networks, or who suffer from discrimination. For example, Kuhn and Mansour (2014) find in their study that Black job seekers are significantly more likely to search for work online than White job seekers in an attempt to compensate for the limited opportunities available to them through "informal" channels (professional, residential networks, etc.).

On the other hand, companies continue to selectively publish their job offers. More importantly, professional networking platforms tend to reinforce the importance of professional networks without changing their exclusive nature. For example, Brenner et al. (2020) study a large dataset of people with full-time jobs to explore their behavior in terms of joining professional social networking sites such as LinkedIn. They find that most people who join these platforms in order to find a new job do so because they already have a professional network whose members are

---

14. From the ITU 2020 report: https://www.itu.int/dms_pub/itu-s/opb/pol/S-POL-BROADBAND.21-2020-PDF-E.pdf.

active on the platform. It thus seems that these platforms encourage segregation in human interactions, ultimately favoring the most qualified.

In this context, the impact of online portals and platforms on the geographic inequalities in access to employment, has not been extensively explored. Partial empirical evidence suggests that spatial mismatch remains a pervasive problem, even for those who have access to the Internet and the digital literacy to use online job search tools. On the labor demand side, there is no evidence that the proliferation of online job search portals and recruitment platforms has significantly increased the size of labor markets, at least not for all types of workers. On the job seeker side, the Internet age does not appear to have improved the poor access to employment that workers face when they live further away from those jobs. Marinescu and Rathelot (2018) use 2012 data from the largest online job search site in the United States, CareerBuilder.com, to assess the impact of distance on the application behavior of job seekers in the United States. They show that workers who use online job search tools are also not looking to apply for distant jobs. In fact, the authors report that these workers are 35% less likely to apply for jobs located 10 miles from their current residence. One interpretation of this result is that by improving local job opportunities, the relative ratio of job opportunities to costs (in terms of transportation, health care, etc.) in searching a larger geographic area decreases. In doing so, workers, especially the less educated, are exposed to the power of local corporate monopsony, which translates into lower quality jobs (lower pay, higher skills requirements for a given position (Macaluso et al. 2019)).

4.6.2. *Telework: a new order?*

The European Framework Agreement of July 16, 2002 between the European Trade Union Confederation (ETUC), the Union of Industrial and Employers' Confederations of Europe (UNICE/UEAPME) and the European Centre of Enterprises with Public Participation and of Enterprises of General Economic Interest (CEEP) provides a definition of telework encompassing most academic approaches as well as legislation: telework is a "form of organising and/or performing work, using information technology, where work, which could also be performed at the employers premises, is carried out away from those premises on a regular basis. The agreement concerns teleworkers with an employment contract and does not deal with self-employed telework". Telecommuting is therefore different from working from home. On the one hand, it requires a salaried relationship with an employer who has premises, and the use of information technology (an artist painting in his studio is not a teleworker). On the other hand, telework can be done outside the home in a third place (such as a coworking space, for example).

With the advent of network technologies, analysts in the 1980s saw the firm implementation of telework on the horizon. Supiot (1996), in the introduction to a special issue of the *Revue internationale du travail* (the journal of the International Labour Organization), "Regards croisés sur le travail et son devenir", stated: "The futuristic horizon of a population of autonomous teleworkers connected to the Internet is unlikely to ever be reached" (Supiot 1996). However, available pre-Covid statistics, both from the OECD and developing countries, show an expansion of telework. For example, in Europe, according to the Labour Force Surveys, 11.5% of employees were teleworking in 2019, compared to 7.5% 10 years earlier (Milasi et al. 2020). This practice is concentrated in sectors and professions where tasks are based on the use of digital or digitizable technologies, such as the information technology sector or legal professionals. However, for the vast majority, telework is only done occasionally – this is the case, for example, with teachers, who represent the professional category with the highest proportion of teleworkers.

Despite its relative marginality, telework has been the subject of many empirical studies. All of this work suffers from the problem of establishing causal identification, as telework can largely be chosen. The picture of working conditions is mixed, with, for example, a possible better work/life balance, but also greater isolation (for a review, see ILO 2020).

Hook et al. (2020) and O'Brien and Yazdani Aliabadi (2020) survey the extensive literature on the impact of telecommuting on housing and commuting. The first striking result is the persistence of such commutes. Ory and Mokhtarian (2006), using California data, describe a particularly illuminating dynamic: people who move after telecommuting move closer to their workplace on average, while those who take advantage of their move to telecommute move much farther – on average 30 km from their physical workplace! One interpretation is that, as teleworkers gain experience, they abandon the illusion that they won't have to travel frequently to their employer's premises.

Panel studies in the United States, the Netherlands and Sweden attempt to identify a net causal effect of telecommuting (for workers who do or do not change their residential area, and for those who do or do not change jobs when telecommuting). If commuting to work remains, the time or distance traveled increases significantly by 5–15%, especially for workers living in suburban areas. In the Netherlands, for example, telecommuting means that people accept 5% longer commute times on average, and each additional day of telecommuting is associated with a 3.5% increase in distance traveled (de Vos et al. 2018).

All in all, like job portals and platforms, telework, at least until 2019, was far from abolishing distances; it did, however, allow a number of workers, mainly qualified and in expanding sectors, which already had opportunities to access a (quality) job, to benefit from a significantly larger labor market.

The lockdowns and other travel restrictions during the Covid-19 health crisis provided a remarkable exogenous shock. However, this cannot be used to measure the impact of telework on working conditions or the labor market, because the conditions are so specific (e.g. children were also confined to their homes) and because, above all, the direct effects of the crisis itself in terms of its health, social and economic dimensions are much more prominent.

On the other hand, lockdown has revealed the potential of telework and even more so its extreme heterogeneity. This is striking, for example, for France, according to the large EpiCov epidemiological survey of a representative sample of 135,000 people (Table 4.3): 70% of employed managers and professionals were teleworking in May 2020, compared with less than 7% of blue-collar workers. The predictions of the ex-ante studies (ILO 2020) are broadly confirmed by these ex-post observations.

	Part-time	Full-time
Workers	5.0	1.5
Employees	13.9	20.7
Intermediate professions	18.8	28.0
Executives and intellectual professions	22.8	57.3
Craftspeople, tradespeople	13.3	7.9
Farmers	4.8	0.6
All	15.8	28.1

Interpretation: In May 2020, 28.1% of those who had worked the week before the survey reported having teleworked exclusively, while 15.8% had done so partially.

Scope: People aged 15 years or older who worked at least one hour in the week preceding the survey in metropolitan France, Martinique, Guadeloupe and La Réunion.

Table 4.3. *Share of teleworkers by occupation (in %) after 2 months of lockdown in France, May 2020 (source: Inserm-Drees, EpiCov survey, wave 1)*

Will the Covid-19 crisis sustain telecommuting? The gain in experience and investment, both by workers and employers, suggests that it will. If telecommuting is expanded in a major and sustained way, then spillover effects may emerge

(O'Brien and Yazdani Aliabadi 2020). They would benefit workers not concerned by telework, with ambiguous effects on geographical inequalities of access to employment or of job quality. For example, the possible peri-urbanization of teleworkers would free up housing in employment-dense neighborhoods for workers with more than one job. This would free up housing in job-dense neighborhoods for workers with less financial and educational capital. The reduced congestion brought about by telework would also allow those who have to work in the office to reduce the burden of commuting, in traveling greater distances for the same amount of time, and thus expand their employment opportunities.

4.6.3. *Microwork: equal access but exploitation?*

Microwork (otherwise known as "click work", micro-jobbing or crowd-working) is the archetype of an apparent disappearance of the physical dimension in access to employment, both in terms of geography and identification of the employer or person in charge. With a simple Internet connection, any worker around the world can perform small digital tasks that are then outsourced to digital platforms. A wide range of tasks is offered and requires very different skill levels, from the most basic to the most specialized: from translating or writing pieces of computer code to simply labeling images. Clickers are essential to artificial intelligence (AI), as they feed learning data enriched by humans. AI itself will not be able to replace humans in these micro-tasks for several decades. Microwork is therefore likely to continue to expand in the coming years, especially as needs increase, for example, for long-term objectives, such as autonomous vehicles. Estimates of the number of workers involved are difficult, but potentially number in the hundreds of millions; researchers estimate that there are at least 200,000 microworkers in France (Tubaro et al. 2020).

The first specific surveys underline that microwork allows people who are far from employment to gain access to an activity. Thus, according to data collected by the International Labor Office (Berg et al. 2019), in both advanced and developing countries, one-third of microworkers were unemployed, and one-third were female microworkers caring for children, disabled or dependent persons, who may find it difficult to hold down a "normal" job.

In the absence of any geographical anchor, click workers undertaking such activities do not have any social protection offered by local laws. This does not mean that the geographical dimension is absent: fundamentally, they participate in a global market where they are in competition[15]. The levels of remuneration are low, far below the minimum wages in their place of residence (when they exist), whether in advanced or developing countries. This weakness is not due to the fact that the tasks are without significant added value. As a result of major network effects and non-regulation, the micro-labor segment is concentrated, dominated in particular by the first mover, Amazon Mechanical Turk (AMT). The micro-labor market is thus probably highly monopsonic. In an empirical study on AMT alone, Dube et al. (2020) estimate that microworkers only receive about 20% of the value they create[16]. In conclusion, the elimination of the physical dimension in micro-labor produces an increase in the size of the labor market (at a global or regional level), without affecting the importance of the geographical dimension in access to employment. Indeed, working conditions, state protections and assistance, and real wages vary according to where workers live, and it is these geographic inequalities that determine workers' ability to access micro-labor. Increased competition without the necessary protections thus has negative consequences in terms of an unequal access to jobs, at least to good quality jobs.

4.7. Conclusion

Both behavioral models of migration and amenities convey optimistic visions. For the former, residential mobility tends to blur the geographical heterogeneity of employment opportunities within an area of free legal movement of people, that is, essentially within one country. For the latter, differences in terms of employment or remuneration do not reinforce inequalities but, on the contrary, compensate for inequalities in the local supply of amenities.

This chapter has analyzed the weight of geographical processes within countries on the inter-individual inequalities[17] in access to employment in its various dimensions – unemployment, status, alignment with aspirations and skills, working conditions and remuneration, etc. In doing so, it has identified a multiplicity of socioeconomic mechanisms supported by an impressive body of empirical literature in geography, economics and sociology. They question and often refute the relevance of the assumptions and predictions of these models.

---

15. This borderless nature remains, even if the necessary skills, such as language skills, limit the pool of click workers to essentially one geographical area.
16. It is worth recalling that the share of labor in value added is estimated at between 40% and 70% in most OECD market economies, both emerging and developing.
17. Aggregate inequalities between territories are dealt with in a work by M. Talandier and J. Tallec, to be published in 2022 in the same collection on geographical inequalities.

In particular, they show that, for large segments of the population, the place of residence and the place of work (if any) are not the result of a free choice, or are not even chosen. Overall, the constraints on residential mobility or on commuting follow gradients that reinforce social scales of all kinds, including generational, ethnic, educational, patrimonial or gender-based ones. For example, the prevalence of a male career in the residential choice of a mixed couple limits employment opportunities for the woman; the domestic work of a mother forces her to search for employment in a geographically restricted area, again reducing her opportunities and exposing her to the risk of monopsonic employers. Whether alone or within a household, workers do not have the freedom of residential choice that would allow them to improve their employment opportunities; monetary barriers, discrimination, gentrification and urban segregation disproportionately keep the least qualified, the youngest and people from minority groups from areas rich in high-quality jobs or transportation infrastructure. Far from the initial models which, in fact, do not see space as a source of inter-individual inequalities, this chapter therefore highlights their significance.

From a methodological point of view, should we then enrich the behavioral models of residential migration by integrating the joint residence of couples, discrimination, social networks, etc.? Rather than a cumbersome formal model whose predictions would necessarily be ambiguous and without practical significance, we would argue for further structural, quantitative and qualitative research on the mechanisms of geographical inequalities in access to employment. Notably since, far from erasing physical space, we have seen that the boom in professional networking platforms and the materialization of telework in the wake of technological change, as well as shocks such as Covid-19, are bringing out new interactions between geography and the social characteristics of individuals in terms of employment opportunities. At the same time, the increasing availability of big data, especially on travel and on localized job offers, should reinforce the potential for the production of empirical knowledge.

Two issues are currently insufficiently explored. On the one hand, strategies aimed to reduce inequalities in access to employment in a specific territory – for example, an urban area – can exacerbate competition between territories, ultimately contributing to an increase in inequalities. On the other hand, such strategies, which are often local, and employment policies, which are often centralized, must be linked.

However, the vast body of knowledge, some of which has been articulated in this chapter, could be used empirically. Ex ante simulations and ex post evaluations can be carried out, at different scales, of the impact of planning, housing and transport policies on the inequalities of access to employment.

4.8. References

Askenazy, P. (2018). The changing of the French labor market, 2000–2017. IZA World Labor [Online]. Available at: https://doi.org/10.15185/izawol.412.

Askenazy, P. (2021). *Share the Wealth: How to End Rentier Capitalism*. Verso, Brooklyn.

Åslund, O., Östh, J., Zenou, Y. (2010). How important is access to jobs? Old question – Improved answer. *J. Econ. Geogr.*, 10, 389–422.

Bastiaanssen, J., Johnson, D., Lucas, K. (2020). Does transport help people to gain employment? A systematic review and meta-analysis of the empirical evidence. *Transp. Rev.*, 40, 607–628 [Online]. Available at: https://doi.org/10.1080/01441647.2020.1747569.

Becker, G.S. (1974). A theory of social interactions. *J. Polit. Econ.*, 82, 1063–1093 [Online]. Available at: https://doi.org/10.1086/260265.

Berg, J., Furrer, M., Harmon, E., Rani, U., Silberman, M.S. (2019). Les plateformes de travail numérique et l'avenir du travail : pour un travail décent dans le monde en ligne. Report [Online]. Available at: https://www.ilo.org/wcmsp5/groups/public/-dgreports/-dcomm/-publ/documents/publication/wcms_721011.pdf.

Blanchard, O. and Katz, L. (1992). Regional evolutions. *Brook. Pap. Econ.*, 1, 1–75.

Bonnet, C., Garbinti, B., Solaz, A. (2015). *Les conditions de vie des enfants après le divorce*. Insee Première, Paris.

Bosch, M., Carnero, M.A., Farré, L. (2010). Information and discrimination in the rental housing market: Evidence from a field experiment. *Reg. Sci. Urban Econ.*, 40, 11–19 [Online]. Available at: https://doi.org/10.1016/j.regsciurbeco.2009.11.001.

Bound, J. and Holzer, H.J. (2000). Demand shifts, population adjustments, and labor market outcomes during the 1980s. *J. Labor Econ.*, 18, 20–54.

Brandtner, C., Lunn, A., Young, C. (2019). Spatial mismatch and youth unemployment in US cities: Public transportation as a labor market institution. *Socio-Econ. Rev.*, 17, 357–379 [Online]. Available at: https://doi.org/10.1093/ser/mwx010.

Brenner, S., Sivrikaya, S.A., Schwalbach, J. (2020). Who is on LinkedIn? Self-selection into professional online networks. *Appl. Econ.*, 52, 52–67 [Online]. Available at: https://doi.org/10.1080/00036846.2019.1638497.

Büchel, F. and Battu, H. (2003). The theory of differential overqualification: Does it work? *Scott. J. Polit. Econ.*, 50, 1–16 [Online]. Available at: https://doi.org/10.1111/1467-9485.00251.

Calvó-Armengol, A. and Jackson, M.O. (2004). The effects of social networks on employment and inequality. *Am. Econ. Rev.*, 94, 426–454 [Online]. Available at: https://doi.org/10.1257/0002828041464542.

Chetty, R., Hendren, N., Kline, P., Saez, E. (2014). Where is the land of opportunity? The geography of intergenerational mobility in the United States. *Q. J. Econ.*, 129, 1553–1623.

Christian, T.J. (2012). Trade-offs between commuting time and health-related activities. *J. Urban Health Bull. N.Y. Acad. Med.*, 89, 746–757 [Online]. Available at: https://doi.org/10.1007/s11524-012-9678-6.

Clark, W.A.V., Huang, Y., Withers, S. (2003). Does commuting distance matter? Commuting tolerance and residential change. *Reg. Sci. Urban Econ.*, 33, 199–221 [Online]. Available at: https://doi.org/10.1016/S0166-0462(02)00012-1.

Compton, J. and Pollak, R.A. (2007). Why are power couples increasingly concentrated in large metropolitan areas? *J. Labor Econ.*, 25, 475–512 [Online]. Available at: https://doi.org/10.1086/512706.

Conley, T.G. and Topa, G. (2007). Estimating dynamic local interactions models. *J. Econom., Analysis of Spatially Dependent Data*, 140, 282–303 [Online]. Available at: https://doi.org/10.1016/j.jeconom.2006.09.012.

Cooke, T.J. (2011). It is not just the economy: Declining migration and the rise of secular rootedness. *Popul. Space Place*, 17, 193–203 [Online]. Available at: https://doi.org/10.1002/psp.670.

Diamond, R. (2016). The determinants and welfare implications of US workers' diverging location choices by skill: 1980–2000. *Am. Econ. Rev.*, 106, 479–524.

Donni, O. and Ponthieux, S. (2011). Approches économiques du ménage : du modèle unitaire aux décisions collectives. *Trav. Genre Soc.*, 26, 67–83.

Elhorst, J.P. (2003). The mystery of regional unemployment differentials: Theoretical and empirical explanations. *J. Econ. Surv.*, 17, 709–748.

Frank, R.H. (1978). Why women earn less: The theory and estimation of differential overqualification. *Am. Econ. Rev.*, 68, 360–373.

Gautié, J. (2020). *Le salaire minimum et l'emploi*. Presses de Sciences Po, Paris [Online]. Available at: http://journals.openedition.org/lectures.

Ghani, E., Goswami, A.G., Kerr, W.R. (2016). Highway to success: The impact of the golden quadrilateral project for the location and performance of Indian manufacturing. *Econ. J.*, 126, 317–357 [Online]. Available at: https://doi.org/10.1111/ecoj.12207.

Gimenez-Nadal, J.I. and Molina, J.A. (2016). Commuting time and household responsibilities: Evidence using propensity score matching. *Journal of Regional Science*, 56(2), 332–359.

Gobillon, L., Selod, H., Zenou, Y. (2007). The mechanisms of spatial mismatch. *Urban Stud.*, 44, 2401–2427.

Gobillon, L., Magnac, T., Selod, H. (2011). The effect of location on finding a job in the Paris region. *J. Appl. Econom.*, 26, 1079–1112 [Online]. Available at: https://doi.org/10.1002/jae.1168.

Groenewold, N. (1997). Does migration equalise regional unemployment rates? Evidence from Australia. *Pap. Reg. Sci.*, 76, 1–20.

Hall, M., Crowder, K., Spring, A., Gabriel, R. (2018). Foreclosure migration and neighborhood outcomes: Moving toward segregation and disadvantage. *Soc. Sci. Res.*, 70, 107–114 [Online]. Available at: https://doi.org/10.1016/j.ssresearch.2017.11.006.

Hansson, E., Mattisson, K., Björk, J., Östergren, P.-O., Jakobsson, K. (2011). Relationship between commuting and health outcomes in a cross-sectional population survey in southern Sweden. *BMC Public Health*, 11, 834 [Online]. Available at: https://doi.org/10.1186/1471-2458-11-834.

Hassan, R., Zang, X., McDonnell-Baum, S. (1996). Why families move: A study of residential mobility in Australia. *Aust. N.Z.J. Sociol.*, 32, 72–85 [Online]. Available at: https://doi.org/10.1177/144078339603200107.

Hellerstein, J.K., McInerney, M., Neumark, D. (2011). Neighbors and coworkers: The importance of residential labor market networks. *J. Labor Econ.*, 29, 659–695 [Online]. Available at: https://doi.org/10.1086/660776.

Hellerstein, J.K., Kutzbach, M.J., Neumark, D. (2014). Do labor market networks have an important spatial dimension? *J. Urban Econ., Spatial Dimensions of Labor Markets*, 79, 39–58 [Online]. Available at: https://doi.org/10.1016/j.jue.2013.03.001.

Hervouët, V. (2001). La sémantique périurbaine : ou comment se repérer dans un dédale de mots et d'expressions. Working document, Université de Nantes, Nantes.

Hook, A., Court, V., Sovacool, B.K., Sorrell, S. (2020). A systematic review of the energy and climate impacts of teleworking. *Environ. Res. Lett.*, 15, 093003 [Online]. Available at: https://doi.org/10.1088/1748-9326/ab8a84.

Hu, L. (2019). Racial/ethnic differences in job accessibility effects: Explaining employment and commutes in the Los Angeles region. *Transp. Res. Part Transp. Environ.*, 76, 56–71.

Hunt, G.L. (1993). Equilibrium and disequilibrium in migration modelling. *Reg. Stud.*, 27, 341–349.

ILO (2020). Working from home: Estimating the worldwide potential (Policy Brief). International Labour Organisation (ILO), Geneva.

Ioannides, Y.M. and Loury, L.D. (2004). Job information networks, neighborhood effects, and inequality. *J. Econ. Lit.*, 42, 1056–1093.

Jahn, E. and Neugart, M. (2020). Do neighbors help finding a job? Social networks and labor market outcomes after plant closures. *Labour Econ.*, 65, 101825 [Online]. Available at: https://doi.org/10.1016/j.labeco.2020.101825.

Jouffe, Y., Caubel, D., Fol, S., Motte-Baumvol, B. (2019). Dealing with inequality in mobility: Tactics, strategies and projects for poor households on the outskirts of Paris. *Cybergeo Eur. J. Geogr.* [Online]. Available at: https://doi.org/10.4000/cybergeo.33479.

Kain, J.F. (1965). The effect of the Ghetto on the distribution and level of nonwhite employment in urban areas. RAND Corporation, Santa Monica.

Kline, P. and Moretti, E. (2013). Place based policies with unemployment. *Am. Econ. Rev.*, 103, 238–243.

Korsu, E. and Wenglenski, S. (2014). Distance physique, proximité sociale et inégalités devant le chômage. In *Ségrégation et justice spatiale, sciences humaines et sociales*, Fol, S., Lehman-Frisch, S., Morange, M. (eds). Presses universitaires de Paris Nanterre, Nanterre.

Kroft, K. and Pope, D.G. (2014). Does online search crowd out traditional search and improve matching efficiency? Evidence from craigslist. *J. Labor Econ.*, 32, 259–303.

Krugman, P. (1991). Increasing returns and economic geography. *J. Polit. Econ.*, 99, 483–499 [Online]. Available at: https://doi.org/10.1086/261763.

Kuhn, P. and Mansour, H. (2014). Is internet job search still ineffective?. *Econ. J.*, 124, 1213–1233.

Kuhn, P. and Skuterud, M. (2004). Internet job search and unemployment durations. *Am. Econ. Rev.*, 94, 218–232.

Layard, R., Nickell, S., Jackman, R. (2009). *Unemployment: Macroeconomic Performance and the Labour Market*. Oxford University Press, Oxford.

Le Barbanchon, T., Rathelot, R., Roulet, A. (2020). Gender differences in job search: Trading off commute against wage. *Q. J. Econ.*, 136, 381–426 [Online]. Available at: https://doi.org/10.1093/qje/qjaa033.

Lee, B.S. and McDonald, J.F. (2003). Determinants of commuting time and distance for Seoul residents: The impact of family status on the commuting of women. *Urban Stud.*, 40, 1283–1302 [Online]. Available at: https://doi.org/10.1080/0042098032000084604.

Macaluso, C., Hershbein, B., Yeh, C. (2019). Concentration in U.S. local labor markets: Evidence from vacancy and employment data. Meeting Papers, Society for Economic Dynamics.

Mang, C. (2012). Online job search and matching quality. Working document, Ifo Institute – Leibniz Institute for Economic Research at the University of Munich, Munich.

Manning, A. and Petrongolo, B. (2017). How local are labor markets? Evidence from a spatial job search model. *Am. Econ. Rev.*, 107, 2877–2907.

Marinescu, I. and Rathelot, R. (2018). Mismatch unemployment and the geography of job search. *Am. Econ. J. Macroecon.*, 10, 42–70.

McQuaid, R.W. and Chen, T. (2012) Commuting times – The role of gender, children and part-time work. *Res. Transp. Econ., Gender and Transport: Transaction Costs, Competing Claims and Transport Policy Gaps*, 34, 66–73 [Online]. Available at: https://doi.org/10.1016/j.retrec.2011.12.001.

Milasi, S., González-Vázquez, I., Fernández-Macías, E. (2020). Telework in the EU before and after the COVID-19: Where we were, where we head to (science for policy brief). *JRC, European Commission*, Geneva.

Molho, I. (2001). Spatial search, migration and regional unemployment. *Economica*, 68, 269–283.

Moretti, E. (2011). Local labor markets. In *Handbook of Labor Economics*, Card, D., Ashenfelter, O. (eds). Elsevier, Amsterdam.

Nafilyan, V. (2019). Gender differences in commute time and pay: A study into the gender gap for pay and commuting time, using data from the annual survey of hours and earnings. Report, Office for National Statistics, London.

Nisic, N. (2017). Smaller differences in bigger cities? Assessing the regional dimension of the gender wage gap. *Eur. Sociol. Rev.*, 33, 292–3044 [Online]. Available at: https://doi.org/10.1093/esr/jcx037.

O'Brien, W. and Yazdani Aliabadi, F. (2020). Does telecommuting save energy? A critical review of quantitative studies and their research methods. *Energy Build*, 225, 110298 [Online]. Available at: https://doi.org/10.1016/j.enbuild.2020.110298.

Ory, D.T. and Mokhtarian, P.L. (2006). Which came first, the telecommuting or the residential relocation? An empirical analysis of causality. *Urban Geogr.*, 27, 590–609 [Online]. Available at: https://doi.org/10.2747/0272-3638.27.7.590.

Parish, W.L. and Hao, L., Hogan, D.P. (1991). Family support networks, welfare, and work among young mothers. *J. Marriage Fam.*, 53, 203–215 [Online]. Available at: https://doi.org/10.2307/353144.

Parks, V. (2004). Access to work: The effects of spatial and social accessibility on unemployment for native-born Black and immigrant women in Los Angeles. *Econ. Geogr.*, 80, 141–172.

Peach, C. (1996). Good segregation, bad segregation. *Plan. Perspect.*, 11, 379–398 [Online]. Available at: https://doi.org/10.1080/026654396364817.

Pellizzari, M. (2010). Do friends and relatives really help in getting a good job? *Ind. Labor Relat. Rev.*, 63, 494–510.

Pissarides, C.A. and McMaster, I. (1990). Regional migration, wages and unemployment: Empirical evidence and implications for policy. *Oxf. Econ. Pap.*, 42, 812–831.

Schleicher, D. (2017). Stuck! The law and economics of residential stagnation. *Fac. Scholarsh. Ser.*, 78–154.

Skora, T., Rüger, H., Stawarz, N. (2020). Commuting and the motherhood wage gap: Evidence from Germany. *Sustainability*, 12, 5692 [Online]. Available at: https://doi.org/10.3390/su12145692.

Supiot, A. (1996). Perspectives on work: Introduction. *International Labour Review*, 135(6), 603–614.

Topa, G. (2001). Social interactions, local spillovers and unemployment. *Rev. Econ. Stud.*, 68, 261–295 [Online]. Available at: https://doi.org/10.1111/1467-937X.00169.

Topa, G. (2019). Social and spatial networks in labour markets. *Oxf. Rev. Econ. Policy*, 35, 722–745 [Online]. Available at: https://doi.org/10.1093/oxrep/grz019.

Tubaro, P., Le Ludec, C., Casilli, A.A. (2020). Counting "micro-workers": Societal and methodological challenges around new forms of labour. *Work Organ. Labour Glob.*, 14, 67–82 [Online]. Available at: https://doi.org/10.13169/workorgalaboglob.14.1.0067.

Tyndall, J. (2017). Waiting for the R train: Public transportation and employment. *Urban Stud.*, 54, 520–537 [Online]. Available at: https://doi.org/10.1177/0042098015594079.

de Vos, D., Meijers, E., van Ham, M. (2018). Working from home and the willingness to accept a longer commute. *Ann. Reg. Sci.*, 61, 375–398 [Online]. Available at: https://doi.org/10.1007/s00168-018-0873-6.

Weinberg, B.A. (2004). Testing the spatial mismatch hypothesis using inter-city variations in industrial composition. *Reg. Sci. Urban Econ*, 34, 505–532.

5

The Perception of Inequality and Poverty in the Most Segregated, Affluent Neighborhoods

Serge PAUGAM
Centre Maurice Halbwachs, CNRS, EHESS, ENS, Paris, France

In the urban fabric of large metropolises, the borders of poverty correspond almost symmetrically to the borders of wealth (Selimanovski 2008). The upper social categories are at least as highly concentrated in the most affluent neighborhoods as the poorest are in the stigmatized neighborhoods of the urban periphery (Musterd 2006; Préteceille 2006; Le Roux et al. 2017). The segregation suffered by the underprivileged strata of the population corresponds, as an almost identical mirror image, to the self-segregation of the richest, who are sometimes grouped together in what might be called "golden ghettos" (Pinçon and Pinçon-Charlot 1989, 2007). The traditional upper middle class along with the new elites of globalization (Wagner 1998) occupy and defend reserved spaces in large metropolises to preserve their identity and social status.

In most large cities, spatial segregation has increased significantly over the past few decades. The "upper-class neighborhoods" seem to be increasingly cut off from the other neighborhoods. Based on a detailed socio-professional typology of the neighborhoods of the Paris metropolis, Edmond Préteceille has been able to demonstrate that not only do the upper classes have significant weight in the most affluent neighborhoods relative to the price of land and real estate, but they are also increasingly highly concentrated there. His work has led to the conclusion that the social exclusivity of the upper-class neighborhoods has been reinforced over the last few decades, both in terms of their socioeconomic profile (Préteceille 2018; Préteceille and Cardoso 2020) and their ethno-racial characteristics, with immigrants from Africa or Asia being virtually absent from the majority of these neighborhoods, even though their presence is increasing in the city as a whole. This process of self-segregation among the upper classes has played a part in increasing inequality and weakening social cohesion on an urban scale. In other words, the gap has widened between the upper classes, who have real economic power, and the other social classes, including the middle classes, who are increasingly forced to live in more economically accessible areas on the outskirts.

Affluent neighborhoods have become increasingly exclusive because of how the market works. The price of commercial real estate, and of home ownership more generally, is the first link in the process of social selection in wealthy neighborhoods. Some property owners in these affluent neighborhoods have seen their real estate assets increase by enormous amounts, sometimes within a decade or two, as they have watched their less affluent tenant neighbors leave. But the market does not entirely explain this process of spatial concentration of the richest. Michel Pinçon and Monique Pinçon-Charlot (1989), sociologists looking at the bourgeoisie and the upper class, have studied how high society constitutes a dense network of associations, committees, councils and circles. The objective of these, in addition to the pleasure of meeting in an affinity-based environment, is to maintain close relations with both the holders of economic power and the representatives of political power, in particular to preserve the quality of their living spaces in terms of the maintenance of public spaces and the enhancement of their heritage, but also in terms of the exclusion of populations considered undesirable (Pinçon and Pinçon-Charlot 2007). Social attachment to a place can translate into collective mobilizations[1] (Sébastien 2018). In the case of wealthy neighborhoods, these appear as strategies that are sometimes discreet, often hidden, but nonetheless effective in defending the interests of their inhabitants.

---

1. The concept of social attachment, inspired by the sociology of Emile Durkheim, starts with the different types of bonds that attach individuals to each other and to society. These bonds ensure, in an unequal way, protection and recognition in four distinct spheres of moral life (domestic, associative, professional and civic). This concept of social attachment makes it possible to analyze how they intersect in each individual throughout the socialization process, and how each society contributes to this by setting and regulating the rules of collective life (Paugam 2016; Paugam et al. 2020). Social attachment to a place aims to explore how these ties intersect at the scale of a territory and maintain collective memory.

Often inspired by American work on urban segregation, research carried out over the last 20 years has made it possible to better analyze both the mechanisms of the socio-spatial confinement of the poor and the parallel mechanisms of affinity aggregation of the rich. Yet, curiously enough, this research has not intersected. It is striking to note, for example, that the relationship of the upper social categories to poverty has very rarely been studied as such. This may seem all the more surprising given that, on the basis of research on the first half of the 19th century, the historian Louis Chevalier established that urban inequalities could be explained by the bourgeois elite's perceptions of the working classes, which were seen as dangerous classes (Chevalier 1958). By referring to workers in deprived neighborhoods as "barbarians" or "savages", and by reducing the working-class condition to biological traits and physical behaviors, the bourgeois elite and its observers of the time did indeed maintain in the consciousness of their contemporaries the idea that social separatism was justified as a state of emergency when faced with insalubriousness and criminality[2].

The constitution of the urban "self" of the upper social categories has been studied over the last 20 years almost exclusively from the angle of affinity aggregation motivated solely by the interests of the accumulation of different types of capital. However, it has recently been observed that this residential choice of the most affluent is also motivated by particular representations of urban poverty, by a specific relationship with the precarious working-class categories[3]. Thus, two processes reinforce one other: the affinitive aggregation of the rich is in fact supplemented by what might be called a discriminatory segregation of the poor (Cousin 2014). While studies have shown that a low preference on the part of the upper categories to live next to those who resemble them is enough to make the space ultimately segregated (Schelling 1971, 1978; see Chapter 6), it seems legitimate to ask how the rich justify their choice to live in a segregated

---

2. The opposite social relationship, of the poor with regard to the rich, has not been the subject of such in-depth historical studies. Pierre Birnbaum, however, has studied in a more general way the myth of the "privileged" versus the "people", something that has been widely disseminated since the end of the 19th century (Birnbaum 1979). This perspective deserves to be re-examined today on the basis of direct surveys of the populations of deprived neighborhoods.
3. In his survey on redeveloped neighborhoods of the Paris region, characterized by a population of business executives and engineers, particularly in Courbevoie and Levallois-Perret, Bruno Cousin was able to verify that the inhabitants talk about teenagers from outside the neighborhood, who meet in the wooded alleys or public gardens of these residential spaces, and whom they spontaneously associate with suburban youth gangs and popular juvenile delinquency (Cousin 2014).

neighborhood, and whether this choice is the result of a clearly expressed desire to free themselves from the presence of those social categories considered inferior.

Following a presentation of studies on the perception of poverty and the rationale for localized and comparative research based on in-depth interviews with residents of highly segregated, affluent neighborhoods, this chapter analyzes how these residents describe their neighborhoods in terms of the moral values they attribute to them. We then examine how they manage to free themselves from the proximity of the working classes, by protecting themselves from the risk they attribute to them of insecurity and possible physical contamination, due to their behavior which is deemed to run contrary to the rules of cleanliness and bodily hygiene. Finally, it seems essential to question how these privileged categories living in inward-looking neighborhoods justify the social inequalities and poverty.

5.1. Studying the perception of poverty

When we look at the issue of poverty, our spontaneous reflex is to start by defining who the poor are, so that we can count them, study how they live and analyze the evolution of their situation over time. However, research on the social representations of poverty, i.e. the meaning that individuals give to this phenomenon according to their lived experiences and the processes of exchange and interaction that characterize life in society, are more rare. If, in line with Max Weber, we can consider social representations as a vector of individual action, it is important to study in greater depth what "floats in the heads of real men" (Weber 1971), especially when they see and try to explain the phenomenon of poverty, especially since each society adopts policies to address poverty, which shape its particular meaning and specific function (Simmel 1908; Gans 1972; Paugam 1991).

5.1.1. *A perception that varies in time and space*

Historians have tried to explain how the social relationship to poverty has changed over the centuries (Polanyi 1983; Geremek 1987; Castel 1995) and sociologists have succeeded in demonstrating that the explicit or underlying functions attributed to the system of assistance to the poor have varied greatly over the course of the 20th century, in particular according to the phases of development of industrial society and economic conditions (Katz 1986, 1989; Paugam 1993; Piven and Cloward 1993; Gans 1995). Thus, using the example of the United States, Frances Fox Piven and Richard A. Cloward have established that the main function of welfare is to regulate the temporal eruptions of civil disorder during phases of recession and mass unemployment. This function then disappears in phases of economic growth and political stability, to be replaced by a completely different function, that of encouraging the poor to join the labor market by reducing the benefits they had previously received, sometimes drastically (Piven and Cloward 1993). In the first phase, the poor are seen as victims, and the challenge is to prevent them from rising up against the existing social system; in the second phase, they are seen as potentially lazy, and only a policy of "moralization" is deemed likely to transform their behavior. These analyses focus on economic cycles and their consequences for the organization of welfare, but they inevitably encompass several dimensions and do not directly address the perception of poverty. Upstream of these changes in welfare policies, however, we can hypothesize that there is a transformation of the representations of poverty (Paugam 1993). Policies intervene in the wake of events that influence public opinion and change perceptions.

It is important here to clarify what we mean by the "perception of poverty". Building on recent work by social psychologists, we can distinguish between collective representations and social representations (Moscovici 1982). For Durkheim (1960), the former are different to individual representations and imply a strong stability in their transmission and reproduction. They endure through generations and exert a constraint on individuals. The latter imply, on the contrary, both a greater diversity of origin, both in individuals and in groups, and the possibility of evolution under the joint influence of the mechanisms of reproduction and acquisition during the many interactions of social life. By perception of poverty, we mean the social representations of poverty, which means that we admit that there are many such representations within a single society – and, a fortiori, when comparing different societies – and the possibility of their evolution according to the economic situation.

Since the mid-1970s, a great deal of attention has been paid to representations of poverty in Europe (Riffault and Rabier 1977; Rigaux 1994; Paugam and Selz 2005; Paugam 2013); the main studies have focused on the statistical and comparative use of Eurobarometers. Of all the questions asked in these surveys, one in particular concerns the causes of poverty. It distinguishes between two traditional and radically opposed explanations of poverty: one that emphasizes the laziness or unwillingness of the poor, and one that emphasizes, on the contrary, the injustice that abounds in society. The laziness explanation refers to a moral idea based on a sense of duty and work ethic. In this explanation, the poor are somehow blamed for not taking enough care of themselves, and therefore the government should not help them more. According to this approach, each individual is responsible for themselves, and they can only escape poverty through their own fortitude. The explanation of poverty by injustice, on the contrary, refers to a more global conception of society. The poor are above all victims of a system that condemns them. In this spirit, the public authorities have a duty to help the poor in order to achieve greater social justice. Thus, the laziness and injustice explanations correspond to contrasting opinions, the ideological and political meaning of which is not lost on anyone. It has thus been possible to trace the evolution of the laziness and injustice explanations by country since 1976 (Paugam and Selz 2005). These two explanations vary, in fact, both by country and by survey period. If we compare, for example, France and the UK, it appears that the laziness explanation is always, whatever the reference period, more often given in the UK than in France. In order to interpret these differences, one should take into account not only the type of welfare state but also the way in which inequalities are discussed in each country, which is related to past experiences in the fight against poverty, to the actors involved in this field and, more generally, to the modes of social intervention (van Oorschot and Halman 2000). It is also striking to note how strongly the injustice explanation of poverty varies over time. In nine out of 11 countries, it peaked in 1993, at a time when economic conditions were very unfavorable, with a very high unemployment rate in most countries and a very low, even negative, growth rate. The injustice explanation for poverty decreased sharply in 2001 in all countries except Greece, where it stabilized at a high level. Finally, it rose sharply in 2009 in all countries, a rise that can be seen as an effect of the 2008 financial crisis (Paugam 2013).

Of course, these analyses do not allow for a sufficiently granular level of interpretation at the level of a specific urban unit or a particular social stratum. This is why localized surveys based on in-depth interviews are valuable and complementary.

5.1.2. *How do the wealthy justify their choice to reside in a segregated neighborhood?*

Analyzing the social relationship to poverty at the more detailed level of territory than that of the nation, in particular the urban district, makes it possible to introduce additional hypotheses. In particular, it offers the possibility of studying the relationship between urban segregation and the process of social distancing from the populations most exposed to poverty. The literature on urban segregation is extensive – particularly in the United States – and it is not possible to present it in detail here. Those works emphasize that the permanent causes of urban segregation are to be found not only in the discriminatory practices observable in the housing market but also in the stereotypes of poverty that are conveyed among the middle and upper classes and, particularly in the United States, among the white population (Farley et al. 1994; Massey and Denton 1995).

To analyze the link between the perception of poverty and urban segregation, this chapter draws primarily on a recent comparative survey of three metropolises: Paris, São Paulo and Delhi (Paugam et al. 2017, see Box 5.1). The general premise of this survey is that differences in individual and local resources, in access to them, and in the measurable effects of segregation are important but that they must be analyzed in relation to contemporaries' awareness of social and urban inequalities and the conclusions they draw from them to inform or justify their practices. Studying representations of poverty among the upper social categories who have chosen to live in a self-segregated neighborhood involves analyzing the relationship between concrete self-contained practices and representations of the world of poverty. These representations may be based, as we shall see, on the notion of insecurity and the representation of the poor as a danger to people and property (risks of theft, physical or verbal aggression, etc.), but also on the fear of being somehow contaminated by lifestyles considered culturally undesirable or intolerable in the public space. Children are often considered to be the first potential victims of this cultural contamination, against which it is advisable to protect oneself by exercising strict control over who they spend their time with. Thus, living in a neighborhood "protected" by the high social level of its residents and the prices of the real estate market could correspond not only to a search for prestige and a strategy of social reproduction, but also to a desire to distance oneself from the poor and to seek a local order free of all the problems and costs that the upper classes associate with an open and socially mixed space.

In this type of survey, the quality of the interviews is highly dependent on the interviewer's attitude toward the interviewee and their ability to put the interviewee at ease. In their daily lives, the interviewees do not have to report on their practices to a stranger. The statements made by the interviewees in this experimental and artificial setting cannot, therefore, be considered as the direct and spontaneous expression of their factual actions or of the real motives that lead them to act in a particular way. However, this investigative technique, which comes under the heading of comprehensive sociology, takes the approach of studying lived experiences and constitutes an excellent means of identifying the processes that create and rationalize the meaning of the latter. In this survey, the aim was therefore to gain a general understanding of how the most segregated upper classes consider the poor, establish a moral boundary toward them or not and justify the social order of the structure of class and the socio-spatial order of the city.

The sociological survey conducted in 2012–2013 in the major metropolises of Paris, São Paulo and Delhi (PSPD survey) is based on a qualitative and comprehensive approach. It is based on 80 in-depth – or semi-structured – interviews per metropolis, i.e. 240 in total, with people living in highly segregated affluent neighborhoods. This number, which may seem rather high at first glance, was justified by the need to have a sample in each metropolis to take into account the variety of neighborhoods and reach the various components of the elite in satisfactory proportions. What are the characteristics of these three metropolises? What are the neighborhoods in which the survey was conducted? By choosing the Paris metropolis, which, like other European metropolises, is still strongly affected by tensions and urban revolts in the suburbs, and two other metropolises located in emerging countries characterized by strong economic growth and the development of mass consumption, the objective was to compare the representations of poverty among the upper social classes in contrasting economic and social contexts. On the one hand, there is insecurity and social malaise in an environment of job shortages for the least qualified and immigrant populations. On the other hand, there is economic take-off in a society where inequalities inherited from the colonial context and traditional forms of domination have long deprived the vast majority of the population of the possibility of escaping from poverty and hoping for social ascension. Thus, while the Parisian metropolis is confronted with new inequalities that can be considered a threat to social cohesion, the metropolises of São Paulo and Delhi are making great strides in catching up in terms of economic development and are offering certain segments of the population new opportunities to improve their living conditions. What these three metropolises have in common, however, is that they are all, each in their own way, the scene of profound changes that are gradually redefining social relations. In each of them, the upper classes may feel the need, as a result of these changes, but for possibly different reasons, to group together in selected and sometimes secure residential spaces. The selected metropolises are also very different from one another in terms of the history of their urbanization and the real estate market.

In each metropolis, the choice of neighborhoods was made following a pre-survey. Visits to several neighborhoods and a comparative analysis of them based on ethnographic observations, statistical indicators and historical or sociological documents made it possible to determine the choice, using similar selection criteria in each metropolis. In the end, 12 of the most privileged areas in the three metropolises were chosen for investigation: they correspond to the top two levels (out of 18) of the hierarchical typology of Parisian neighborhoods constructed by Préteceille (2003), to the top level (out of 16) of the typology developed by Préteceille and Cardoso (2008) to describe São Paulo, and to the most luxurious districts of Delhi identified, in the absence of precise data on their inhabitants, by mobilizing several indirect indicators of their socio-professional and economic levels.

The districts selected in the three metropolises are historical districts that are very well known at the city or metropolitan level. They are distinguished in particular by the price of real estate. Their geographical delimitation is self-evident to the inhabitants and has never been raised as a concern for them. In Delhi, these are the neighborhoods of Sunder

Nagar, Chattarpur Farms, Noida 15-A and Gurgaon, and in São Paulo the neighborhoods of Higienópolis, Morumbi, Jardins and Alphaville. In Paris, two of the four selected neighborhoods are located in the 5th and 16th arrondissements and correspond, respectively, to much superior types of space ("bourgeoisie space with a slight predominance of intellectual categories" and "bourgeoisie space with a predominance of company managers and executives") taken from in the middle of other similar bourgeois spaces. Another neighborhood, located in the commune of Ville-d'Avray and composed of a mixture of single-family homes and multi-family housing, although occasionally bordering on average areas, was also mainly integrated into the territories of the western part of Île-de-France that are characteristic of the upper classes. Finally, a fourth district was chosen in the commune of Le Vésinet (Yvelines), in order to add an area located a little further from the center of Paris to the three others. This district is the oldest example of a suburban bourgeois housing estate in the agglomeration.

Once the neighborhoods in each metropolis were selected, the next step was to recruit the people to be interviewed. Several methods were used. For the Île-de-France survey, it was possible to rely, for each of the three neighborhoods located, respectively, in the 5th and 16th arrondissements and in Ville-d'Avray, on lists of residents belonging to an upper-class household who had already agreed to respond to a previous questionnaire survey (the "Health, Inequalities and Social Divisions" survey, SIRS). In the commune of Le Vésinet, the interviewees were recruited mainly through direct contact in public spaces in the commune (in parks, on the streets, in front of shops and after mass, etc.) by the survey coordinator. In the neighborhoods of the other two metropolitan areas, the "snowball" technique was most often used. This technique consists of asking the interviewees to indicate other people they know who might be willing to be interviewed, based on initial contacts in the neighborhood. Thus, by first selecting neighborhoods with a very high concentration of high-income households and then selecting residents of these neighborhoods characterized by their particularly high standard of living, the PSPD survey was able to reach the upper-class minority living in the better neighborhoods of the three cities studied.

Box 5.1. *Investigating uptown Paris, São Paulo and Delhi*

5.2. The constitution of a moral boundary

What is the point of the richest people being free of the presence of categories considered socially inferior in their neighborhoods and therefore fighting any public policy aimed at promoting social diversity? The answer is to ensure the best chances for social reproduction. To achieve this, they feel it is necessary to build what might be called a moral boundary.

5.2.1. *An idealized self-contained bubble*

The upper classes living in these highly segregated neighborhoods most often agree on the foundations of a moral order in accordance with their representation of the territory in which they live. This moral order appears, according to Durkheim (2012), to be the product of the individuals' attachment to social groups and to society as a whole. It is based first of all on a spirit of discipline, which implies a consensus on what constitutes good and respectable ways of behaving toward one another and, conversely, on the behaviors which must be outlawed because they are unanimously considered to be in breach of the etiquette, way of speaking and interpersonal skills which characterize the bourgeois *ethos*. The defense of a moral order thus very often refers to a strategy of class distinction based on the idea of the superiority, or even the predisposition, of the rich to create and transmit to their children a complete and rigorous moral education, which they consider to be distinct from other strata of society. The rich neighborhood residents interviewed in the PSPD survey were almost unanimous in expressing their belief that they are socially, and especially morally, superior to other segments of the population. Their shared feeling of residing where they should, in accordance with their social status, allows them to live in harmony with one another and their fellow human beings, and to avoid the tensions, misunderstandings or altercations that they sense are inevitable in the presence of other social classes. They thus openly recognize the advantages of self-segregation. The world in which they live is, according to them, incomparable because it is based on specific moral values. Thus, the defense of a moral order may refer to a strategy of class distinction understood in a broad sense, i.e. based on the idea of the superiority of the rich and their predisposition to create and perpetuate a moral education distinct from other strata of society. In other words, the strategies of distinction of the upper classes, which the work of Bourdieu (1979) has shown to be inscribed in cultural practices, are also based on various forms of justification of their moral superiority (Lamont 1995). These are translated in the discourse by the definition of a kind of social barrier, to take up the metaphor of the barrier and the level proposed by Goblot (1925) in his study of the French bourgeoisie. This metaphor is still particularly suggestive today, since the segregated bourgeois neighborhood is most often presented as a space protected by a symbolic barrier designed to make it clear to potential intruders that they do not belong there, since the latter brings together people who are most often united and supportive in preserving the superiority of their social level.

For households with children, living in a "good" neighborhood also provides access to a "good" school and, consequently, to a "good" education (see Chapter 1). In the representations of the people interviewed, the social composition of the school is one of the major criteria for determining its quality, given that there is no doubt in the minds of the parents that their children will progress more quickly if they are surrounded by children of a comparable social level. The school is at the heart of the neighborhood and is the center of gravity in terms of the social world of children and adolescents. It is therefore essential for parents to ensure that they also have the best possible chance of associating with peers who share the same interests and moral values. While school choice has also become a central issue for the middle classes, who most often wish to avoid the "school on the periphery" (van Zanten 2001), the analysis of the effects of school mapping, which is intended to distribute pupils according to their place of residence, nevertheless leads to the observation that the upper classes generally benefit most from this. In the most widespread representations, the self-contained "bubble" mentality is associated with school performance and is therefore a necessary part of it (Oberti 2007).

While social relations in this type of neighborhood are highly intertwined, this does not mean that all residents are intrinsically linked. What happens in the neighborhood may, however, be what Sampson (2012) calls "collective efficacy", that is, a combination of mutual trust and shared expectations of social control. What unites the inhabitants of a self-segregated neighborhood presupposes the existence of a consensual normative framework, the common reference to values deemed essential. It is not necessary for everyone to know each other; it is enough to share the certainty that they can trust each other, possibly come together to address problems that affect the neighborhood as a whole, and even develop collective strategies to defend specific interests concerning order, security and the well-being of residents.

5.2.2. *A moral order within neighborhoods*

Nor should the wealthy, segregated neighborhood be seen as perfectly homogeneous in terms of their values. Dissonant voices can sometimes be heard.

In the wealthy bourgeois neighborhoods of Paris, such as the 16th arrondissement for example, some inhabitants espouse resolutely progressive values that are explicitly opposed to the conservative tendencies of the majority of the inhabitants. This causes them to feel disgusted with what they often consider to be hypocritical and socially dominant behavior. In other words, the widespread belief among elites that they share with their neighbors a community of values and interests based on the same class membership – which predisposes them to maintain a moral order that is considered superior – does not preclude struggles for social distinction within the bourgeoisie.

Thus, in each metropolis, there is both a more or less strong desire for the social enclosure of wealthy neighborhoods within themselves, in the form of self-segregation practices that are all the more effective because they correspond to strategies that are most often skillfully developed by most of the inhabitants, and also, in some neighborhoods more than others, a desire to guard against the risk of leveling down, especially when newcomers introduce habits that are not entirely in keeping with the traditional bourgeois ethos.

5.3. Keeping out the working class

While social cohesion is considered by the wealthiest as a guarantee of social peace in their neighborhood, most of them nevertheless share the conviction that this guarantee is entirely relative and that it is absolutely necessary to remain vigilant in the face of all disruptive threats from the outside. One of the challenges is, for example, preventing the construction of social housing in these bourgeois neighborhoods or communities. However, the French law of December 13, 2000, known as the "SRU" (solidarity and urban renewal) law, obliges municipalities of a certain size to have a social housing stock equivalent to 25% of all dwellings ("Duflot law" of 2013). This measure, considered to be one of the key elements of a housing policy that is both supportive and Republican, is nonetheless strongly contested by the administrators of these upmarket communities, who see in it the risk of an awkward cohabitation with lower social categories. Some municipalities, under pressure from wealthy and influential families, have opted to pay very high fines out of the municipal budget. This is how some municipalities have maintained a very low rate of social housing (less than 3%, for example, in Neuilly-sur-Seine, a very bourgeois city, where former president Nicolas Sarkozy was mayor from 1983 to 2002, whereas the neighboring municipality of Nanterre, with a working-class tradition, has more than 50%). Let us also recall here the massive, relentless and well-publicized rallying in 2016 among the inhabitants of the 16th arrondissement of Paris against the project to build a shelter for the homeless and refugees on the edge of the Bois de Boulogne. This determination is the expression of a fierce desire on the part of the inhabitants of these privileged neighborhoods to preserve their inner circle by pushing the poorest people to the margins of society and the urban periphery. It is therefore a question of keeping out the working classes and the problems they are likely to bring to the neighborhood.

5.3.1. *Distrust and repulsion of the poor*

The security threat has reached its height in metropolises like São Paulo. Not only is income inequality highest there (the Gini index is 0.56, compared to 0.42 in

Paris), but crime rates are also very high[4]. In the PSPD survey, insecurity as the first thing respondents mention when asked about poverty. Protecting themselves from the poor, who are perceived as dangerous, becomes their daily struggle, as it involves constant vigilance. The rich live in a climate of real tension and adopt protection strategies in all acts of daily life. They rarely walk within their neighborhoods, and even less so in other parts of the city. They very rarely take public transport, preferring the safety of their own car, which is sometimes armored. Some even say they prefer not to go out in public spaces such as restaurants, or avoid going there late at night if they do. Cultural outings are sometimes out of the question. They do not go to the movies, preferring their home theaters. There are even stickers that identify the cars of neighborhood members who are allowed to drive near public places, such as schools.

Faced with the threatening nature of their urban environment, the wealthy take refuge in the comfort of the domestic interior, which must reflect their social status and the norms that accompany it. They also place great importance on the building in which they live. The search for signs of ostentation goes hand in hand with the sophistication of the means of securing the space. The more secure the space is and the more ostentatious the signs of wealth, the more satisfied the inhabitants are. Condominium meetings are often an opportunity to outbid each other in this area. Risk is everywhere, so social life is more limited. Among the people interviewed, some admit to being very isolated in their neighborhood, many say they do not know their neighbors, and most of them retreat to their domestic space and family bonds. The rich often choose an affluent neighborhood because they want to be surrounded by people of the same social status, political opinion and cultural level – it is important to them that their children attend socially homogeneous private schools – but the general context of insecurity drastically limits their relationships within it, compared to what may exist in some neighborhoods of Paris or Delhi. There are, however, variations from one neighborhood to another. When the neighborhood is more homogeneous, as in the case of the Jardins district, the members of São Paulo's patrimonial bourgeoisie nevertheless manage to recreate a significant and dense sociability among themselves, notably through their regular participation in very selective and exclusive clubs.

The issue of dirtiness and lack of hygiene is also present but it is usually a secondary factor. The people interviewed rarely talk about the *favelas*, even though they are sometimes located near their homes. It is another world that they know very little about and to which they feel totally alien. It would be inconceivable that they

---

4. For example, at the time of the survey, the homicide rate per 100,000 was 25.2 in Brazil, compared to 5.5 in India and only 1 in France (source: United Nations Office on Drugs and Crime, 2012 data).

might enter these *favelas*. On the other hand, they willingly speak of the poverty of the city center, associating the dirtiness of the latter with the insecurity which reigns there. The "Cracolândia", a crack house located in the city center next to the new theater (Sala São Paulo), is often cited by the interviewees as a place of real repulsion. In this urban area, the concentration of the poor and homeless frightens them, but also disturbs them, if only because of the smell of garbage and excrement that stains the streets. It is a very real face of São Paulo, of which they are fully aware, but which they try to ignore by all means, carefully avoiding going there, even though some recently restored cultural places, such as the Municipal Theater or the great Mário de Andrade Library, are located there and should logically attract them.

Any contact between the rich and the working classes is made through the intermediary of domestic workers, and the issue of hygiene is also raised on this occasion. Several people interviewed admitted to exercising strict control over their domestic staff to ensure their absolute cleanliness and irreproachable habits in this area. This is a hiring requirement and would be a reason for immediate dismissal. The fear of being contaminated is therefore very real and leads to constant surveillance, especially in the handling of kitchen utensils and foodstuffs. In order to justify this, the upper classes invoke a benevolent attention – of a paternalistic nature – even mentioning the civilizing mission that they have with the poor people they encounter in this way.

More generally, if one were to summarize the representations of poverty among members of the São Paulo elite, one would have to emphasize the social function of violence. It is indeed the permanent insecurity that allows the rich to legitimize their concern for distancing themselves from and protecting themselves from the social categories that are considered threatening. But this protective withdrawal is more a withdrawal into the domestic sphere than a withdrawal into the neighborhood. In this respect, the apartment building is similar to a fortress, where security criteria are combined with esthetic criteria to signify the social prestige of the households that live there. Social life remains limited. While there are exceptions and specific places of bourgeois sociability in certain neighborhoods, for many of the people interviewed, this mostly plays out in the private sphere. Family bonds are the preferred ties of proximity, given that they are easy to rely on. In order to ensure the comfort of domestic life, domestic workers from working class categories are selected, educated and often more or less integrated into the family in a domination–protection relationship.

The metropolis of Delhi has many similarities with the metropolis of São Paulo in terms of the reaction to the presence of the poor in the urban space. While violence is lower in Delhi than in São Paulo and is less of a concern overall, the issue of insecurity is nonetheless crucial. Several interviewees explained that their neighborhood is the primary guarantor of their safety. Living in a wealthy neighborhood, inaccessible to the poor or other categories of the population, is seen as a source of protection. The rich have the city map in mind and know how to distinguish the safe zone – which one of them even calls his "comfort zone" – from other areas deemed unattractive, even when they involve middle-class or even upper-middle-class neighborhoods. The residence space is most often fenced in on two levels: the gated community and the home. The security system is generally similar in complexity to that of the wealthy neighborhoods of São Paulo. It is also important to note the insecurity that specifically affects women, due to the frequency of sexual assaults. This concern, which is mentioned in a discreet way by women, also causes anxiety among husbands with regard to their wives and among fathers with regard to their daughters. Insecurity also refers to the chaotic nature of transport and the numerous traffic accidents that most of the interviewees attribute above all to the incapacities and incivilities of drivers deemed "uncivilized". Finally, some people are concerned about the probable frustration of domestic workers with the lavish spending of their bosses, and some of them even worry about the threat of social revolt. In other words, the insecurity felt by the rich is widespread and is reflected in a daily vigilance that leads them to reduce the urban space to a few enclaves and to move, as some say, "from island to island".

This distrust of the potentially dangerous poor, who live in areas that should be avoided at all costs, is nevertheless coupled with an additional apprehension, which in Delhi takes on considerable proportions with regard to the dirtiness and lack of hygiene that characterize most of the public spaces in the metropolis. Some interviewees insist on the disgust they feel toward the insalubrity, the dirtiness and the disastrous state of the infrastructure. Of course, many are used to it and no longer pay much attention to it, simply avoiding those areas considered repugnant, where the people are heavily concentrated and live in a misery perceived as appalling and repulsive. As in São Paulo, the elite selects the places that are possible to frequent and those that should be avoided. Old Delhi, but also the eastern and western districts generally, inspire a strong sense of disgust. But surprisingly, this spatial ostracism also affects certain areas in the South, such as urban villages, middle-class "colonies" and crowded markets. Their inhabitants are perceived to be uncivilized, both noisy and not respectful toward the environment. Faced with this unhealthy environment, the elite protect themselves on a daily basis by further shrinking their vital urban perimeter. In other words, the issue of hygiene is omnipresent in the attitudes and perceptions of the rich with respect to the poor, and sometimes even toward other strata of the population, and it constrains their geographical practices and mobilities. The lack of cleanliness of public spaces and certain semi-public or private spaces is mentioned again and again to justify the distancing of specific, but ultimately quite numerous, fringes of the population. In a much more radical way than in São Paulo, the criteria for demarcation, both spatial and social, are based on a certain idea of hygiene and the more or less civilized character of the different social groups.

5.3.2. *A growing feeling of insecurity in the rich neighborhoods of Paris*

It is worth noting right away that these two reasons are less often mentioned by the rich in the Paris metropolis. This does not mean that the Parisian elite is not concerned about its security. In Paris, as elsewhere, the feeling of insecurity is even on the rise, as shown by the growing expectations for increased video surveillance at the entrances to private residences, but also in urban spaces in general. In stores and public places, there are increasing numbers of security guards. Finally, the discussion about security, in Paris as elsewhere, is spreading through the supply of services and equipment – security is a flourishing market – as well as in the manifestos of political parties, both left and right. Although the Parisian elite is not immune to this trend, it is rare for them to mention insecurity as a fundamental concern and to call for preventive measures that would restrict freedom of movement and circulation. The Parisian interviewees regularly take public transport, whether it be the bus, the metro or the RER, which is unthinkable for most of the Brazilian or Indian interviewees[5]. In Paris, public spaces, where people from different social backgrounds potentially meet in a continuous flow, are not experienced as a threat but rather as a common good that is accessible to all and should remain so, and as the true symbol of and location for urban life. It is true that some people, especially women, report that they avoid taking public transport late at night, especially when dressed up for a night out, or that they do not wear valuable jewelry on the metro, but these precautions seem basic, if not commonplace, as they seem to correspond to widespread practices in many social strata (see Chapter 2).

This relative tranquility of daily life in Paris does not mean that the interviewees are unaware of the specificity of the "working-class" neighborhoods of Paris and the metro stations that serve them, but since these neighborhoods are not the places they regularly frequent, they do not constitute a particular problem for them. In other words, living in a wealthy district of the Paris metropolis is rarely mentioned as the result of the imperative need to protect oneself from the insecurity linked to the

---

5. The segregation of wealthy Île-de-France residents is weaker during the day than at night, as their daily movements lead them to mix with other social groups. Even so, the rich remain more highly segregated in Île-de-France than the poor, regardless of the time of day (Le Roux et al. 2017).

supposed danger of the poor. The security threat refers more to a widespread feeling that runs through the whole of society (Castel 2003), before being directed toward a specific group of the population, in this case the poor. On the other hand, when the threat is perceived as coming closer to home, as was the case in the 16th arrondissement of Paris after the decision to build a shelter for refugees just near the Bois de Boulogne, many inhabitants do not hesitate to mobilize collectively to show fierce hostility toward underprivileged populations, who are said to be likely to disturb the neighborhood and to represent a danger to them and their families. The question of insecurity immediately comes to the fore. But it is not a major problem so long as it can be put at a distance. As long as the rich feel protected by their own privacy and by the spatial configuration of their neighborhoods, which distances them geographically from working-class neighborhoods, they generally do not feel in danger.

Moreover, in the interviews conducted in Paris, the issue of a lack of hygiene among the poor and the risk of contamination is even more rarely put forward than that of their dangerousness. Most of the interviewees considered Paris to be a generally clean city. It is striking to note that a fairly recurrent problem, at least in the 16th arrondissement, and to a lesser extent in the fifth arrondissement, is linked above all to the presence of dog excrement on the sidewalks, a nuisance that is not due to the undesirable presence of the poor but rather to the practices of the dog owners living in the neighborhood. Hygiene does not seem to be a major concern of the bourgeoisie with respect to the poor, as it was in the 19th century. The picture described by Chevalier (1958) no longer corresponds to reality. That said, some interviewees mentioned the inconvenience they sometimes experience on public transport at busy times, when crowding becomes oppressive for them, when bodies are stuck together and the smell of perspiration spreads. But these people themselves often put these inconveniences into perspective, and only a few people mentioned the risk of illness (otherwise benign, such as the common cold or the flu[6]). Moreover, if certain practices are condemned, such as leaving rubbish lying around or tearing open plastic garbage bags to get at their contents, these criticisms are not directed at the poor in general, but at certain categories considered negligent, careless and irresponsible young people and immigrant populations, particularly from the East, considered dirty and poorly educated. In other words, apart from these sporadic annoyances, the question of hygiene seems to have been resolved overall, and in any case does not constitute a major source of unease among the upper classes of the Paris metropolis living in the most exclusive and formerly bourgeois neighborhoods. This is largely explained by the history of urbanization and health reforms. Unlike São Paulo and Delhi, Paris has undergone a profound

---

6. The PSPD survey was conducted before the Covid-19 pandemic.

and structural reorganization since the 19th century, based on planning that is both hygienic and safe, leading to the expulsion of the poor to the periphery or to specific districts far from the bourgeois neighborhoods. The process of radical expulsion of the poor that we are observing today in Delhi and São Paulo actually existed in Paris a century and a half earlier. It is therefore easier for the people interviewed in Paris, compared to those interviewed in the other two cities, to be more measured in their views of the poor, since the latter appear to them to be further away overall, thereby lowering the risk of being directly affected by their supposed nuisances. It would probably have been different if we had interviewed rich people living in less segregated neighborhoods or in the immediate vicinity of poor neighborhoods: the concern for the safety and protection of the poor would certainly have been much more prevalent.

The representations that underlie the rationalization of the undesirability of the poor are therefore organized differently in the three metropolises. Issues of insecurity and hygiene appear less central in Paris. The rich use these arguments less frequently to justify their self-segregation practices, not because these issues are totally absent from their concerns, but mainly because the spaces they frequent or through which they transit within the Parisian metropolis appear to be generally protected from these risks, which are considered major in the other two metropolises. In contrast, in São Paulo and Delhi, poverty is used as a deterrent to the rich, and the arguments of the dangerousness and lack of hygiene of the poor are mentioned without restraint. But while these two motifs are jointly used in both cities, they do not have equal importance. In São Paulo, the feeling of insecurity is much more intense, while in Delhi, the issue of the lack of hygiene is prevalent.

5.4. Justifying class inequality and poverty

Beyond the evocation of the undesirability of the poor, the rationalization of social inequalities invokes another narrative register to justify self-segregating practices in urban space. The latter is more constructed than the former, in the sense that it goes beyond the spontaneous repulsion of the poor. It appeals to a conception of the social order based on arguments that are mostly ideological and that, around the naturalization of poverty and determined conceptions of merit, mobilize a sense of justice and social and social cohesion (Reis and Moore 2005).

5.4.1. *The neutralization of compassion*

The theme of worthiness and shaming of the poor, for example, can be intertwined with the naturalization of poverty, especially since laziness can be attributed to a cultural trait or naturalized type of personality. In Delhi's affluent neighborhoods, the naturalization of poverty takes place first of all under a religious register. According to the theory of karma, the poor are born poor because of their actions in previous lives (Weber 2003). Beyond this religious dimension, there is a widespread belief that social groups, because of their caste and class culture, or regional origin, cannot mix (Naudet 2014). Thus, the poor are naturally disposed to certain ways of life. Note that, in its extreme form, the naturalization of poverty can even lead to its negation: people designated as "poor" are so in relation to other social categories; they are not poor if one considers that they belong to another world, characterized by specific criteria of family organization and social integration. Rich people in Delhi often show their disdain and contempt for the poorest without restraint. This is class racism based on the belief that the poor are a separate humanity and that, under these conditions, separatism is the best solution. This racism translates into a radical opposition to any program of social mixing, especially in the school system, because of the supposed impossibility of the poor to interact with other social strata and, a fortiori, with the elite. Some rich people even go so far as to admit that, for them, in the event of a serious accident, it would be more appropriate to rescue their fellows rather than the poor, since the latter are less valuable. Empathy toward the poorest remains marginal and, when it appears, it is often only under the hypocritical veil of the absolute refusal of the egalitarian principle. It is true that people who have lived in Western countries sometimes find it difficult to fully support the unequal order of their country, but the culture of class separatism is so pervasive that they find it impossible to change it, especially as it benefits them and reinforces their status. The naturalization of poverty is very present in India, but it is part of a much more extensive process of naturalization of the social order.

The theory of karma does not imply an unsurpassable assignment to the social position of birth, since a certain redemption is possible according to past or present acts. It thus maintains a certain connivance with the ideology of merit: everyone is judged to be responsible for their own actions. It is thus striking to note a certain porosity between the religious reference which founds the argument of the naturalization of poverty and the reference to meritocracy – hence the regular denunciation of the laziness and dishonesty of the poor. Some interviewees lament the total lack of energy for work that they observe in many poor people. Others attack profiteering beggars. These observations very quickly lead to a radical questioning of all social programs intended to reduce poverty, of which there are very few in India, or of all the policies of positive discrimination based on the establishment of quotas, particularly in universities. Some see this not only as an injustice, but also as a risk of degeneration with respect to the Indian elites. More generally, the interviews revealed a relatively consensual adherence to the neoliberal ideology and the meritocratic principle on which it is based. In other words, in the case of India, the naturalization of poverty, and more generally of the social order, which takes extreme forms, constitutes a major argument in favor of the self-segregating practice of the rich, but it does not prevent its relatively flexible and effective adaptation to the ideology of merit and, consequently, its contemporary anchoring in neo-liberalism as it unfolds at the international level. The Indian elites thus appear to be both traditional and, at the same time, in step with the dominant ideology that guides global capitalism.

This process of naturalization of poverty is also found in Brazil in the discourse of the inhabitants of the upper-class neighborhoods. The latter see the poor as a population so marginal to society, so far outside of civilization, that they must either be kept out by a sophisticated system of security (fencing off private space, video surveillance systems, permanent security guards at the entrances to buildings, etc.), or their education must be started from scratch, which is what is envisaged when it comes to turning them into domestic workers (Giorgetti 2015). A traditional relationship of domination, partly inherited from the time of slavery (abolished quite late in this country), tinged with benevolent paternalism, is then grafted onto this perception of inferiority, deemed natural to the poor. Unlike in Delhi, the naturalization of poverty and inequality is not formulated in a religious register. Interviewees very often explain inequality as primarily a natural process. Many refer to an individual's talent or IQ to explain their "success" (or lack thereof). Their reasoning is then most often stated in biological terms, sometimes even based on scientific studies, and invokes the mechanism of natural selection. One interviewee relies on personal observation and points out that inequalities among siblings can be very high despite the fact that everyone has received the same education, which he believes proves that the differential abilities are biological. The naturalization of poverty results in its normalization. There is no need to be offended by this, since people are born unequal and, if they remain unequal, it is primarily a sign of fate. Compassion for the suffering of others may nevertheless occasionally manifest itself, at the sight, for example, of very young children in the bosom of destitute mothers abandoned on the street, but it is somehow very quickly neutralized, both by mechanisms of rationalization based on the shared belief in the natural inevitability of this type of situation, and on processes of convincing oneself that nothing can be done to stop it. People can deplore it deep down, without being overly moved by it, since there are so many scenes of misery, which merely express the reality of the social order, which is undoubtedly severe but nevertheless ordinary, and which becomes "normal" through habit.

However, it should not be concluded that all the upper classes in the metropolis of São Paulo share exactly the same beliefs on this point. In particular, there are variations between the four neighborhoods we studied. In the neighborhood where the old patrimonial bourgeoisie is the most concentrated, the Jardins District, biological determinism is the most common. On the other hand, in Higienopólis and Morumbi, where the more artistic and intellectual professions tend to live, the interviews revealed a greater tendency to include the effect of social environment in the causes of poverty and, therefore, of the inequalities resulting from the environment and education. We also sometimes find a kind of interpenetration of the biological and social arguments to explain the persistence of poverty. But despite these differences, the naturalization of poverty and inequality is still common in São Paulo, although its ideological basis is different and more difficult to grasp than in Delhi. While many interviewees rely on naturalizing conceptions of poverty (biologization of differences, prejudice against *"Nordestinos"*, etc.), the direct expression of racism remains taboo. These repertoires are latent. The concern to appear "politically correct" has undoubtedly led many respondents to measure, understate or even censor their remarks.

To justify inequality and poverty, the elite of São Paulo also draws on the register of meritocracy. This type of argument is actually, at least partially, compatible with that of naturalization. When people attribute their success and social superiority to their work or to that of their parents, they are in fact only implying that the poor do not show as much determination in their lives, as much dedication to work, and that this can also be seen as a trait of their personality. In other words, it is possible to "naturalize" merit. When the São Paulo interviewees mobilize this register, it is more often than not to persuade themselves – and the interviewer – that they cannot be held responsible for the plight of others. The income gap between rich and poor is so wide in this country that it requires the former to justify and exonerate themselves. It is striking to note that many of the interviewees feel this need intensely, as if there were still a bad conscience in them that could only be dispelled by argumentative self-persuasion. Drawing on their personal or family history, they recount episodes alluding to the courage, the temerity and the will to succeed that they or their ancestors have shown in the course of their lives, in order to convince themselves that they owe nothing to society and that it would even be absurd to think that they could be, even if only indirectly, responsible for the misery that is rampant around them. They often derive a sense of pride, of personal or family glory, which they do not try to conceal. What they have acquired, they claim, is above all down to merit and to the law of natural selection, which rewards the most gifted and the most tenacious. The idea that the poor could be victims of a fundamentally inegalitarian and unjust system is, on the contrary, foreign to them – given that they make no mention of this. Some even regard them as parasites.

Such unanimity in the self-justification of their supposed merit leads to a discourse of fierce hostility toward the national anti-poverty program (known as *Bolsa Família*) promoted by the government since the presidency of Lula and that of Dilma Rousseff. Thus, the arguments defended are not unfamiliar; they are derived directly from their perception of poverty and inequality. The poor who receive this type of aid are destined to become even lazier and harder to discipline. They are, by the very fact of receiving state assistance, encouraged to turn away from the ethos of work, saving and foresight.

5.4.2. *Controlled victimization of the poor*

In the Parisian metropolis, well-off residents living in wealthy neighborhoods talk about poverty in significantly different terms. While many recognize inequalities at birth – physical beauty, abilities, artistic gifts, character traits and so on – Parisian interviewees almost always, and far more frequently than those in Delhi, emphasize social determinism. For most of them, the social and familial aspect is absolutely the major factor, while that of natural talent, on the contrary, is rather negligible. Thus, in the neighborhoods studied, there is a tendency, depending on the individual, to sociologize poverty – in other words, to see it not as the effect of an inevitable natural process, but primarily as the effect of unequal opportunity. The absence or low level of education, the difficulty of finding a job, especially when one is poorly qualified, the fact of living in neighborhoods where difficulties are concentrated and where the infrastructure is lacking, and the cramped conditions of housing that deprive children of sufficient space to work are all factors put forward to explain the reproduction of poverty and inequality. For example, one of the interviewees stated that the poor have been "parked" against their will in spaces that have become conducive to all kinds of excesses and reprehensible behavior. In many interviews, we also find forms of denunciation of the dysfunctions of public action in all the areas that contribute to reinforcing the mechanisms of social reproduction, particularly in terms of employment, training and urban planning. These arguments are more about the victimization of the poor than the naturalization of poverty.

However, one should not jump to conclusions too quickly. In fact, an in-depth analysis of the interviews reveals elements of explanation that borrow from the language of the culture of poverty. The poor are partly what they are because of their cultural habits, including lack of courage and willpower, lack of appetite for effort and discipline, and inappropriate or even reprehensible practices, such as alcoholism, excessive fertility, neglect of children, and so on. In this culturalist register of the explanation of poverty, populations of foreign origin appear to be the ideal target of stigmatization. Roma populations, in particular, are mentioned to highlight certain specific features of this cultural poverty, but families of sub-Saharan or Maghreb origin are also mentioned, since it seems obvious to some interviewees that they are not sufficiently integrated into French society, if only because they do not have a sufficient command of the language and, under these conditions, are unable to integrate into the world of work and support the academic success (and therefore the social mobility) of their children.

Yet, strikingly, these culturalist and moralist arguments are only revealed at the margin of a discourse which remains organized overall around structural problems and the many widespread factors they give rise to. The economic crisis and the level of unemployment are mentioned as an extreme form of injustice that primarily affects the weakest and least qualified. The contextual factors linked to globalization, and sometimes even the nature of capitalism, complete the picture and mitigate the direct responsibility of the poor for the accumulation of their misfortunes. Some interviewees even have a sympathetic view of the poor, who are forced to live in overcrowded, unsanitary areas, cut off from opportunities and experience "suffering from a distance" (Boltanski 1993).

While the tendencies toward the naturalization of poverty remain relatively subtle in the remarks of the interviewees of the Parisian metropolis, compared to those of the two other metropolises, the question of merit is also approached there in a more nuanced way. The upper classes living in the four districts selected are often divided between recognizing the need to support the poor, in the name of a principle of national solidarity, and denouncing what they see as the excesses that lead many recipients of social assistance to fail to take sufficient responsibility for themselves. Almost all of the interviewees approve of policies such as the *Revenu de solidarité active* (RSA), as well as the efforts of the State to combat poverty. However, they often deplore the lack of effectiveness, and especially the low efficiency of these measures. They do not want the social state to be withdrawn, but rather to be improved.

On the other hand, the general approval of the principle of solidarity with the poor does not prevent restrictive moral arguments from being introduced, which have often been commented on and debated in the media in recent years. Some interviewees, for example, link poverty to the failure of families to educate and care for their children – hence the proposals put forward by certain right-wing politicians to suspend family allowances to parents whose children are regularly absent from school or are prosecuted for delinquency. The argument visibly appeals to certain Parisian interviewees. By mentioning it, they are simply subscribing to a universe of moral values and a belief system based on the importance of the family and education. In some interviews, we also find traces of neo-liberal ideology, in the form of a denunciation of the excess of regulatory constraints and social benefits charges that would weigh on companies and hamper their ability to hire the personnel they need (and thus reduce unemployment). This register also indirectly leads to the questioning of a generalized inertia, which the poor are seen as partly responsible for, in the sense that some of them may be satisfied with social benefits without really looking for work. In some interviews, the guilt-tripping of the poor and the unemployed appears as an underlying theme, without constituting the ultimate and sufficient explanation for poverty (interviews that are fully, or almost fully, based on guilt-tripping are extremely rare).

To sum up, in Paris, the well-off inhabitants of wealthy neighborhoods most often declare themselves in favor of solidarity with the poor, and sometimes make it their job to ensure it, but remain attached, despite everything, to the base of moral values with which they have always identified – the essential role of family education, the virtue of effort and work (now often mixed in with the neoliberal valorization of individual initiative and self-reliance) and the valorization of merit – which they would like to see inculcated more systematically in the poor. In other words, if the victimization of the poor at least partially explains the support of the upper classes for the welfare state, and even motivates their commitment to solidarity in certain cases, it cannot offer a full explanation for it, since it seems obvious to them that an excess of assistance can lead the poor to be complacent with regard to their situation.

It is thus striking to note that the upper classes encountered in Paris, unlike those interviewed in São Paulo and Delhi, often have a rather nuanced discourse on the poor, from which can emerge both the justification of "solidarism" and the social state as a guarantor of a minimum level of social cohesion and the justification of the statutory inequalities necessary for the organization and proper functioning of society. In both cases, it is in the name of an idea of belonging to a social whole composed of different and complementary parts that one avoids both the excessive guilt-tripping of the poor – which does not mean that this tendency is totally absent in social representations – and their victimization, which would justify a conception of social justice based on absolute egalitarianism. This ambivalence can be understood by pointing out that, in the representations conveyed by the Parisian interviews, the poor are not considered to be outside the social system, even if they are in some way the last layer of it. But if all categories, however different, are recognized as having the right to a social status that is acceptable in terms of the principle of civic equality, this does not imply social leveling. This is why individual merit continues to be mobilized to justify socioeconomic differences. Thus, it is not a question of accusing all poor people of laziness, because they may have extenuating circumstances linked to their living conditions, but of valuing those who compensate for their constraints through their work.

We can therefore speak of a controlled victimization of the poor. In this sense, it leads to the maintenance, often without explicitly formulating it, of a system of tolerance with regard to statutory inequalities, especially when it is seen as a condition of economic and social regulation based on the interdependence of functions and individuals. This does not prevent some of the interviewees, once they have conceded that the poor have extenuating circumstances, from sometimes vehemently denouncing the risk of assistance, especially since this register has become more common in recent years, particularly in the ranks of the French right, which has used it as a political argument to defend the value of work. Controlled victimization is therefore coupled with a muted sense of guilt-tripping.

5.5. Conclusion

The challenge inherent in social sciences, and in particular in comprehensive sociology, is to interpret the behavior of men and women living in society on the basis of their social perceptions and their lived experiences, according to their position in social and geographical space. In other words, it is a question of exploring individual consciences in all that relates to the specificity of social relations, the hierarchies and the distinctions between groups, the statuses and social roles, the relations of power and domination, as well as the forms of relegation or social disqualification. In this perspective, studying the perception of poverty is a thread that can be drawn to analyze not only poverty as such but the overall social structure and the relationship that different social groups have with a population deemed to be poor. Thus, it is interesting to study more specifically what rich people living in segregated – and relatively inward-looking – neighborhoods think of the poor. This chapter assumes that the analysis of urban segregation can be enriched by an in-depth study of representations of poverty – and inequality – and the discourses that the richest inhabitants of metropolitan areas living in exclusive spaces use to justify their concrete and spatial practices of seeking to be in their own self-contained bubble.

On the basis of a comparative survey carried out in the rich neighborhoods unanimously considered to be the most upmarket and the most segregated in three large metropolises, we have been able to study several complementary dimensions: the establishment of a social distance through the production of a moral order considered superior by the inhabitants themselves; the desire to protect oneself from the poor, a category often associated with a dangerous and/or repulsive class; the justification of an inferiority deemed natural or deserved by the poor and, symmetrically, the superiority of the richest, as well as the neutralization of compassion toward the most disadvantaged strata of society. The comparative analysis has brought out both the transversal character of these perceptions and rationalizations in the neighborhoods studied, but also the specificity of the representations according to the configuration of each metropolis. Beyond the neighborhood, it is indeed the metropolis as a whole that must be taken into account, since the neighborhoods are distinguished from one another within an urban mosaic that encompasses them all and also has its own specificities in relation to the forms and configurations of the socio-spatial division specific to other cities. The characteristics of each of these metropolises, in terms of insecurity, crime, insalubrity, maintenance of public space, urban infrastructure and transport, distribution of wealth, etc., provide elements of explanation. The history of the city, of its urbanization and of its institutions helps to shape the arguments put forward by the people interviewed.

At the end of this review, it is clear that the perception of poverty by wealthy people living in the most segregated neighborhoods is an explanatory dimension of urban segregation. When they talk about their neighborhoods, the wealthy emphasize the benefits of their bubble for themselves and their families, and most often express a clear desire to keep at bay the segments of the population that pose the greatest threat to their peace of mind and the maintenance of their privileges. However, this observation deserves two nuances.

First, while the survey was exclusively conducted in the most segregated affluent neighborhoods to facilitate a comparison between the three metropolitan areas, this does not mean that the results can be extrapolated to all affluent neighborhoods. Urban sociology has made it possible to distinguish between several types of neighborhoods. The neighborhoods selected in the survey correspond to what are often called "uptown neighborhoods", characteristic of patrimonial bourgeoisie and a secular class. To this very easily identifiable type, we can add at least two others, not taken into account in the survey. On the one hand, the type that Cousin (2013) described as "refounded neighborhoods", made up of high-end residential buildings built over the last two decades and populated mainly by business executives working in the business centers. On the other hand, there are the so-called "gentrified" neighborhoods, composed of formerly working-class areas now made up of senior executives, but also, and this distinguishes them from the "refounded" neighborhoods, of intellectual categories, middle-class professionals, artists and liberal professionals. Research outside of the PSPD survey has analyzed the variations of the "bubble" in these three types of neighborhoods in Paris and its agglomeration and has verified whether or not the social ties of these categories are anchored in the territory of residence, using the SIRS survey[7] ("Health, Inequalities and Social Divisions") (Cousin and Paugam 2014). In the former (the "uptown neighborhoods"), the "bubble" is more family and community based. By surrounding themselves with relatives who they can rely on, who share the same values and whom they can trust, the inhabitants of these neighborhoods often have the feeling of living in a peaceful village, where they feel completely safe. They also know that their children will have "good relationships" from an early age and will benefit from a protective environment. These neighborhoods are also those in which religious practice is strongest. In the neighborhoods inhabited by senior executives ("refounded" neighborhoods), the local anchoring is more individualistic in nature. Although their inhabitants want to be surrounded by people of the same social status, which is supposed to ensure peace and security, it is not essential for them to cooperate in social life, especially since their professional life is busy and does not really allow for investment in neighborhood relations. It is a sort of "everyone in their own home" (Cousin 2014). Finally, the inhabitants of gentrified neighborhoods appreciate, and sometimes seek, a less socially compartmentalized social life, but they prefer contact between relatives, if only to defend the interests of gentrification. They do not neglect relationships with neighbors, but they do not seek to form families or communities, which would be perceived as a sign of conservatism. Fewer of them also like their neighborhoods, which suggests that some of them have chosen this residential option as a stopgap[8]. These three types of neighborhoods thus refer to three forms of appropriation of the local territory and the constitution of symbolic boundaries between the different fringes of the elites. They correspond to three distinct forms of intersecting social bonds at the origin of different strategies of social reproduction and distinction. Thus, there are contrasting ways of considering social withdrawal and the constitution of a moral boundary. We can therefore put forward the hypothesis that the perception of poverty is also, at least partially, differentiated.

Second, discrimination against the poor is not limited to the upper social classes. It is a process that can spread to many layers of society, especially among the middle

---

7. The SIRS survey was conducted longitudinally in 2005, 2007 and 2010 in 50 neighborhoods in Paris and the inner suburbs, with a total sample of 3,000 households. The neighborhoods were chosen based on Edmond Préteceille's typology (2003), in order to diversify the different types of urban social spaces.

8. This type of neighborhood has been the subject of numerous surveys in France, but also abroad. In the South End, a gentrified neighborhood in downtown Boston, where a certain social and ethnic mix still exists, Sylvie Tissot found, for example, that the associations are almost exclusively composed of white, property-owning members, and that there is even a discreet selection process at the entrance, proof of the determination of the upper classes to control the spaces and the contours of their neighborhood (Tissot 2011).

classes. To the traditional question about the causes of poverty, a recent French survey[9] allows us to analyze the variations between professions and socio-professional categories (SPCs): (1) the explanation of poverty by laziness remains in the minority (13.8%) and concerns more self-employed people, employees, retired people (except former executives and intermediate professions) than the upper categories; (2) among executives and higher intellectual professions, there are strong variations according to status, with public service executives explaining poverty much more by injustice than business executives (52%, compared to 37.8%); (3) employees are not a homogeneous group either, with civil servants explaining poverty proportionally more often by injustice than others, especially private sector employees; (4) retired former farmers are more likely to explain poverty by laziness than other retirees; (5) business executives and intermediate professions (in the private sector) are distinguished by the fact that they consider poverty to be an inevitable phenomenon in the modern world[10]. These findings make it possible to qualify the analyses produced by the PSPD survey. If there is a mechanism of discrimination against the poor, which can take many forms and appear in a concentrated way in certain rich neighborhoods when events occur that make it even more visible, it can neither be exclusive to these neighborhoods nor represent an absolute obstacle to any expression of solidarity. Among executives and higher intellectual professions in France – who do not all live in segregated neighborhoods – the explanation of poverty by injustice is, in this case, much more frequent than the explanation by laziness.

5.6. References

Birnbaum, P. (1979). *Le peuple et les gros. Histoire d'un mythe.* Grasset, Paris.

Boltanski, L. (1993). *La Souffrance à distance.* Métailié, Paris.

Bourdieu, P. (1979). *La distinction : critique sociale du jugement.* Éditions de Minuit, Paris.

Castel, R. (1995). *Les métamorphoses de la question sociale. Chronique du salariat.* Fayard, Paris.

---

9. Dynegal-GEMASS/CMH/PACTE survey (2013). The use of this nationally representative base was carried out in Paugam et al. (2017) with respect to pre-submitted data (i.e. 3,913 individuals).

10. This survey also made it possible to verify that there are no major variations in the response to this question depending on the size of the city, with the exception of the Paris metropolitan area, where the explanation of poverty by injustice is statistically significantly more marked than in rural areas and in medium-sized cities or regional metropolises.

Castel, R. (2003). *L'insécurité sociale. Qu'est-ce qu'être protégé ?* Le Seuil/La République des Idées, Paris.

Chevalier, L. (1958). *Classes laborieuses, classes dangereuses à Paris pendant la première moitié du XIXe siècle.* Plon, Paris.

Cousin, B. (2013). Ségrégation résidentielle et quartiers refondés. Usages de la comparaison entre Paris et Milan. *Sociologie du travail*, 55(2), 214–236.

Cousin, B. (2014). Entre-soi mais chacun chez soi. L'agrégation affinitaire des cadres parisiens dans les espaces refondés. *Actes de la recherche en sciences sociales*, 204, 88–101.

Cousin, B. and Paugam, S. (2014). Liens sociaux et déclinaisons de l'entre-soi dans les quartiers de classes supérieures. In *L'Intégration inégale. Force, fragilité et rupture des liens sociaux*, Paugam, S. (ed.). Presses Universitaires de France, Paris.

Durkheim, E. (1960). *Les formes élémentaires de la vie religieuse.* Presses Universitaires de France, Paris.

Durkheim, E. (2012). *L'éducation morale.* Presses Universitaires de France, Paris.

Farley, R., Steeh, C., Krysan, M., Jackson, T., Reeves, K. (1994). Stereotypes and segregation: Neighborhoods in the Detroit area. *American Journal of Sociology*, 100(3), 750–780.

Gans, H.J. (1972). The positive functions of poverty. *American Journal of Sociology*, 78(2), 275–289.

Gans, H.J. (1995). *The War Against the Poor.* Basic Books, New York.

Geremek, B. (1987). *La potence ou la pitié. L'Europe et les pauvres du Moyen-Âge à nos jours.* Gallimard, Paris.

Giorgetti, C. (2015). Comment les catégories supérieures de Sao Paulo parlent de leurs employés domestiques ? Analyse d'un rapport de classe. *Brésil(s). Sciences humaines et sociales*, 8, 73–96.

Goblot, E. (1925). *La barrière et le niveau. Étude sociologique sur la bourgeoisie française moderne.* Librairie Félix Alcan, Paris.

Katz, M.B. (1986). *In the Shadow of the Poorhouse. A Social History of Welfare in America.* Basic Books, New York.

Katz, M.B. (1989). *The Undeserving Poor. From the War on Poverty to the War on Welfare.* Pantheon Books, New York.

Lamont, M. (1995). *La Morale et l'Argent. Les valeurs des cadres en France et aux États-Unis.* Métailié, Paris.

Le Roux, G., Vallée, J., Commenges, H. (2017). Social segregation around the clock in the Paris region. *Journal of Transport Geography*, 59, 134–145.

Massey, D.S. and Denton, N.A. (1995). *American Apartheid*. Descartes & Cie, Paris.

Moscovici, S. (1982). Des représentations collectives aux représentations sociales : éléments pour une histoire. In *Les représentations sociales*, Jodelet, D. (ed.). Presses Universitaires de France, Paris.

Musterd, S. (2006). Segregation, urban space and the resurgent city. *Urban Studies*, 43(8), 1325–1340.

Naudet, J. (2014). Postface : Les sociodicées ou la justification des privilèges. In *Justifier l'ordre social*, Jaffrelot, C., Naudet, J. (eds). Presses Universitaires de France, Paris.

Oberti, M. (2007). *L'école dans la ville : ségrégation, mixité, carte scolaire*. Presses de Science Po, Paris.

van Oorschot, W. and Halman, L. (2000). Blame or fate, individual or social? An international comparison of popular explanations of poverty. *European Societies*, 2(1), 1–28.

Paugam, S. (1991). *La disqualification sociale. Essai sur la nouvelle pauvreté*. Presses Universitaires de France, Paris.

Paugam, S. (1993). *La société française et ses pauvres. L'expérience du revenu minimum d'insertion*. Presses Universitaires de France, Paris.

Paugam, S. (2013). Les cycles de la solidarité envers les pauvres. In *L'avenir de la solidarité*, Castel, R., Duvoux, N. (eds). Presses Universitaires de France, Paris.

Paugam, S. (2016). Poverty and social bonds: Towards a theory of attachment regimes. In *Rescuing the Vulnerable: Poverty, Welfare and Social Ties in Modern Europe*, Raphael, L., Stazic, T., Altahmmer, B. (eds). Bergham Books, New York.

Paugam, S. and Selz, M. (2005). La perception de la pauvreté en Europe depuis le milieu des années 1970. Analyse des variations structurelles et conjoncturelles. *Économie et statistique*, 383–385, 283–305.

Paugam, S., Cousin, B., Giorgetti, C., Naudet, J. (2017). *Ce que les riches pensent des pauvres*. Le Seuil, Paris.

Paugam, S., Beycan, T., Suter, C. (2020). Ce qui attache les individus aux groupes et à la société. Une comparaison européenne. *Swiss Journal of Sociology*, 46(1), 7–35.

Pinçon, M. and Pinçon-Charlot, M. (1989). *Dans les beaux quartiers*. Le Seuil, Paris.

Pinçon, M. and Pinçon-Charlot, M. (2007). *Les Ghettos du Gotha. Comment la bourgeoisie défend ses espaces*. Le Seuil, Paris.

Piven, F.F. and Cloward, A.C. (1993). *Regulating the Poor. The Functions of Public Welfare.* Vintage, New York.

Polanyi, K. (1983). *La grande transformation. Aux origines politiques et économiques de notre temps.* Gallimard, Paris.

Préteceille, E. (2003). La division sociale de l'espace francilien. Typologie socioprofessionnelle 1999 et transformations de l'espace résidentiel 1990–1999 [Online]. Available at: https://halshs.archives-ouvertes.fr/halshs-00130291/document.

Préteceille, E. (2006). La ségrégation contre la cohésion sociale : la métropole parisienne. In *L'Épreuve des inégalités*, Lagrange, H. (ed.). Presses Universitaires de France, Paris.

Préteceille, E. (2018). Dynamique et diversité des classes moyennes dans la métropole parisienne. In *Les Bobos n'existent pas*, Authier, J.-Y., Collet, A., Giraud, C., Rivière, C., Tissot, S. (eds). Presses universitaires de Lyon, Lyon.

Préteceille, E. and Cardoso, A. (2008). Río de Janeiro y São Paulo: ¿Ciudades duales? Comparación con París. *Ciudad y Territorio – Estudios Territoriales*, 40(158), 617–640.

Préteceille, E. and Cardoso, A. (2020). Socioeconomic segregation and the middle classes in Paris, Rio de Janeiro and São Paulo: A comparative perspective. In *Handbook on Urban Segregation*, Musterd, S. (ed.). Edward Elgar Publishing, Cheltenham/Northampton.

Reis, E. and Moore, M. (eds) (2005). *Elite Perceptions of Poverty and Inequality.* Zed Books, London/New York.

Riffault, H. and Rabier, J.J. (1977). The perception of poverty in Europe. Report, European Commission, Brussels.

Rigaux, N. (1994). The perception of poverty and social exclusion in Europe 1994. Report, European Commission, Directorate General for Employment, Industrial Relations and Social Affairs, Brussels.

Sampson, R.J. (2012). *Great American City: Chicago and the Enduring Neighborhood Effect.* University of Chicago Press, Chicago.

Schelling, T.C. (1971). Dynamic models of segregation. *Journal of Mathematical Sociology*, 1(2), 143–186.

Schelling, T.C. (1978). *Micromotives and Macrobehavior.* Norton, New York.

Sébastien, L. (2018). L'attachement au lieu, vecteur de mobilisation collective ? *Norois*, 238–239.

Simmel, G. (1908). *Zur Soziologie der Armut, Soziologie.* Duncker & Humblot, Leipzig.

Tissot, S. (2011). *De bons voisins. Enquête dans un quartier de la bourgeoisie progressiste.* Raisons d'agir, Paris.

Wagner, A.-C. (1998). *Les nouvelles élites de la mondialisation. Une immigration dorée en France*. Presses Universitaires de France, Paris.

Weber, M. (1971). *Économie et société*. Plon, Paris.

Weber, M. (2003). *Hindouisme et bouddhisme*. Flammarion, Paris.

van Zanten, A. (2001). *L'école de la périphérie : scolarité et ségrégation en banlieue*. Presses Universitaires de France, Paris.

6

Modeling Inequalities in Geographical Space

Clémentine COTTINEAU[1,2]
[1] Centre Maurice Halbwachs, CNRS, Paris, France
[2] Technische Universiteit Delft, The Netherlands

6.1. Introduction: different modeling formalisms for different purposes

Neither the level of inequalities nor the trend of their evolution are random or accidental. They are the result of economic, political, social and spatial processes that build up over time, fueled by the interactions and strategies of multiple actors, not least collective institutions, whether public or private. As a result, there are multiple "explanations" for inequalities, and at least as many ways to detect them through quantitative analysis. Modeling inequalities, from the most abstract to the most descriptive, can thus account for observed trends, illustrate the (expected or unexpected) effect of a particular policy measure or even include interactions between agents or between agents and their geographical environment in the production and reproduction of inequalities. In this chapter, it is neither a question of reviewing all the models dedicated to inequalities in geographical space nor a question of producing a manual for modeling inequalities. Rather, the ambition is to present, on the one hand, different modeling approaches (statistical, spatial and agent-based), and what they bring to different inequality modeling objectives; on the other hand, it is to present some salient examples and important results from existing models dedicated to inequalities in geographical space.

Since a model is defined as a simplified representation of reality for a particular purpose, the question arises, as with other models: "why model" (van der Leeuw

Inequalities in Geographical Space,
coordinated by Clémentine COTTINEAU and Julie VALLÉE. © ISTE Ltd 2022.

2004; Epstein 2008; Edmonds et al. 2019) inequalities among individuals in geographical space? The purpose of the model – whether it is to explain, predict or illustrate a theory, for example – conditions the formalism and precision with which the system in question is represented, as well as the choice of entities and interactions present in the model. This is similar to generalization in cartography, which corresponds to the selection and simplification of the elements chosen to appear on a map (Cottineau et al. 2019). With regard to the modeling of inequalities in geographical space more specifically, the first decision is based on the type of inequality to be studied: economic, health, education, etc. The second branch on the decision tree depends on the place occupied by space in the description and explanation of these inequalities. Thus, while a series of mathematical models attempt to simplify the description of inequalities (particularly income inequalities) in order to be able to map them and eventually draw conclusions in terms of spatial distribution (section 6.2), multilevel and geographically weighted regression (GWR) models combine the effect of the relative location and the geographical affiliation of individuals in the estimation of inter-individual inequalities (section 6.3). With simulation models, the aim is to model the process by which inequalities are created, by including geographical space in the rules of action and change of agents' attributes (section 6.4). There are, of course, a number of other models, especially equilibrium models from economics (see Chapter 4), which we felt were too specific and insufficiently spatialized to be included in this chapter. Here, we shall reduce the focus to the graphical, statistical and generative modeling of inequalities in geographical space.

6.2. Inequality in the distribution of economic resources and in its spatial distribution

In the introduction, we defined inequality as the existence of systematic, significant and perceived differences in the distribution of social resources (e.g. wealth, health, education) between individuals because of certain characteristics (e.g. gender, age, ethnicity). These inequalities between individuals can be translated into space when privileged individuals are concentrated in certain places and disadvantaged individuals in a distinct set of places. However, these spatially translated inequalities are distinct from spatial inequalities, which would concern, for example, unequal exposure to certain nuisances or unequal access to certain resources (resulting from the distribution of facilities and services over a territory). These two types of inequalities are obviously linked to the presence of rare and valuable facilities (historical monuments, blue and green spaces, renowned hospitals) or, on the contrary, to infrastructures with negative externalities (wastewater treatment plant, motorway, cemetery) which condition the location (residential, for example) of favored or disadvantaged individuals, while modifying the potential access of populations to different resources. However, it seems more judicious to distinguish between them in the analysis in order to better understand the dynamics at work.

We therefore first discuss models for describing inequalities in the distribution of economic resources (section 6.2.1), before detailing a method for describing inequalities in space, namely through mapping (section 6.2.2). Third, we evoke the models of spatial inequality and social discontinuity in space (section 6.2.3).

6.2.1. *Lorenz/Gini, Pareto and Theil in economics: three distinct models*

In the field of economic inequality, and typically income inequality, the most widely used mathematical model is the Lorenz curve and its associated index: the Gini coefficient. The model implemented by Lorenz in 1905 is graphic and aims to represent the concentration of wealth in relation to the concentration of the population within a given area. By indicating the percentage of the population classified by increasing wealth on the x-axis, and the percentage of wealth held by the corresponding population on the y-axis, the Lorenz curve is a convex curve (or straight line) between the origin (0;0) and the coordinates (1;1). Indeed, 0% of the population always holds 0% of the wealth and 100% of the population always holds 100% of the wealth. Between these two known points, the convexity of the curve indicates the extent of the concentration of wealth in a small number of hands, and thus the degree of (mathematical) inequality in the distribution of income. A straight curve indicates a perfectly egalitarian distribution, since each proportion of the population has an equivalent proportion of the total wealth, whereas an extremely convex curve indicates a very high concentration of wealth. In the example in Figure 6.1, which has a particularly convex curve, we find that the poorest 80% of the population hold only 20% of the total wealth. Conversely, the richest 20% of individuals hold 80% of the wealth.

In 1914, Gini found the Lorenz curve and made it famous (Alacevich and Soci 2017) by creating a concentration index bounded between 0 and 1, which corresponds graphically to the area marked in yellow in Figure 6.1, between the Lorenz curve and the blue dotted line indicating equality, divided by the total area of the right-angled triangle below the line of equality (i.e. 1/2). The higher the Gini index, the greater the concentration of wealth, and therefore the greater the economic inequality. The modeling of inequality is unidimensional here. It does not account for possible asymmetries in the distribution, is not decomposable and gives more weight to transfers around the mode of the distribution than to transfers between extremes. These characteristics make the Gini index, according to general consensus among economists (Alacevich and Soci 2017), a very imperfect indicator for summarizing empirical distributions of wealth and income. Yet it is one that is indispensable because of its simplicity and its adoption by the majority of economic and social scientists, as well as in reports by international institutions on economic inequality.

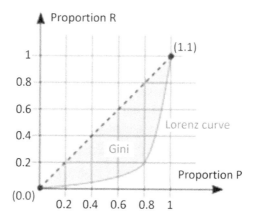

Figure 6.1. *A graphic model of wealth inequality: the Lorenz curve, where R represents wealth and P represents the population. For a color version of this figure, see www.iste.co.uk/cottineau/inequalities.zip*

Concentration indicators constructed from tax and wealth data have been revived by Piketty (2001). They correspond to particular points on the Lorenz curve: for example, the share of wealth held by the richest 1% or by the poorest 50%. These indices are simple to use and more intuitive than other aggregate measures, while describing the same trends in inequality. In this case, the concentration indices covary positively and significantly with the Gini index, the Atkinson index[1] and the 90:10 ratio, that is, the ratio between the value of the last and the first decile of wealth or income (Leigh 2007). In contrast, the use of the share of income captured

---

1. The Atkinson index (1970) is a normative inequality index that is based on a utility function representing the degree of society's aversion to inequality. This function makes it possible to give a different weight to the effect of a wealth transfer between rich and poor on the inequality index, depending on the direction of the transfer. The Atkinson index varies between 0 and 1 and is written as follows: $A = 1-(y_e/\mu)$, where y_i = the income of an individual i; $\mu = (\Sigma_i\ y_i) / n$; and $y_e = y\ |\ [nU(y) = \Sigma_i\ U(y_i)]$.

by the top 1% is questionable, according to Reynolds (2012), because these incomes are elastic (i.e. sensitive to economic conditions) and are calculated before redistribution[2]. Their share in overall income therefore decreases sharply during crises, which does not reduce structural inequalities.

While the Lorenz curve and the Gini coefficient reflect the concentration of wealth in relation to an egalitarian reference model (the equivalence line between % population and % wealth), the Pareto model, which precedes them, is quite different. Resulting from the mathematical generalization of a series of empirical observations, the Pareto model for describing the distribution of wealth is that of a power law. Indeed, by collecting individual wealth figures in different countries of the world, Pareto showed that there is a decreasing and scalar mathematical relationship between the probability P for an individual to hold a wealth X greater than x, and the ratio between this level x and the minimum level of wealth x_m, such that: $P(X > x) = (x_m/x)^\alpha$, where α is a scale parameter interpreted by Pareto as an indicator of the level of inequality. Here, the geometric progression of wealth levels in the distribution is thus the empirical model used: a far cry from the egalitarian model of Lorenz and Gini. Paretian distributions are only compared to each other synthetically with α to determine an order of levels of inequality (much like the rank-size distribution in urban studies).

The Theil index applies the physical model of entropy and information theory to the distribution of economic quantities. This measure, which is broad enough to reflect inequality, segregation and information redundancy, is mainly used to decompose inequality into inter-group and intra-group variations. Thus, analyses show that national affiliation "explains" about two-thirds of inequalities between individuals in the world, but that this share has recently been decreasing with the considerable rise of giants such as China, Brazil and India (Sala-i-Martin 2006).

Compared to the study of economic inequalities resulting from the distribution of a single variable (wealth or income) within a population, the analysis of social, health or education inequalities, for example, involves putting two variables in relation to each other. The difference in means or concentration indices between groups are often used to illustrate differences in resources or access by social or demographic group, using statistical tests of significance, such as t-tests. For example, Kakwani et al. (1997) measure health inequalities by comparing the level of perceived health according to the income level in the Netherlands in 1980–1981.

---

2. This argument can be applied to other indices, although synthetic indices and reports are less sensitive to it.

They observe, by studying averages and standardized averages, that individuals report better health as their income decile increases. Based on a t-test between concentration indices similar to the Gini index (crossing the cumulative proportion of income and an ordinal health indicator), they confirm the existence of health inequalities to the benefit of the richest, even when the demographic structure of the sample is taken into account, and all the more so when the health variable is subjective.

> Developed mainly by geographers, statisticians and sociologists to describe sociospatial segregation (Apparicio 2000), spatial inequality indices can be classified into three groups.
>
> In the first group, we find spatialized versions of the inequality indices presented above, such as the Gini or Theil index, in which we replace the distribution of wealth population groups with the distribution of different social groups between geographical units.
>
> In the second group, we find variations on Duncan and Duncan's (1955) dissimilarity index, which expresses the proportion of individuals who have to change geographical unit (by moving to another neighborhood, for example) in order to move from the observed situation to a situation of equitable distribution of the social groups considered in a given space (groups of different levels of education in a city, for example). This indicator of spatial inequality is the simplest and most frequently used measure, particularly for measuring ethnoracial segregation in American literature.
>
> In the last group, there are indices developed by geographers such as Morrill (1991), Wong (1993), Reardon and O'Sullivan (2004), which include "spatial parameters such as distance between spatial units, area" (Apparicio 2000, §17) or the contiguity of spatial units in measuring inequalities. Although more complicated to calculate and more demanding in terms of spatial data and analysis, these indicators provide a more accurate account of the spatial structure of inequalities.

Box 6.1. *Spatial inequality indices*

All of the indices presented so far are a-spatial but they can be used to compare geographical units between them. Thus, inequality between regions and countries is most often analyzed by comparing the values of their indices (George 1981), possibly over time, or by breaking down the global Theil index into two components: international and intranational inequality (Sala-i-Martin 2006). Geographical space can be taken into account in inequality indices in two ways:

either by using spatial indices (Box 6.1) or by mapping inequalities and modeling them graphically (section 6.2.2).

6.2.2. *Mapping socioeconomic inequalities and graphical modeling*

The most basic form of spatialization of inter-individual inequalities is to map the aggregate values (e.g. mean, median, sum) of a social resource and to consider, in the manner of social inequalities, geographic units as groups whose (significant) differences in values indicate the presence of location-related inequalities. Examples of this form of representation can be found in most atlases dedicated to inequalities (e.g. Le Bras 2014), whether they are economic, gender, or health related. However, depending on the adequacy of the discretization choice for quantitative variables, the impression offered by the color patches on the map can be misleading or uninformative about the level and dispersion of inequalities represented (Bell et al. 2019). A second option for spatializing inequality is to map not the aggregate values but the value of an inequality index of the social resource in question, its distribution pattern, or the result of a typology within the geographic units represented. This is the case, for example, with the mapping of national Gini indices or the share of the wealthiest 1% (Figure 6.2), or with maps of socio-residential inequalities (e.g. François and Ribardière 2004). In the latter case, the use of graphical models of spatial inequality is explicitly mobilized to interpret the maps. In particular, the authors describe the specialization of Île-de-France communes in the residence of more or less well-off households according to the sectoral model, identifying a "sector" of well-off communes from the center of Paris to the southwest of the region, and several sections specialized in the residence of poor households in the inner suburbs. The center-periphery model is used to distinguish between communes specialized in middle-class residence (pericentral areas), and the poor periphery of the eastern margins of Seine-et-Marne. Local discontinuities are also highlighted by changing the scale of analysis from the commune to the IRIS (*îlots regroupés pour l'information statistique*, that is, a homogeneous sub-municipal territorial unit with approximately 2,000 inhabitants).

As this example suggests, the description of spatial patterns lends itself to the use of spatial models of inequality, as well as to the analysis of spatial discontinuities. In the following section, we discuss the classical models of the organization of urban societies, popularized by American sociologists and geographers in the last century, to describe the process of segregation, before turning to the identification and interpretation of discontinuities in homogeneous areas.

a) Gini coefficient, national income

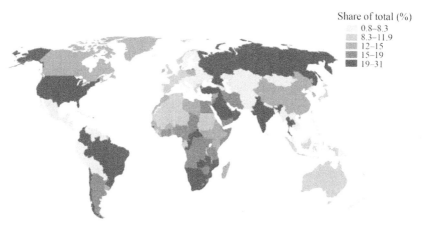

b) Share of the wealthiest 1% in national income

Figure 6.2. *Global mapping of economic inequality indices (source: World Inequality Database, latest available year 2020[3]). For a color version of this figure, see www.iste.co.uk/cottineau/inequalities.zip*

The zonal, or concentric, model describes the spatial distribution of a phenomenon in terms of distance to a center. In the original version by Park and Burgess (1925), the concentric zones represent relatively homogeneous areas in terms of population (by social and migratory origin) in Chicago. This model is used

---

3. Available at: wid.world.fr.

to represent the urban structure in which migrants circulate, from the center to the suburbs as they integrate into American and Chicago society. It has since been reused to describe the spatial distribution of urban functions (production in the center vs. residence in the suburbs) and urban forms (high-rise buildings in the center vs. detached houses in the suburbs). The sectoral model, attributed to Hoyt (1939), combines an axial dimension with the concentric model to represent the historical dependence of certain urban sectors on the presence of industries or wealthy residences along a transport axis (initially the railroad) during the development of a city. The multiple nuclei model proposed by Harris and Ullman (1945), suspending the assumption of isotropy of urban development, allows for more complex and variable patterns than Burgess's initial model, including secondary centers and areas of varying size.

The contribution of factorial ecology by Bell and Shevky (1955) was to combine these models to represent different dimensions of spatial organization of the population in a city. The concentric model would represent the different stages of the life cycle, with young adults living closer to the center and activity, families moving away from the center as the number of children increases, and the elderly returning to more central locations as their households shrink. The sectoral model would correspond to economic specialization, while the multiple nuclei model would describe concentrations of populations on an ethnic basis. This approach was operationalized by Berry and Kasarda (1977) on metropolitan areas by means of factor analysis, which also made it possible to rank the importance of these urban organization factors in the various cities.

In terms of spatial inequalities, these models aim to show that beyond the apparent complexity of cities and individual experiences, there are recurrent structural configurations in urban organizations. The proximity of industry to the homes of disadvantaged households, for example, indicates unequal access to a green environment as well as to the city as a whole (industrial and transport infrastructures often create barriers). These models are based on the presence of discontinuities between areas, but do not acknowledge them. On the contrary, some works (Grasland et al. 1997; François 2002; Roberto and Hwang 2015) put the notion of discontinuity at the heart of the analysis of spatial distributions of society. This notion allows for:

> [...] understanding both the intensity of the separation that is forged in the neighborhood and the factors of social division of the space, because of the links that articulate them. Discontinuities, when they are defined in a multidimensional way (administrative and political limits, morphological or accessibility breaks, cognitive categories) and

when their trajectories in space and time are taken into account, therefore become a rich concept to read the urban and segregation in cities [...] At least two theoretical configurations can be identified: polarization and fragmentation. Polarization refers to simple partitions of the city where large homogeneous areas are separated by gradients. Taken to the extreme, this situation leads to a dual structure as described for many large cities and transposed without nuance to other cities. Fragmentation corresponds to a more complex spatial structure in which group concentrations are fragmented and dispersed in the city. Yet conventional measures of segregation cannot capture these spatial configurations, which are nonetheless decisive because of the contextual effects they generate. (Duroudier 2014, pp. 136–137)

These spatial models (polarization, sectorization, fragmentation, etc.) of inequality thus make it possible to describe the economic organization of societies in geographical space in a simplified manner, to identify recurring patterns – the center–periphery relationship in cities, a North–South gradient on an international scale between egalitarian and inegalitarian countries – as well as strong local discontinuities (between regions, neighborhoods, or residential blocks).

Although useful for describing the distribution of resources in a population and in geographical space, the analysis of (a-spatial) inequality indicators and spatial models of their distribution do not account for the effect of individuals' location on their economic and social characteristics. One way to model these effects is through multilevel and GWR statistical models.

6.3. Statistical regression models: estimating the effects of geographic location on inequality

We present the functioning of each regression model in detail before discussing its contribution and limitations for the study of inequalities in geography.

6.3.1. *Description of the models*

Two families of statistical models are discussed below: multilevel models and geographically weighted models. These are the most suitable for taking into account the geographical organization of individuals in the statistical explanation of their inequalities.

6.3.1.1. *Multilevel models*

Multilevel models are regression models applied to hierarchical data. They are increasingly used in social and educational sciences (Goldstein 1987). Unlike classical ordinary least squares (OLS) regression models, multilevel models have two variance components, one generally at the level of the individual (level 1) and the other at a higher level (level 2) in which the level 1 individuals are contained. These models combine individual explanatory variables (level 1) with higher level variables (level 2), whose effect applies to individuals belonging to the same higher level group. This higher level classically corresponds to a geographical level (the neighborhood, the community or the country) or to an institutional grouping (e.g. the class or the school in models of educational inequalities). The equation of a multilevel model is written as follows:

$$y_{ij} = \beta_0 + (\beta_1 + u_{1j}) * x_{ij} + u_{0j} + \varepsilon_{ij}$$

where i refers to a level 1 individual (e.g. a student), j refers to the level 2 set to which they belong (e.g. their school), y refers to the characteristic whose distribution we seek to explain (e.g. income, level of academic achievement, life expectancy), and x refers to the vector of lower level explanatory variables introduced into the model (e.g. the student's age, income, and parents' education). β_0 is the *intercept* at the origin, u_{0j} is the level 2 residual for set j and ε_{ij} the level 1 residual for individual i, with these two types of residuals being uncorrelated and each following a normal distribution. Finally, the vector of coefficients β_1 can be associated with a vector u_{1j} to differentiate the slope of the regression according to the membership of the individual i to a set j.

Depending on the implementation chosen, a multilevel model can thus allow you to vary the *intercepts* of the regression according to the groups j ($u_{0j} \neq 0$), to vary the slopes of the regression lines according to the groups j ($u_{1j} \neq 0$), or both. When applied to political, school and health data, these models can suggest neighborhood effects on important individual characteristics, including the intraclass correlation (ICC), which is the share of inter-individual variance attributable to top-level membership. Indeed, when the residuals of the geographical groups are significantly different, they make it possible to isolate a (geographical) belonging effect in the variation of the levels of school or health performance, thus suggesting that, all else being equal regarding individual variables, the place of residence plays a distinct role in the lives of individuals, through a composition effect, the action of peers or the more general physical and social environment (see Chapter 1). Examples of such results are given in section 6.3.2.

A variant of multilevel models estimates cross-level interactions. These cross-level interaction effects can measure the influence of higher level variables in the variation of regression slopes between higher level groups. The equation of a multilevel model with cross-level interactions is written as follows:

$$y_{ij} = \beta_{0j} + (\beta_{1j} + u_{1j}) * x_{ij} + u_{0j} + \varepsilon_{ij}$$

with:

$$\beta_{0j} = \gamma_{00} + \gamma_{01} * w_j$$

$$\beta_{1j} = \gamma_{10} + \gamma_{11} * w_j$$

where w_j represents the vector of top-level explanatory variables j (e.g. school size and specialization in the example of school inequality), γ_{00} corresponds to the intersection at the origin (*intercept*) common to all observations in the model. γ_{01} is the change in *intercept* of group j induced by a variation in the variable w. γ_{10} corresponds to the change in slope of the variable w induced by a variation in *intercept* at the group level. Finally, γ_{11} is the inter-level interaction effect, i.e., the change in slope of the individual variable induced by a change in slope of the higher level variable. Like the interactions between variables of the same level, the inter-level interactions allow us to identify the effects of variables that depend on other variables. In the field of inequalities, these interactions can be presented, for example, in the form of variable relationships between the level of education for women and men, for residents of areas with high unemployment rates and for others. Multilevel models with interlevel interactions – which are quite similar to variable slope models – therefore require working with sufficiently large samples, and with a sufficient proportion of total variance attributable to differences between higher level entities (ICC), to obtain significant effects (Mathieu et al. 2012).

6.3.1.2. *Geographically weighted models*

GWR models are regression models applied to localized data in which spatial autocorrelation is assumed. "GWR is a relatively simple technique that extends the traditional regression framework [...] by allowing local variations in rates of change so that the coefficients in the model rather than being global estimates are specific to a location" (Brunsdon et al. 1996, p. 284). The value of a variable at a given point in space is thus assumed to vary systematically with the characteristics of the given point, as well as with the characteristics of neighboring points in geographical space. In other words, what happens at a point depends on the characteristics of the surrounding spaces. The technical implementation of geographically weighted models aims precisely at delineating the "surrounding" space and quantifying its weight in the explanation. The equation of a GWR model is written as follows:

$$y_i = \beta_{i0} + \beta(i) * x_i + \varepsilon_i$$

where y_i represents the characteristic y, whose distribution is sought to be explained (e.g. income, educational attainment, life expectancy) for an individual located at point i. x_i representing the vector of explanatory variables, β_{i0} represents the intersection at the origin for point i and ε_i, the residual at point i (the residuals being independent and distributed according to a normal distribution with a mean of zero). The central element of this model is the continuous neighborhood function $\beta(i)$. This function determines which observations are included in the regression for each point. Most applications of this model use a distance decay function around i to select these observations, but other functions are possible (Brunsdon et al. 1996). They share defining weight matrices between localized individuals. When the function restricts the neighborhood to very close observations, it generates a high variability of the estimated coefficients. On the contrary, a function that would systematically include all observations would not differ from an OLS regression model without a spatial component.

A GWR model will therefore produce as many estimates of *intercepts* and coefficients associated with the explanatory variables as there are localized individuals i. This model thus makes it possible to analyze the cases in which the spatial autocorrelation of the observations makes it possible to better explain the observed unequal patterns. They are particularly useful for revealing situations in which the direction and intensity of the relationship between two variables vary in different regions of the area. In addition, these continuous neighborhood function models make it possible to extrapolate the value of the coefficients associated with the explanatory variables to points not covered by empirical observations (Brunsdon et al. 1996). "To calibrate a GWR model at any one location, data is 'borrowed' from nearby locations and weighted according to the distance each nearby location is from the regression point [...] Hence, not only does GWR identify spatial heterogeneity in processes but it also takes advantage of the spatial dependence in data – thus tying together the two main distinguishing features of spatial analysis" (Fotheringham et al. 2017, p. 1248). Their implementation, however, is more expensive (in computation, choice[4], data, and interpretation), but is justified in

---

4. "GWR's simplicity fuels its popularity, which is reflected by its implementation in a number of software packages including the ESRI ArcGIS suite of tools, five R packages: spgwr (Bivand et al. 2013), gwrr (Wheeler 2013), GWmodel (Lu et al. 2014; Gollini et al. 2015), McSpatial (McMillen 2013) and lctools (Kalogirou 2019), two Python packages: PySal (Rey, Anselin 2010) and mgwr (Oshan et al. 2019) and standalone implementations such as GWR3 (Charlton et al.

complex situations. The principles and differences between the classical, multilevel and geographically weighted models are summarized in Figure 6.3.

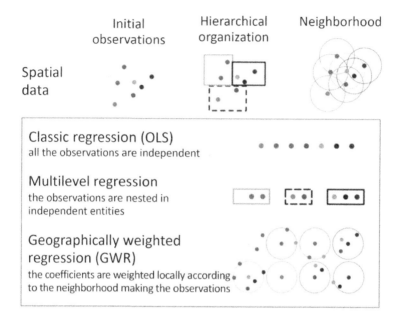

Figure 6.3. *Data organization and principles of classical, multilevel and geographically weighted regression. For a color version of this figure, see www.iste.co.uk/cottineau/inequalities.zip*

A multiscalar variant of GWR models has been proposed by Yang (2014). The MGWR method allows for a different scale to be associated with each explanatory variable, by varying the parameters of the neighborhood function (thereby expanding or contracting the area of influence of the neighbors on the estimate of the locally regressed quantity) for each variable. "That is, the bandwidths indicating the data-borrowing range can vary across parameter surfaces" (Fotheringham et al. 2017, p. 1249). The equation for an MGWR model is written as follows:

$$y_i = \beta_{i0} + \beta_{i,bwj} * x_{ij} + \varepsilon_i$$

2003), GWR4 (Nakaya 2015) and MGWR 1.0 (Li et al. 2019). Each software package has a standard GWR option complemented by a variety of alternative GWR forms and associated tools. No single package provides a fully comprehensive choice to the user although the GWmodel package comes closest" (Comber et al. 2020, p. 3).

where *bwj* is the *bandwidth* parameter of the associated neighborhood function for explanatory variable j, and $\beta_{i,bwj}$, the parameterized neighborhood function for the localized observation i. This model implements more degrees of freedom and is slower to calibrate (five to ten times slower in the simple simulations of Fotheringham et al. (2017)). However, it allows variables that represent processes acting at different scales to be included in the same regression by estimating the optimal spatial magnitude for each explanatory variable. In order to choose the most appropriate regression for each situation, Comber et al. (2020) recommend starting the analysis of a spatial dataset with a simple regression model such as OLS and then using a multiscale geographically weighted regression (MGWR) model. If the residuals of this regression appear not to be spatially autocorrelated, OLS is sufficient. If the estimated *bandwidths* for each variable are similar, then a geographically weighted regression (GWR) is more appropriate. If the residuals are spatially autocorrelated and the amplitudes are varied, then MGWR is the formalism that will give the best results.

6.3.2. *Important results of the analysis of inequalities by statistic models*

Using data from the well known U.S. Equality of Educational Opportunity survey, which stemmed from the 1966 Coleman Report, Borman and Dowling (2010) show, using a hierarchical model in which level 1 is the student and level 2 is the school, that 40% of the variance in student academic outcomes can be explained by the differences between schools. The ethnoracial composition (as a percentage of African Americans) of the school has a 1.3 times greater effect than being African American or not on academic outcomes, while the effect of average financial resources of the pupils' parents in a school are about three times greater than the resources of the student's own parents in predicting individual academic success. Because attendance at one school compared to another is generally based on residential location (see Chapter 1), these results suggest that the residential choices of affluent households (as well as the lack of choice among poorer households) significantly influence the level of societal and ethnic inequalities in education in the United States.

In a very comprehensive protocol including 400,000 students in the English public system in 2006, the different schools they attended during their schooling and the neighborhoods in which the schools are located, Leckie (2008) implements a multilevel model with random slopes. He finds that the strength of the negative relationship between school mobility and final exam scores depends strongly on the timing and nature of school changes (compulsory between primary and secondary school, or non-compulsory). In this case, it is mainly students changing schools outside the primary–secondary transition, outside the summer vacations or without changing residence, who progress less quickly than others. "Accounting for pupil mobility also reveals that schools and neighbourhoods are more important than shown by previous analysis" (Leckie 2008, p. 537). The correlations between the top-level regression lines, on the other hand, help to qualify the synthetic results used to evaluate or rank schools, whether in terms of academic achievement or reduction in inequalities (social, gender, need) among students. Indeed, it shows that a school's performance is not uniform for all types of school audiences. In this case, the correlation between the "school effect" of non-disadvantaged girls with good academic results and the "school effect" of disadvantaged boys with poor academic results is only 0.22.

By more explicitly spatializing their use of multilevel models, Roscigno et al. (2006) show, using a fixed-slope multilevel model, that students living in inner-city and rural areas of the United States have a systematically lower level of academic performance and a systematically higher probability of dropping out of school than their compatriots residing in peri-urban areas, given the same individual characteristics. The authors attribute these geographical differences to deficits in educational investment by families and schools lacking economic resources in the inner cities and the countryside, but also to the political and cultural orientations conveyed by the political and economic actors present, which would be less conducive to the educational success of all students.

In the field of health, Diez-Roux et al. (2000, p. 684) show that high levels of inequality in US states are detrimental to lower income individuals with respect to their risk of blood pressure and obesity (BMI index), but these risks are negatively and weakly associated with for individuals with high incomes. In other words, all else being equal, the economic inequalities measured in the different states reinforce the inequalities in health, with poor individuals more affected by the risks of a sedentary lifestyle, obesity and stress in the more unequal states, and on the contrary, wealthy individuals less at risk in these same states. These results reinforce the conclusions of Wilkinson and Pickett (2009), who conclude using simple multilevel models that individual incomes do not explain all the differences in health between individuals, but that economic inequalities (adversely) affect the health of all the geographical communities concerned (see Introduction). By associating the place of residence with the space used daily by more than 1,500 Île-de-France women, Vallée et al. (2010) show, using a multilevel model with interaction effects, that women residing in neighborhoods with characteristics that do not favor the use of health care services (low average income and low density of practitioners, for example) tend to neglect cervical cancer screening more systematically than women from other neighborhoods, especially since their daily activity space is limited to their single neighborhood of residence.

Finally, in a paper discussing the incidence of the first wave of Covid-19 in the United States, Mollalo et al. (2020) draw on the results of GWR and MGWR models to show that the positive relationship between the Covid-19 incidence rate and the level of population inequality in US counties is most apparent "in the tri-state area (i.e. New York, Connecticut, and New Jersey states), Massachusetts, and in parts of the Western United States, particularly in Nevada, Idaho, and Utah" (Mollalo et al. 2020, p. 5), while the relation is more tenuous, if not absent, in the rest of the country. They find the same result for median household income level, which has a strong positive correlation with greater Covid-19 prevalence only in these areas of the country.

6.3.3. *Limitations of the analysis of inequalities in geographical space by statistical models*

Despite the type of strong results that statistical modeling of inequalities in geographical space produces, there are a number of criticisms of the use of these methods to highlight the effects of spatial and geographical context on educational or health inequalities between individuals.

First, although multilevel modeling can take into account the common membership of some individuals in neighborhoods, regions and schools, statistical regression is still a modeling framework that assumes the independence of observations considered at a given level (Figure 6.3). Thus, even when the hierarchical aspect of the data is taken into account, the higher level units are still considered independent. In particular, their spatial organization (the proximity between two neighborhoods, for example) remains excluded from the model. Multiscale geographically weighted modeling can compensate for this weakness when the residuals are effectively autocorrelated. For this type of modeling, however, the cost of implementation is sometimes prohibitive (Fotheringham et al. 2017), while the level of expertise required to evaluate the model and interpret its results leads some authors to publish incomplete, inadequate or erroneous analyses (Comber et al. 2020).

Second, there is strong endogeneity between the top and bottom levels, which is not accounted for by the model (Manski 1993). "Individual characteristics are often considered to be the property of individuals, whereas they are also determined by where they live. Similarly, the context whose characteristics can be measured at a given time, in a given territory, is strongly associated with the composition of the population residing there. It is therefore illusory (or somewhat artificial) to hope to distinguish perfectly between individual and contextual characteristics and to dissociate compositional effects from contextual effects" (Vallée 2009, §32). This endogeneity is added to the risk of attributing to one level a share of the effects of the other level by over- or underestimating the model (*ibid.*).

Third, Salgado et al. (2014) mention the homogeneity of the effects estimated by multilevel models, with level 2 variables applying uniformly across all level 1 individuals in the same way, whereas the group in which a peer effect applies – for example, in the school setting – would be the group of friends rather than the class or even the school as a whole. The use of regression models with varying slopes or with cross-level interactions may mitigate this limitation. However, the issue of multiple scales at which context effects operate is crucial. Models with more than two levels are certainly possible, but particularly costly and demanding. Moreover, the levels at which data are available are often arbitrary: "A weakness of the multilevel approach is that it does not really look at the impact of scale upon segregation but upon the amount of segregation that can be attributed to the various levels of the model. The problem is that [...] one level is usually a mixture of scales because the areal units that comprise it vary in shape and size" (Harris 2017, p. 442).

Finally, Salgado et al. (2014) emphasize that the choice of *proxies* used as variables at the neighborhood, regional, or school level can obscure the causal processes linking individuals to their geographic unit or institutional grouping. For example, when the school is introduced as a top-level variable in a model of individual school performance, it is difficult to know whether the effect being modeled is that of peers within the school, of teachers' and families' educational investment, or of economic and cultural resources available to students outside the school. Identifying specific variables for each mechanism and collecting corresponding data is often a challenging task (Hanushek et al. 2003). This limitation is not unique to multilevel or geographically weighted modeling, but rather to statistical modeling in general.

While statistical models describe the reality captured by empirical data and make it possible to identify privileged associations between variables without presuming causality between them, simulation (in particular agent-based), by generating causal configurations, makes it possible to produce demonstrations of causal possibility, without it being possible to prove the identity between the simulated process and the empirical process having resulted in a similar configuration. These two approaches are therefore more complementary than alternative, as suggested by the studies that combine them. For example, Salgado et al. (2014) use the estimates from multilevel models on educational inequalities as a standard from which to estimate the quality of the agent-based model. In Cottineau's thesis (2014), variations in urban growth in the different regions of the former Soviet Union are identified by multilevel analysis, in order to build the generative mechanism that will be introduced into the multilevel model to represent the (causal) effect of different regional demographic regimes (level 2) on the demography of cities (level 1).

6.4. Simulation models to explain and illustrate the dynamics of inequalities in geographical space

Thus, whereas the models of inequality that we have seen so far have served to organize empirical data in such a way as to describe inequality or to isolate its factors and geographical scales, the models that we present here are designed to "recreate" in silico situations of inequality on the basis of causal processes applied to synthetic societies (i.e. artificial societies that exist only in the simulation). We restrict the type of simulation to two formalisms that are particularly well adapted to the consideration of geographical space: cellular automata and agent-based models, whose differences and common points are presented in Box 6.2.

In other words, we simulate a society of agents subject to rules of action based on hypotheses chosen by the modeler (according to empirical regularities and theoretical propositions). We then analyze the consequences of the interactions between agents and between agents and their environment on the level of inequalities, and their distribution in space, in order to identify which mechanisms are "candidates for explaining" the inequalities observed in real societies. These candidate mechanisms correspond to the rules of action that allow us to simulate the artificial society closest to real societies (according to a series of pre-determined indicators). We present three examples of agent-based models simulating inequalities in geographical space: a model of segregation (Schelling), two models of unequal access to localized resources and three models of eviction/gentrification.

> **Cellular automata** (CA) were developed in the 1940s in Los Alamos by researchers in mathematics and computer science (Ulam, Von Neumann). Considering the computing power of computers at the time, their operation is quite simple. They are presented as a grid of cells (typically squares) with two properties: each cell contains a value of its own (whether it is a color, a type or a number) and is affected by the value of the cells in its neighborhood (whether it is the four cells located above, below and on each side – Von Neumann's neighborhood – or the eight cells located surrounding the cell – Moore's neighborhood). The animation of a cellular automaton comes from the implementation of two types of action rules: the rules of change of the cell according to its own value, and the rules of change related to the values of the neighboring cells. Although simple in their principle and implementation, cellular automata allow the simulation of a wide range of geometric patterns and spatial dynamics. For example, with only two possible states as cell values and five change rules, Conway's (1970) "game of life" produces a range of patterns, some of which are stable, some oscillatory, some dynamic, and some ephemeral, depending on the starting spatial configuration (Gardner 1970). In geography, these simulations have been popularized by Batty (1997), White (1998) and Frankhauser (1998) for their ability to simulate certain structures (notably fractals) of urban growth.
>
> **Agent-based models** (ABMs) are extensions of cellular automata. Indeed, the "agents" of these models can be immobile cells arranged on a grid, but can also be represented by point, linear or surface mobile entities. In most of the agent-based models developed in geography since the 1990s (Bura et al. 1996; Batty et al. 1998), mobile agents interact with each other and with a spatial environment that can itself be a cellular automaton. Rules of change are then defined for mobile agents: (1) according to their own dynamics; (2) according to their interactions with other agents; (3) according to their spatial situation (interaction with cells, for example). The main advantage of agent-based modeling compared to other forms of simulation is that it allows the representation of heterogeneous, mobile agents with objectives and potentially with memory. Its main disadvantage results from this flexibility: it is indeed expensive to evaluate the simulated results, in terms of robustness and sensitivity.

Box 6.2. *Cellular automata and agent-based models*

6.4.1. *Agent-based models of spatial segregation: Schelling and its variants*

Schelling's model (1971, 1978) is one of the most well known examples of agent-based simulation in the social sciences. Designed by Schelling in the 1960s using a checkerboard, and then transcribed by his numerous successors into digital form, this very simple model involves two qualitatively different populations (often symbolized by a different color or shape) moving in a very abstract housing market.

The objective of the agents is to "reside in a dwelling" (i.e. to settle on a location corresponding to a cell of the checkerboard or the numerical environment) whose neighbors satisfy a diversity criterion chosen for the whole population. In this case, the agents are given a percentage that corresponds to the maximum share of their environment that neighbors of different color or shape can represent without the agents getting upset (i.e. they do not change their state in the simulation). If the proportion of different neighbors exceeds this percentage, then the agent "decides" to change its cell of residence and looks for one that is free, either randomly in most computer-implemented simulation models (e.g. the model available by default in the NetLogo software example library; Tisue and Wilensky (2004)), or as close as possible to the cell it leaves in the original version of the model. The simplest version of Schelling's model consists of a square-shaped, small "city" (a few dozen cells organized in a checkerboard pattern). The capacity of the cells is generally uniform, with a maximum of one agent per cell, and only part of them is occupied at the beginning of the simulation (according to a percentage that is an important parameter of the model), which allows disgruntled agents to move to unoccupied cells during the simulation. The main conclusion of this very simple model in the field of modeling inequalities in geographical space is that the interplay of local interactions and the reduced perception of the agents lead to the production of a collective situation of spatial segregation, even when the agents are individually relatively tolerant (they can, for example, accept being surrounded by neighbors who are 60% or 70% different from them). Indeed, as soon as 30% intolerance is reached, the model converges towards segregated patterns (Gauvin et al. 2009). The presence of many vacant spaces further favors this separation of groups in space. Although Schelling's model does not claim to represent the mechanism by which the housing market promotes urban segregation, it does tend to prove that it is not necessary to introduce conscious segregation or discriminatory mechanisms between populations to produce patterns of inequality in the distribution of individuals in space.

This model has been the subject of numerous criticisms and as many variations in implementation. Note, for example, the variations introduced in the 1990s by Portugali et al. (1994), who vary the maximum tolerance levels between the two simulated population groups, or by Benenson (1999), who introduces differences in economic status between agents, which accentuates or balances the effects of individual preferences in the location of individuals. Flache and Hegelsmann (2001) introduce irregularity into the grids and partitions of the model space, without leading to significant changes in the behavior of the model. Benenson and Torrens (2002) introduce the geometry of residential buildings and their capacity in the model, in order to better take into account the proximities between agents and the morphology of the city, whereas Laurie and Jaggi (2003) introduce differences in scope in the perception of agents. Fossett and Dietrich (2009) modify Schelling's classic model to measure the sensitivity of the shape and size of city cells on the level of segregation obtained. In 2012, Hatna and Benenson (2012) produced a version of Schelling's model allowing for the simulation of a population composed of a majority and a minority, rather than two equal-sized groups, while Banos (2012) introduced reticular structures between cells into the model to compare the effect of network shapes on the observed levels of segregation at the end of the simulation. In this case, the author shows that simulation environments following fractal networks favor group segregation in the space. Spielman and Harrison (2014) vary the urban density and location preferences of agents as a function of their individual characteristics, using empirical data from the 19th century. Raimbault et al. (2019) focus on the sensitivity of the model to initial spatial conditions. They implement Schelling's model on "cities" whose spatial distribution of densities corresponds to configurations close to those of European cities, that is, non-uniform and varied (monocentric, polycentric, discontinuous cities). They show that the effect of the model's parameters (i.e. the individual tolerance level of agents and the city's vacancy rate) is the same regardless of the city's density profile, although discontinuous and polycentric cities favor systematically higher final segregation levels. Finally, Forsé and Parodi (2019) reveal the fragility of the model's results by revealing an implicit assumption: "Schelling's model neglects [...] moves made for reasons other than intolerance [...] Taking these other moves into account, we would spontaneously observe the disappearance of homogeneous neighborhoods that are only transitory formations. Schelling's conclusion is therefore very fragile because, basically, he stops the film at the moment when, by accident, homogeneous neighborhoods have formed" (Forsé and Parodi 2019, p. 101).

6.4.2. *Two agent-based models of the emergence of inequalities linked to the distribution of resources in space*

The Sugarscape model is one of several environment-society interaction models that help explain the formation of inequalities between individuals and between settlement nuclei, based on artificial societies embedded in their physical environment (Schmitt and Pumain 2013). Initially proposed by Epstein and Axtell (1996), who were pioneers in social simulation, agent-based models are designed to study the interactions between plausible mechanisms of emergence of the economy and differentiation between individuals in a society. Its configuration is very simple and can be completed by more elaborate versions of the model. Agents evolve in a landscape characterized by the non-uniform presence of a renewable resource (sugar). They can collect this resource, store it or use it for their survival. This collection depends on their perception, which varies from one individual to another (some see further than others). The amount of sugar needed for survival (or metabolism) also varies from one individual to another. The uneven distribution of sugar across the landscape, combined with differences in individual vision and metabolism, is enough to produce an economically unequal society, in which levels of wealth (measured in sugar) vary greatly between individuals, some of whom have a very large amount of sugar and others not enough to survive. The measure on which the evaluation and comparison of the model outputs is based on is therefore generally, as in the NetLogo implementation of Li and Wilensky, the Gini index, the measure which here summarizes the inequalities of sugar-wealth between agents.

As with Schelling, the simplicity of the initial model has led to a significant number of additions and complementary mechanisms. This is particularly true of the authors of the original model, who have adapted Sugarscape from its most simple form to a model in which the behavior of agents approximates the empirical diversity of interactions between members of a society. "Over time, the repertoire of agent behaviors grows to include movement, resource harvesting, sexual reproduction, combat, culture transmission, exchange, trade, inheritance, credit, pollution, disease spread, and immune resistance" (Schmitt and Pumain 2013, §8). Comparing the impact of the initial spatial configuration in Schelling's and Sugarscape's models, Raimbault et al. (2019) show that Sugarscape's simple implementation is highly sensitive to the initial distribution of the resource in the emergence of inequalities between individuals, to the point that the model outputs can be modified more strongly by changing the initial spatial conditions than by changing the values of the model parameters (minimum and maximum sugar production capacity of the cells, number of agents, etc.).

In the Auchincloss et al. (2011) model, the inequalities modeled between individuals are those related to their diet. They emerge as a result of income differences among individuals in a segregated environment, through the supply of healthy food in shops which adapt to the local residents' demand. The model effectively simulates two types of agents: households and food stores. Households are distributed in two categories of equal size: rich households and poor households. They have a preference (continuous between 0 and 1) for healthy food, which is distributed either randomly or conditionally to their category (rich/poor), depending on the simulated scenarios. The food stores are distributed in two equally sized categories: those selling healthy food and those selling unhealthy food. Half of the stores are simulated as selling their food cheaply, and the other half selling their food at high prices, with the price being assigned either randomly or conditionally to their category (healthy/unhealthy) depending on the simulated scenarios. The space is simulated in a very abstract way, by a torus (i.e. a space folded on itself to remove edge effects) of 50 × 50 square cells. Households are randomly distributed or isolated by income level in two distinct zones of the space according to the scenarios, while stores are randomly distributed or isolated by the type of food sold (healthy or not) in two distinct zones of the space according to the scenarios. No agent moves between these zones during the simulation. The dynamics of the model revolve around the relationship between households and stores. Households evaluate the stores they visit based on price, accessibility and the match between the food sold and their preference, and distribute their spending among the stores that score highest. Stores respond to household spending by closing if the number of customers is too low, while new stores (possibly with different prices and food) may replace them at the same locations. Auchincloss et al. (2011) show, using this model and different scenarios, that in the absence of other factors, income-related nutrition inequality results from the segregation of wealthy households and healthy food stores in separate areas from poor households and unhealthy food stores. When households have a preference for healthy food, regardless of income level, the diets of the poorest appear consistently more healthy than in the other scenarios, although inequality persists between rich and poor. Finally, the authors show that only favorable preferences and accessible cheap stores can overcome the differential introduced by household segregation, thus demonstrating the structural importance of agents' inscription in their environment on food inequalities in relation to possible changes in their behavior.

6.4.3. *Three models simulating spatial relegation dynamics*

The last type of simulation model of inequalities between individuals in geographical space that we wish to present in this chapter concerns the process of spatial relegation, that is, the forced displacement of poor populations from certain urban neighborhoods, following the chosen displacement of more affluent social fractions who, by investing in mixed, poor and/or degraded neighborhoods, contribute to the physical urban renewal, and subsequently to the social replacement of these neighborhoods. Three models are focused on this dynamic that modifies urban space through the interaction between economically unequal individuals.

The first model (O'Sullivan 2002) is a cellular automaton, that is, a model in which the geographical location of the agents is fixed and resembles a cell. The author models the spatial relegation process from the point of view of buildings and housing, focusing on the *rent gap* hypothesis (Smith 1979). The rent gap, or the gap between potential land rent and current land revenues, is one of the elements of economic theory involved in explaining the urban and social renewal of urban neighborhoods. O'Sullivan explores the geographical and temporal aspects of these economic mismatches between the use value of housing and its potential value, due to its location. His model is more refined in terms of spatial representation than most conventional cellular automata, which are constructed as regular grids of identical square cells. The cells it represents are the centroids of buildings, whose neighborhoods are constructed according to a proximity graph rather than by contiguity. Each cell has four possible states: for sale, not for sale, looking for a tenant or rented. The transition between these four states is conditioned by the characteristics of the building (particularly its degree of deterioration) and the income of the occupants, the demand available for buying and renting, as well as by an indicator of the status of the neighborhood, but also contains an element of stochasticity (i.e. chance). The model is able to reproduce the dynamics of physical and economic deterioration of the neighborhood, followed by gentrification, using the example of Hoxton in East London. Its representation of inter-individual inequalities in geographical space is therefore rather mechanical and impersonal, since the dynamics of the model are played out at the level of the buildings and their objective characteristics. The author suggests, however, that the neighborhood status parameter is crucial in determining the dynamics of the model, since it updates at each point in time the composition of the neighborhood according to the income of the residents present at a given moment, and thus determines the income of potential new owners and renters. According to O'Sullivan himself, this parameter should rather be treated as an exogenous factor in connection with the representation of other neighborhoods in the city for a more realistic simulation: "A fairer application would imply that the neighborhood presented here in a larger model of the urban system" (O'Sullivan 2002, p. 270). Indeed, this parameter can be interpreted as an element of neighborhood reputation, that is, an important element of the social dynamics of gentrification in theory.

The second model is a hybridization between a cellular automaton representing the dwellings of a neighborhood according to a regular grid of square cells, and an agent-based model representing individuals moving between these dwellings and "animating" the social, economic and urban space. Torrens and Nara (2007) focus their attention on the functioning of the housing market and represent four scenarios of gentrification that they compare with data from a Salt Lake City neighborhood. The first scenario is that of no change (business as usual), the second represents a change from the point of view of demand (in modeling, the arrival of a group of "gentrifiers" with different economic and social behaviors from those of the initial population), the third is a change from the point of view of supply (by taking into account the rent gap and the undervaluation of the real estate stock at a given time), and the fourth illustrates a combination of scenarios two and three. The rule of action for agents is to decide whether or not to move, to select one of the three housing markets in the city if necessary and then choose a property to move into. The factors influencing this decision depend on their preferences (for a type of dweling, its size, etc.), the characteristics of the home, the characteristics of the neighborhood (accessibility to a shopping mall, a freeway off-ramp, the city center; as well as the surrounding vacancy rate) and their own resources. Torrens and Nara (2007, p. 352) show that only the last scenario, including supply and demand dynamics, can reasonably explain the gentrification dynamics observed in Salt Lake City. Here, the modeling of inequalities in geographical space incorporates competition for neighborhood housing by households, both local and newcomers, with unequal resources. The attractiveness of the housing itself depends on its location with respect to fixed resources (such as downtown and transport routes).

The last model, devoted to the forced displacement of populations in an urban space, is an agent-based model developed by Boeing (2018). The author is interested in the effect of the correlation between individual preferences and economic status in the displacement of low-income groups from areas that are suitable for them. Despite its 13 parameters, the model is much simpler than the previous two, and is designed as a theoretical model rather than as one that can be applied to a particular case. Agents are categorized into three levels of wealth (poor, medium, rich), while the cells available to them are characterized by two dimensions – on the one hand, the presence of abstract amenities functioning as club goods (i.e. whose benefit applies equally to all those who have access to them, without decreasing its stock through the increase in the number of members) and, on the other hand, their level of density. The preference of poor agents is to reside near the amenity they exploit for a living, while the preference of rich agents is to reside near densely populated areas. The land rent increases with the number and income of agents present in a cell, leading occupants who cannot afford to pay the rent to change location. The model leads poor households to form dense clusters around amenities that attract rich households. The dense presence of rich households in turn pushes poor households to the periphery of the cluster, and away from the amenities on which they depend, resulting in an inefficient state of the system. Much like Schelling's model, Boeing's model allows for the reproduction of a stylized fact of inequality between individuals in and through geographical space by simulating a mechanism sufficient to reproduce an empirically observed dynamic, although globally unrealistic by itself.

6.5. Conclusion

This overview of the modeling of inter-individual inequalities in geographical space has made it possible to take into account the diversity of the objectives of the possible models, the diversity of the methodological approaches implemented to meet these objectives, as well as the multiplicity of points of view on the same question (spatial relocation, for example). We have noted that the different families of modeling (cartographic, statistical, generative) should be used in a complementary rather than competing manner. Indeed, the cartographic models synthesize the empirical regularities of the geographical distribution of individual inequalities and suggest factors to be introduced into the statistical models. These describe the relative influence of measurable factors on the distribution of inequalities, and their results feed into the construction and plausibility assessment of generative models. The theoretical results of the simulation can in turn enrich the set of hypotheses to be tested empirically. According to Manzo (2005, p. 39), "the recent literature is beginning to outline a type of quantitative empirical sociology in which variable-based analysis describes, mechanism-based modeling (constructed in terms of methodological individualism) explains, and the simulation dynamically animates (and tests) the supposed mechanisms underlying the observed statistical relationships". In the same way, the variables and mechanisms selected by the different studies are often more complementary than competitors in explaining social and economic inequalities. Thus, some models emphasize the physical aspect of the spatial environment, whereas some other models emphasize its demographic, economic or social composition, to explain inequalities in geographical space. It seems that the diversity of social reality favors a combination of these explanatory registers, which vary according to the case and the time.

6.6. References

Alacevich, M. and Soci, A. (2017). *A Short History of Inequality*. Agenda Publishing, Newcastle upon Tyne.

Apparicio, P. (2000). Les indices de ségrégation résidentielle : un outil intégré dans un système d'information géographique. *Cybergeo*, 134. doi:10.4000/cybergeo.12063.

Atkinson, A.B. (1970). On the measurement of inequality. *Journal of Economic Theory*, 2, 244–263.

Auchincloss, A.H., Riolo, R.L., Brown, D.G., Cook, J., Diez-Roux, A.V. (2011). An agent-based model of income inequalities in diet in the context of residential segregation. *American Journal of Preventive Medicine*, 40(3), 303–311.

Banos, A. (2012). Network effects in Schelling's model of segregation: New evidences from agent-based simulation. *Environment and Planning B: Planning and Design*, 39(2), 393–405. doi:10.1068/b37068.

Batty, M. (1997). Cellular automata and urban form: A primer. *Journal of the American Planning Association*, 63(2), 266–274.

Batty, M., Jiang, B., Thurstain-Goodwin, M. (1998). Local movement: Agent-based models of pedestrian flows. UCL Working Paper [Online]. Available at: https://discovery.ucl.ac.uk/id/eprint/225/1/paper4.pdf.

Bell, W. and Shevky, E. (1955). *Social Area Analysis: Theory, Illustrative Application, and Computational Procedures*. Stanford University Press, Stanford.

Bell, A., Hartman, T., Piekut, A., Rae, A., Taylor, M. (2019). *Making Sense of Data in the Media*. Sage Publishing, Thousand Oaks.

Benenson, I. (1999). Modeling population dynamics in the city: From a regional to a multi-agent approach. *Discrete Dynamics in Nature and Society*, 3(2/3), 149–170.

Benenson, I. and Torrens, P.M. (2004). Geosimulation: Object-based modeling of urban phenomena. *Computers, Environment and Urban Systems*, 28(1/2), 1–8.

Berry, B.J.L. and Kasarda, J.D. (1977). *Contemporary Urban Ecology*. Macmillan Publishing Company, New York.

Boeing, G. (2018). The effects of inequality, density, and heterogeneous residential preferences on urban displacement and metropolitan structure: An agent-based model. *Urban Science*, 2(76) [Online]. Available at: https://doi.org/10.3390/urbansci2030076.

Borman, G. and Dowling, M. (2010). Schools and inequality: A multilevel analysis of Coleman's equality of educational opportunity data. *Teachers College Record*, 112(5), 1201–1246.

Brunsdon, C., Fotheringham, A.S., Charlton, M.E. (1996). Geographically weighted regression: A method for exploring spatial nonstationarity. *Geographical Analysis*, 28(4), 281–298.

Bura, S., Guérin-Pace, F., Mathian, H., Pumain, D., Sanders, L. (1996). Multiagent systems and the dynamics of a settlement system. *Geographical Analysis*, 28(2), 161–178.

Comber, A., Brunsdon, C., Charlton, M., Dong, G., Harris, R., Lu, B., Lü, Y., Murakami, D., Nakaya, T., Wang, Y., et al. (2020). The GWR route map: A guide to the informed application of geographically weighted regression. arXiv preprint arXiv:2004.06070.

Conway, J. (1970). The game of life. *Scientific American*, 223(4), 4.

Cottineau, C. (2014). L'évolution des villes dans l'espace post-soviétique. Observation et modélisations. PhD Thesis, Université Paris 1 Panthéon-Sorbonne, Paris.

Cottineau, C., Chapron, P., Le Texier, M., Rey-Coyrehourcq, S. (2020). Modélisation territoriale incrémentale [Online]. Available at: http://doi.org/10.1002/9781119687290 [see Chapter 4 for the English version].

Diez-Roux, A.V., Link, B.G., Northridge, M.E. (2000). A multilevel analysis of income inequality and cardiovascular disease risk factors. *Social Science & Medicine*, 50(5), 673–687.

Duncan, O.D. and Duncan, B. (1955). Residential distribution and occupational stratification. *American Journal of Sociology*, 60(5), 493–503.

Duroudier, S. (2014). Les divisions socio-spatiales dans les villes intermédiaires des États-Unis. Perspectives de recherche à partir de la notion de discontinuité. *Espace géographique*, 43(2), 134–147 [Online]. Available at: https://doi.org/10.3917/eg.432.0134.

Edmonds, B., le Page, C., Bithell, M., Chattoe-Brown, E., Grimm, V., Meyer, R., Montañola-Sales, C., Ormerod, P., Root, H., Squazzoni, F. (2019). Different modelling purposes. *Journal of Artificial Societies and Social Simulation*, 22(3), 6 [Online]. Available at: https://doi.org/10.18564/jasss.3993.

Epstein, J.M. (2008). Why model? *Journal of Artificial Societies and Social Simulation*, 11(4), 12 [Online]. Available at: http://jasss.soc.surrey.ac.uk/11/4/12.html.

Epstein, J.M. and Axtell, R. (1996). *Growing Artificial Societies: Social Science from the Bottom Up*. MIT Press, Cambridge.

Flache, A. and Hegselmann, R. (2001). Do irregular grids make a difference? Relaxing the spatial regularity assumption in cellular models of social dynamics. *Journal of Artificial Societies and Social Simulation*, 4(4), 6 [Online]. Available at: http://www.soc.surrey.ac.uk/JASSS/4/4/6.html.

Forsé, M. and Parodi, M. (2019). Retour critique sur le modèle de ségrégation urbaine de Schelling. *Émulations-Revue de sciences sociales*, 31, 91–104.

Fossett, M. and Dietrich, D.R. (2009). Effects of city size, shape, and form, and neighborhood size and shape in agent-based models of residential segregation: Are Schelling-style preference effects robust? *Environment and Planning B: Planning and Design*, 36(1), 149–169. doi:10.1068/b33042.

Fotheringham, S.A., Yang, W., Kang, W. (2017). Multiscale geographically weighted regression (MGWR). *Annals of the American Association of Geographers*, 107(6), 1247–1265. doi:10.1080/24694452.2017.1352480.

François, J.-C. (2002). Ressemblance et proximités : un point de vue sur le contexte théorique de la notion de discontinuité géographique. *Cybergeo*, 214.

François, J.-C. and Ribardière, A. (2004). Qu'apporte l'échelon infracommunal à la carte des inégalités de richesse en Île-de-France ? *MappeMonde*, 3(75), 1–8 [Online]. Available at: http://mappemonde-archive.mgm.fr/num3/articles/art04305.html.

Frankhauser, P. (1998). Fractal geometry of urban patterns and their morphogenesis. *Discrete Dynamics in Nature and Society*, 2(2), 127–145.

Gardner, M. (1970). Mathematical games. The fantastic combinations of John Conway's new solitaire game "life". *Scientific American*, 223, 120–123.

Gauvin, L., Vannimenus, J., Nadal, J.P. (2009). Phase diagram of a Schelling segregation model. *The European Physical Journal B*, 70(2), 293–304.

George, P. (1981). *Géographie des inégalités*. Presses Universitaires de France, Paris.

Goldstein, H. (1987). *Multilevel Models in Educational and Social Research*. Oxford University Press, Oxford.

Grasland, C., François, J.-C., Brunet, R. (1997). La discontinuité en géographie : origines et problèmes de recherche. *L'Espace géographique*, 26(4), 297–308.

Hanushek, E.A., Kain, J.F., Markman, J.M., Rivkin, S.G. (2003). Does peer ability affect student achievement? *Journal of Applied Econometrics*, 18(5), 527–544.

Harris, C.D. and Ullman, E.L. (1945). The nature of cities. *The Annals of the American Academy of Political and Social Science*, 242, 7–17

Harris, R. (2017). Measuring the scales of segregation: Looking at the residential separation of white British and other schoolchildren in England using a multilevel index of dissimilarity. *Transactions of the Institute of British Geographers*, 42(3), 432–444.

Hatna, E. and Benenson, I. (2012). The Schelling model of ethnic residential dynamics: Beyond the integrated-segregated dichotomy of patterns. *Journal of Artificial Societies and Social Simulation*, 15(1), 6.

Hoyt, H. (1939). *The Structure and Growth of Residential Neighborhoods in American Cities*. US Government Printing Office, Washington.

Kakwani, N., Wagstaff, A., Van Doorslaer, E. (1997). Socioeconomic inequalities in health: Measurement, computation, and statistical inference. *Journal of Econometrics*, 77(1), 87–103.

Laurie, A.J. and Jaggi, N.K. (2003). Role of "vision" in neighbourhood racial segregation: A variant of the Schelling segregation model. *Urban Studies*, 40(13), 2687–2704.

Le Bras, H. (2014). *Atlas des inégalités. Les Français face à la crise*. Autrement, Paris.

Leckie, G. (2008). Modelling the effects of pupil mobility and neighbourhood on school differences in educational achievement. Centre for Market and Public Organisation, Bristol.

van der Leeuw, S.E. (2004). Why model? *Cybernetics and Systems*, 35(2/3), 117–128.

Leigh, A. (2007). How closely do top income shares track other measures of inequality? *The Economic Journal*, 117(524), F619–F633.

Manski, C.F. (1993). Identification of endogenous social effects: The reflection problem. *The Review of Economic Studies*, 60(3), 531–542.

Manzo, G. (2005). Variables, mécanismes et simulations : une synthèse des trois méthodes est-elle possible ? Une analyse critique de la littérature. *Revue française de sociologie*, 46(1), 37–74.

Mathieu, J.E., Aguinis, H., Culpepper, S.A., Chen, G. (2012). Understanding and estimating the power to detect cross-level interaction effects in multilevel modeling. *Journal of Applied Psychology*, 97(5), 951.

Mollalo, A., Vahedi, B., Rivera, K.M. (2020). GIS-based spatial modeling of COVID-19 incidence rate in the continental United States. *Science of the Total Environment*, 728, 138884 [Online]. Available at: https://doi.org/10.1016/j.scitotenv.2020.138884.

Morrill, R. (1991). On the measure of geographic segregation. *Geography Research Forum*, 11, 25–36.

O'Sullivan, D. (2002). Toward micro-scale spatial modeling of gentrification. *Journal of Geographical Systems*, 4(3), 251–274.

Park, R.E. and Burgess, E.W. (1925). *The Growth of the City: An Introduction to a Research Project*. University of Chicago Press, Chicago.

Piketty, T. (2001). *Les Hauts Revenus en France au XXe siècle*. Grasset, Paris.

Portugali, J., Benenson, I., Omer, I. (1994). Socio-spatial residential dynamics: Stability and instability within a self-organized city. *Geographical Analysis*, 26(4), 321–340. doi:10.1111/j.1538-4632.1994.tb00329.x.

Raimbault, J., Cottineau, C., Texier, M.L., Néchet, F.L., Reuillon, R. (2018). Space matters: extending sensitivity analysis to initial spatial conditions in geosimulation models. *Journal of Artificial Societies and Social Simulation*, 22(4), 10.

Reardon, S.F. and O'Sullivan, D. (2004). Measures of spatial segregation. *Sociological Methodology*, 34(1), 121–162.

Reynolds, A. (2012). The misuse of top 1 percent income shares as a measure of inequality. *Cato Working Paper*, 105. doi:10.2139/SSRN.2226941.

Roberto, E. and Hwang, J. (2015). Barriers to integration: Physical boundaries and the spatial structure of residential segregation. arXiv:1509.02574.

Roscigno, V.J., Tomaskovic-Devey, D., Crowley, M. (2006). Education and the inequalities of place. *Social Forces*, 84(4), 2121–2145.

Sala-i-Martin, X. (2006). The world distribution of income: Falling poverty and... convergence, period. *The Quarterly Journal of Economics*, 121(2), 351–397.

Salgado, M., Marchione, E., Gilbert, N. (2014). Analysing differential school effectiveness through multilevel and agent-based modelling. *Journal of Artificial Societies and Social Simulation*, 17(4), 3. doi:10.18564/jasss.2534.

Schelling, T.C. (1971). Dynamic models of segregation. *Journal of Mathematical Sociology*, 1(2), 143–186.

Schelling, T.C. (1978). *Micromotives and Macrobehavior*. Norton, New York.

Schmitt, C. and Pumain, D. (2013). Modélographie multi-agents de la simulation des interactions sociétés-environnement et de l'émergence des villes. *Cybergeo: European Journal of Geography*, 643. doi:10.4000/cybergeo.25900.

Smith, N. (1979). Toward a theory of gentrification a back to the city movement by capital, not people. *Journal of the American Planning Association*, 45, 538–548.

Spielman, S. and Harrison, P. (2014). The co-evolution of residential segregation and the built environment at the turn of the 20th century: A Schelling model. *Transactions in GIS*, 18(1), 25–45. doi:10.1111/tgis.12014.

Tisue, S. and Wilensky, U. (2004). Netlogo: A simple environment for modeling complexity. In *International Conference on Complex Systems*, 21, 16–21.

Torrens, P.M. and Nara, A. (2007). Modeling gentrification dynamics: A hybrid approach. *Computers, Environment and Urban Systems*, 31(3), 337–361.

Vallée, J. (2009). Les disparités spatiales de santé en ville : l'exemple de Vientiane (Laos). *Cybergeo: European Journal of Geography*, 477. doi:10.4000/cybergeo.22775.

Vallée, J., Cadot, E., Grillo, F., Parizot, I., Chauvin, P. (2010). The combined effects of activity space and neighbourhood of residence on participation in preventive healthcare activities: The case of cervical screening in the Paris metropolitan area (France). *Health & Place*, 16(5), 838–852.

White, R. (1998). Cities and cellular automata. *Discrete Dynamics in Nature and Society*, 2(2), 111–125.

Wilkinson, R. and Pickett, K. (2009). *The Spirit Level: Why Greater Equality Makes Societies Stronger*. Penguin Books, London.

Wong, D.W.S. (1993). Spatial indices of segregation. *Urban Studies*, 30(3), 559–572.

Yang, W. (2014). An extension of geographically weighted regression with flexible bandwidths. PhD Thesis, School of Geography and Geosciences, University of St. Andrews, Fife [Online]. Available at: http://hdl.handle.net/10023/7052.

7

A Critical Reading of Neighborhood-based Policies and their Geography

Julie VALLÉE
Géographie-cités, CNRS, Paris, France

A large number of interventions developed by institutional actors target a small number of circumscribed areas, with the aim of reducing social inequalities. These policies exist in different countries, such as France, the United Kingdom, the Netherlands, Sweden and the United States. In France, we speak of the "*Politique de la Ville*" (and of the "*quartiers prioritaires de la politique de la ville*"). In the United Kingdom, the term "neighbourhood-based policies" refers to Area-Based Initiatives (ABIs) developed within the Neighbourhood Renewal Fund. The term neighborhood-based policies is also used in other countries to designate actions carried out, for example, within the framework of the "Metropolitan Development Initiative" (Sweden) or the "Big Cities Policy" and the "40 Neighbourhoods Programme" (Netherlands). For each of these neighborhood-based policies, the spatial reference is explicit, with a two-level scale: the city, then the neighborhood. However explicit it may be, this reference to geographical space raises more questions than it solves. What goals guide the institutional division of "priority" neighborhoods? Do not the public policies implemented in specific, well-defined territories lead to a watering down of the role of geographical space when they focus on the extreme spatial manifestations of social inequalities, rather than on the structural mechanisms at play? How do the time and the trajectories of neighborhoods and individuals manage to be incorporated (or not) into neighborhood-based policies whose geography is often frozen? These are the three

Inequalities in Geographical Space,
coordinated by Clémentine COTTINEAU and Julie VALLÉE. © ISTE Ltd 2022.

main questions that will be discussed in this critical chapter about neighborhood-based policies and their geography[1].

7.1. A geography plagued by contradictions

Like any institutional division, areas concerned by neighborhood-based policies must ensure the *sustainability of spatial forms of institutional actions* on a territory. In this respect, it is similar to an "investment in form" (Thévenot 1986) in the sense that this division of geographical space (which has an immediate cost for those who design it, but also has benefits for all subsequent periods) must allow for the passage from an indeterminate thing (the areas where action is needeed most) to a "class of shared equivalence" (the priority neighborhoods constructed, designed and instrumented by the actors[2] who find a common interest there). However, this transition to a class of shared equivalence is perhaps even more difficult to achieve for areas targeted in neighborhood-based policies than for other institutional divisions, because the *aim is twofold*: to pinpoint pockets of poverty (in order to offer targeted assistance to poor populations) and to delimit the areas that have an effect on populations (in order to organize rallies and collective actions and to improve local living conditions).

7.1.1. *The dual purpose of "priority" neighborhoods*

Territorial regeneration, which was initially a means of indirectly addressing the issue of exclusion and poverty, has been progressively replaced by an entry into so called "priority" or "critical" neighborhoods (Tissot 2004). This double shift (from poverty to territory, and then from territory to priority neighborhoods) is based on various arguments that make it possible to understand how neighborhood-based policies are currently legitimized and put into practice: (1) intervening in a limited number of neighborhoods is a cost-effective strategy in theory, especially when problems are spatially concentrated and cumulative; (2) modifying some

---

1. Territorially selective policies aimed at rebalancing the economy between countries, regions or metropolises, or those dealing with a specific dimension of social inequalities (e.g. educational inequalities (see Chapter 1) or inequalities in access to employment (see Chapter 4)), will not be explicitly dealt with in this chapter, even though their geography often responds to the same principles and contradictions.

2. Neighborhood-based policies are steered and implemented by various actors (national government services, local authorities, associations and economic agents). These agents, their coordination strategies and their power relations (which vary over time) will not be described in this chapter but have been studied elsewhere (Le Galès 1995; Warin 1997; Estèbe 2005).

neighborhoods and the living conditions they offer to the population appears to be more feasible (and more visible) than intervening directly in populations; (3) targeting neighborhoods is politically more acceptable than targeting populations according to their ethnic or racial profile, especially in countries like France, where universalism is a high priority (Hancock et al. 2016); (4) developing actions in specific neighborhoods makes it possible to propose a response that is in line with citizens' expectations of greater local democracy, and with the expectations of local elected officials of greater local scope for action, as well as a decentralization of means and prerogatives; (5) adapting public action to local specificities appears to be an obligatory step – and even a pledge of modernity – at the beginning of the 21st century, where finely localized data (and the tools to map them) are multiplying[3].

Behind these arguments, however, we can distinguish two different rationales: when public actors decide to implement actions in small and circumscribed areas, their objective may be (1) to reach the poor people or (2) to improve the living conditions of the neighborhoods. However, it is not necessarily the same priority areas that should be targeted, depending on whether the first or the second reasoning is opted for.

In the first case, neighborhood-based policies are a way of restricting the actions to be carried out on areas where there are maximum chances of reaching the target public, because of the spatial segregation processes that lead populations with the same social profile to concentrate in the same place. The geographical space is then merely the revelation of social inequalities: it is a question of identifying the priority neighborhoods as being those which concentrate the "priority" populations in order to carry out targeted interventions for people (help in finding a job, public health prevention campaigns, etc.). This is the *logic behind the "neighborhood-container"* approach.

In the second case, neighborhood-based policies are prompted by the recognition of the role of space on employment, education or health (the "place effects"[4]). The

---

3. It should be noted, however, that this last argument is relatively recent: at the time of the first neighborhood-based policies, the challenge was, on the contrary, to collect and distribute localized data that had been lacking until then. These policies thus played a "pioneering role in the prolific territorial production" that has been observed since the 1980s (Estèbe 2001, p. 25).

4. Neighborhood effects (or place-based effects) refer to different mechanisms by which geographical space affects individuals. These mechanisms can be grouped under four broad rubrics, depending on whether they relate to prevailing social processes among the locally present population: exposure to harmful environments (such as violence, pollution), geographical location (and, by extension, distance to places of power, employment, education, health care, and so on), or institutional patterns, such as those that play into the quality of services or the reputation of neighborhoods (Galster 2012).

challenge is then to list the living conditions of the neighborhoods that have an effect on the employment, education or health of individuals, and to identify the neighborhoods whose living conditions are harmful to the populations that frequent them. This is the *logic behind the neighborhood-agent* approach.

Following the "neighborhood-container" approach, the objective of neighbourhood-based policies would then be to limit the effect of individual poverty on the pathways (educational, professional, health, etc.) of individuals. On the other hand, following the "neighborhood-agent" approach, the objective would be to limit the harmful consequences of *collective* poverty on people's lives. The choice of one or the other of these approaches is often made in terms of a trade-off between *place-based* policies, which focus on the endogenous revitalization of neighborhoods, and *people-based* policies, which are concerned with improving the chances of individuals to escape poverty (Kirszbaum 2009). There is no doubt that these people- and place-based policies complement each other and should go hand in hand (Manley et al. 2013). However, they do not necessarily target the same priority areas. In the first case, the focus will be on neighborhoods with a high concentration of poor people, for whom targeted interventions will be carried out (the neighborhood-container approach). In the second case, the focus will be on the neighborhoods whose deteriorating living conditions are detrimental, particularly for the poorest residents (the neighborhood-agent approach). By formalizing the priority neighborhood as both a population container and an agent with an impact on the population, neighborhood-based policies thus, in a way, "play both sides of the fence", which is not without consequences when it comes to delineating "priority" neighborhoods: *depending on the logic that is favored, the size and shape of the priority neighborhoods will not be the same.*

7.1.2. *Challenges of size and shape*

The *spatial scale* to be used to delineate neighborhoods is a thorny and widely debated issue, both in the literature on *place effects* (Vallée et al. 2015; Petrović et al. 2019) and in the literature on segregation (Andersson and Musterd 2010). The Holy Grail of delineating the neighborhood object is all the more difficult to achieve in neighborhood-based policies because their geography is subject to the tensions between, "on the one hand, the territory, a space of equivalence associated with institutional action and liable to be cut up, and, on the other hand, the locality, the support of a social, economic and political life with multiple components, described from the point of view of its inhabitants or its leaders[5]" (Desrosières 1994, p. 46). This is one of the difficulties of the neighborhood-based policies, which must make it possible to "create standardized, legible and – at least in part – debatable policies while opening up local public arenas where the mobilization of those involved, necessary to deal with both general and specific situations, can be played out[6]" (Estèbe 2001, p. 26).

Spatial grids created by official statistics to disseminate aggregated data (e.g. population censuses) are often used as the basic geographical units for neighborhood-based policies. This is the case for the "Îlots Regroupés pour l'Information Statistique" (IRIS) in France[7], Dissemination Areas (DAs) in Canada, Output Areas (OAs) in the United Kingdom or Census Tracts in the United States. These zonings combine two major trends: (1) one consists of dividing the city into *small portions* – in the literal sense of the French term "quartier" (quarter); (2) the other consists of grouping the inhabitants (neighbors in the literal sense) into *socially homogeneous zones*. These national zonings are, in fact, constructed in order to disseminate census data without violating the principle of confidentiality of personal data. The number of inhabitants per spatial unit varies from country to country: about 2,000 inhabitants per IRIS in France, from 400 to 700 inhabitants per DA in Canada, 310 inhabitants on average per OA in the United Kingdom, and from 2,500 to 8,000 inhabitants per Census Tract in the United States. These elementary grids are also designed to maximize social homogeneity. Aggregate data are made available in built-up areas, with the declared aim (by the statistical bodies responsible for delimiting them) of being as homogeneous as possible with respect to population characteristics, economic status, and living conditions (U.S. Census Bureau) or with respect of tenure of household and dwelling type (Office for National Statistics, UK). This quest for homogeneity refers to the idea that a neighborhood only makes sense if it is socially homogeneous, as if "seduced by the image of the neighborhood in late 20th-century European culture, we tend to believe that if an area is not socially homogeneous it is not a real neighborhood" (Crossick 1993).

The elementary spatial grid created by official statistics is, in fact, much more than a way of formatting data. It is *prescriptive*, insofar as it imposes itself as a

---

5. Original citation: "d'une part le territoire, espace d'équivalence associé à une action institutionnelle et susceptible d'être découpé, et, d'autre part, la localité, support d'une vie sociale, économique et politique aux composantes multiples, décrite du point de vue de ses habitants ou de ses responsables".
6. Original citation: "Construire des politiques normées, lisibles et – pour partie du moins – discutables tout en ouvrant des scènes publiques locales où peut se jouer la mobilisation des acteurs, nécessaire pour traiter des situations à la fois générales et singulières".
7. In France, a new gridded zoning has made available demographic and socioeconomic data aggregated in 200-m squares since 2013.

norm, but also performative, because it channels questioning, processing and interpretations. Rather than using these elementary grids directly, actors and scientists could nevertheless aggregate them in order to delimit neighborhoods that make sense in the eyes of the processes studied (or combated). However, such aggregations are still rare in academic work and institutional approaches, as if it was necessary to choose the smallest and most homogeneous unit possible. Many authors point out that "the strongest context effects are generally those that succeed in defining the immediate environment of ecah indivdiual as precisely as possible" (Maurin 2004, p.43). However, this statement is open to discussion: it is also possible to think that this context effect is strong precisely because it corresponds more to an "aggregated" individual effect than to a place effect as such. Favoring small spatial units makes sense when one reasons according to a neighborhood constructed to be a proxy for the socioeconomic situation of individuals, or a roundabout way of targeting the individuals who live there in the best possible way and at the lowest cost. However, this logic is much more questionable when one considers the neighborhood as an agent-neighborhood in which populations interact. In this case, for what reasons should the geographical space that would make sense for the populations, and have an effect on them, necessarily be designed as a small and socially homogeneous space? A study conducted in Paris (France) has, in fact, shown that in order to obtain a size comparable to that of the neighborhoods perceived by the inhabitants, it would be necessary to aggregate an average of 12 IRIS in Paris and nearly two IRIS in the large peripheral Parisian municipalities with more than 50,000 inhabitants (Vallée et al. 2016). A study conducted in Bristol, UK, also showed that neighborhoods represented by local activists or residents are more socially mixed than areas created automatically on the basis of a criterion of social homogeneity (Haynes et al. 2007). *The "smallest" and "most homogeneous" arguments possible, which were legitimate when applied to the neighborhood-container, become inappropriate when transposed to the neighborhood-agent.*

In all countries where neighborhood-based policies are implemented, priority neighborhoods are defined as socially homogeneous micro-neighborhoods. The zoning instituted in the new neighborhood policy implemented in France in 2014 is a good example as it is based on the spatial concentration of poor people in small spatial areas[8]. When they reason solely according to a neighborhood-container, the actors of neighborhood-based policies then de facto limit the effectiveness of the measures they

---

8. Based on household tax incomes in a 200 × 200 m grid, areas where more than half of the inhabitants are below the low-income threshold were identified and discussions were held with local elected officials in order to adjust, if necessary, the perimeters of priority neighborhoods. For each urban unit, a different low-income threshold was calculated based on the median income of metropolitan France and the median income of the urban unit, in order to be able to isolate areas whose households were out of step with the rest of the urban unit (Darriau et al. 2014).

put in place. Indeed, they implicitly consider that poor households can only interact within a socially limited space: the very fact of wanting to maximize the social homogeneity of neighborhoods is tantamount to denying a priori the effect (and the interest) of social mixing, which is often, however, one of the aims of neighborhood-based policies. Moreover, it is common to point out the risk of stigmatization that the labeling of "priority neighborhoods" could provoke by projecting an image of these neighborhoods and their inhabitants that is symbolically violent. (Hancock et al. 2016). Moreover, by reasoning solely according to a "neighborhood-container" approach, these policies neglect the fringe of the population that does not live in the neighborhoods with a high concentration of poor households, but whose living context is degraded. This criticism has recently gained visibility in France with the mobilization of the *"gilets jaunes"* in the winter of 2018: claims against territorial inequity then emerged "with the idea that the inhabitants of the priority neighborhoods would be unduly privileged, benefiting both from access to the resources of metropolitan development and from more favorable treatment of public authorities, in comparison with rural areas, peri-urban areas, and medium-sized cities that are neglected, or even despised, by the political elites" (Epstein and Kirszbaum 2019, p. 37). Finally, by reasoning on the basis of micro-neighborhoods, whose difficulties are highlighted, a dual vision of geographical space is introduced by artificially reinforcing the territorial fractures between these "isolates" and the rest of the territory, even though one of the aims of these policies is precisely to achieve greater inclusion of neighborhoods – and populations – in the whole territory. We thus find here, in several forms, the *performative effect* that the very choice of a spatial division can have on the phenomenon that is described, measured and on which we want to act. However, as Epstein (2021) points out, it is necessary to carry out counterfactual analyses to estimate the negative effects associated with the inclusion of an area in neighborhood-based policies, and to see whether these negative effects are really less than the benefits that this labeling brings. This question could also be asked differently, if we are interested in the size and shape of the priority neighborhoods: Does this ratio of benefits to negative effects vary according to the spatial delineation of the priority neighborhoods?

The question of the size and shape of priority neighborhoods echoes another question: that of the number of people left out by neighborhood-based policies, even though they are theoretically part of the target. Here, we can make a link to "critical representation", which refers to the representativeness of priority neighborhoods in relation to the location of priority populations (van Gent et al. 2009; Sharpe 2013). This question of representativeness arises as soon as we adopt the "neighborhood-container" reasoning. It can be discussed by combining two indicators: (1) the number of poor people in priority areas compared to the total number of poor people in the country as a whole, i.e. what proportion of the total individuals reached are poor (*completeness* rate); (2) the number of poor people in priority areas compared to the total number of people in priority areas, i.e. what proportion of the target population of poor individuals is reached (*efficiency* rate). These two rates are closely linked: an increase in the completeness rate will automatically decrease the efficiency rate and vice versa.

Studies have estimated this completeness rate. In Sweden, 5% of the country's poor people reside in the 24 neighborhoods targeted by the "Metropolitan Development Initiative" (Andersson 2004); in the Netherlands, 8% of the country's poor people reside in the "40 Neighbourhoods Initiatives" (van Gent et al. 2009); in the United Kingdom, 57% of the country's income assistance recipients reside in the 88 neighborhoods identified as priorities under the "Neighbourhood Renewal Fund" (Tunstall and Lupton 2003). In France, 23% of the country's poor people (below the poverty line) live in the priority neighborhoods (*"quartiers prioritaires de la politique de la ville"*), according to our calculations based on data from the *"Atlas des quartiers prioritaires"* (CGET 2017). Regarding the effectiveness rate, work in the United Kingdom estimates that 15% of residents in neighborhoods targeted by the "Neighbourhood Renewal Project" claim Income Support (Tunstall and Lupton 2003). In France, 43% of the population in the *"quartiers prioritaires de la politique de la ville"* live below the poverty line, according to our calculations based on data from the *"Atlas des quartiers prioritaires"*. The rates of exhaustiveness and effectiveness therefore vary widely across countries. These differences are due to differences in the distribution and concentration of disadvantaged populations at the national and intra-urban levels, but above all to the political and methodological choices made when delimiting priority areas (number of neighborhoods to be retained, spatial grid for analysis, "poverty" indicator taken into account, etc.).

7.2. Reductive policies

After analyzing the way in which "priority" neighborhoods are delimited and the ins and outs of these choices, the aim is to broaden the focus and discuss the *reductive vision of geographical space* conveyed by these neighborhood-based policies, which focus on the concrete forms of urban marginality rather than the generic mechanisms that produce it (Wacquant 2008).

7.2.1. *A diversionary operation*

Neighborhood-based policies become a dangerous subterfuge when they *divert attention from the deep structural causes of inequality*. This diversionary operation – which consists of dealing with problems only where they are most visible – amounts to transforming problems specific to a type of society into problems caused by a certain type of space, and thus confusing problems in the city with problems of the city (Busquet 2009; Garnier 2010). Here, we find the criticism of the uses that can be made from place effects: by giving "a falsely depoliticized vision of urban unequality" when they are merely "the effects of the State inscribed into space" (Wacquant 2008, p. 284; 2009, p. 109), place effects constitute "an instrument of accusation, a veiled form of class antagonism that conveniently has no place for any concern over what happens outside the very neighbourhoods under scrutiny" (Slater 2013, p. 124).

This diversionary operation not only concerns the place effects and the use made of them by neighborhood-based policies: it occurs for all territorial assessments produced upstream. The French term *"diagnostic territorial"* (which is difficult to translate into other languages, but which is similar to *neighborhood assessment* in English) refers to the local assesment of the population's living conditions and needs. The idea of using geographical space as a means of accumulating and relating observations on the social world, by giving it a specific explanatory power, can be found early in the history of public statistics (Desrosières 1994). In France, the term *"diagnostic territorial"* has gradually entered the vocabulary of territorial actors (Jeannot 2001), with a very significant increase in the use of this term since the early 2000s (see Box 7.1). This "golden age" of neighborhood assessment also coincides with the growing competition between territories, brought about by the deployment of local performance indicators, the preferred instruments of New Public Management (Epstein 2015). By pushing local actors to mobilize around a measurable objective of reducing the gaps between neighborhoods, national agencies are promoting competition that is maintained by the granting of funding through selective calls for projects and the awarding of labels and other signs of territorial distinction (Epstein 2015).

The growing awareness of neighborhood assessment on which national and local actors rely, both to describe the world and to act on it, is part of the same logic as that of neighborhood-based policies: *incriminating certain specific territories* and putting them in competition with each other without, however, addressing the *more structural causes of inequalities between territories*.

> Almost non-existent at the beginning of the 21st century, the French term *"diagnostic territorial"*. This is shown by the sharp increase in the number of web pages that include this term, both in absolute terms and in comparison with the older term *"analyse spatiale"*, which is used here as a reference (a term made up of two words and whose semantic field is fairly similar). We can thus see that, as of 2015, the term *"diagnostic territorial"* is more present on the web than *"analyse spatiale"*.

192 Inequalities in Geographical Space

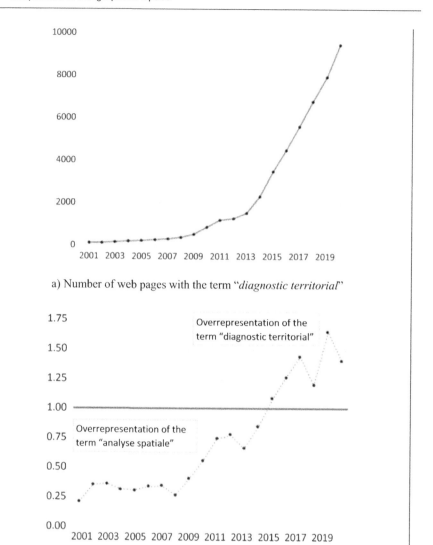

a) Number of web pages with the term "*diagnostic territorial*"

b) Overrepresentation of the number of web pages with the term "*diagnostic territorial*" and the number of web pages with the term "*analyse spatiale*". For a color version of this figure, see www.iste.co.uk/cottineau/inequalities.zip

These figures are the result of a query made in April 2021 via the Google search engine for the number of pages containing the term "*diagnostic territorial*" (and "*analyse spatiale*") year after year (from January 1 to December 31).

Box 7.1. *The golden age of "diagnostic territorial"*

7.2.2. *An impoverishment of the interdependencies between agent and structure*

This diversionary operation can be directly linked to the status afforded to geographical space: by compartmentalizing what relates to the individual, on the one hand, and to the space in which they live, on the other, we come to transform geographical space into a simple medium whose complexity is impoverished. This question is more broadly related to the *agent/structure debate in the social sciences*, and the way in which the choices and actions of individuals result from the structures that they bring about. In the face of the conservative tendency to blame socially excluded groups (e.g. the unemployed, ethnic minorities, or low-income households) for their living conditions and behaviors, researchers working on social inequalities have argued that the behaviors of vulnerable groups are largely explained by the social and spatial structures in which they are embedded. In the late 1980s in the United States, Wilson drew attention in *The Truly Disadvantaged* (1987) to the fact that the effect of individual poverty is greater in neighborhoods with concentrated poor populations. In this case, poor people often face a *double burden*: not only do they have to deal with the multiple problems arising from their own lack of income, but also with the often-deteriorating conditions of the neighborhoods in which they live. By introducing the notion of "concentration effects", Wilson suggested that poor people might be particularly vulnerable to neighborhood effects because they lack the collective resources and "social buffers" that more advantaged people enjoy, which would enable them to overcome the deteriorating conditions of the neighborhoods in which they live. This concentration effect has fueled debates about the overly artificial separation between individual and contextual factors in statistical models (Pickett and Pearl 2001; Frohlich et al. 2002; Bernard et al. 2007). By favoring the distinction between what belongs to the individual, on the one hand, and what belongs to their neighborhood, on the other hand, multilevel regression models have in fact contributed to impoverishing the meaning given to geographical space (see Introduction and Chapter 6).

This debate is important for neighborhood-based policies and their geography. To ignore the *interdependence between individuals and space* is to ignore the *relational dimension of space*. To consider that the space necessarily carries the same weight according to demographic strata (Vant 1986) is to deny the concentration effect highlighted by Wilson's work, but also by more contemporary work on the variable strength of place-based effects according to the socioeconomic profile of individuals. In his work on the effects of social segregation on the academic success of adolescents, Maurin (2007, p. 627) emphasized that "adolescents from modest backgrounds [...] have far fewer means than others to escape from their immediate neighborhood and its control", and that "the immediate neighborhood, the building where they live, represent quite central elements of socialization, particularly for young people from the working classes and, more generally, for all those who have hardly any means of providing themselves with other areas of socialization". In the field of health, the varying strength of place effects has also been studied. A review of the studies dedicated to the variable effect of residential neighborhood on health according to the socioeconomic profile of the individuals underlines a great concordance in the results, with a stronger "neighborhood effect" on disadvantaged, low-skilled or poorly educated individuals, and for different health indicators, such as being overweight, diet quality, alcohol consumption, mortality, perceived health and mental disorders (Vallée et al. 2021). Some authors then conclude that there is a *socially differentiated vulnerability of individuals* with regard to the attributes of their neighborhood of residence (Shortt et al. 2018). In the words of sociologists Pinçon-Charlot and Rendu (1982, p. 683) about the role of distance to cultural facilities, "we are led to note that the categories that possess a certain cultural and educational capital can find in their own dispositions a sufficient incentive to overcome the obstacle of the physical distance that separates them [from cultural facilities][9]".

The *social dimension of place effects weakens the very foundation of neighborhood-based policies*: it questions the very possibility of labeling a neighborhood as a priority since, to use Bourdieu's words in his text on the place effects (1993), the ability to appropriate goods and services in a given area depends on the capital owned and the physical distance to these goods, which also depends on capital. Does this critical reading of neighborhood-based policies mean that we should give up on implementing neighborhood-based policies? Not necessarily. These can contribute to improving the living conditions of individuals locally, but they only make sense if they complement *structural measures of economic regulation and social protection of individuals*, without replacing them.

7.3. Temporal dynamics of priority neighborhoods

If the implementation of neighborhood-based policies can lead to the glossing over of interdependencies between agents and structures, and the structural mechanisms of inequalities that unfold throughout society and geographical space, this *reductionist vision* is all the more likely to develop when *the interrelationships that develop over time between individuals and spaces* are ignored. In line with the

---

9. Original citation: "On est conduit à constater que les catégories qui possèdent un certain capital culturel et scolaire peuvent trouver dans les dispositions qui leur sont propres une incitation suffisante pour surmonter l'obstacle de la distance physique qui les sépare [des équipements culturels]".

authors who call for a relational approach to move away from a fixist approach to geographical space, and to think of it "in terms of interdependence and articulation and no longer in terms of distribution and location" (Berroir et al. 2017, p. 1), it is necessary to pay attention to the temporal dynamics through which the interrelationships between the life course of individuals and the spaces in which they evolve are woven (see Chapter 3). Taking the temporal dimension explicitly into account thus makes it possible to address the issue of the attractiveness (both residential and daily) of priority neighborhoods, which is one of the stated objectives of neighborhood-based policies.

7.3.1. *Residential trajectories*

Let us begin by considering temporal dynamics from the perspective of residential trajectories, distinguishing between the two different ways in which they feed the debate on neighborhood-based policies. The first incorporates residential trajectories, but in a negative way, since it is a matter of "controlling" the fact that individuals do not choose their place of residence by chance (selective mobility), and that the measurement of place effects on the behavior of residents using cross-sectional surveys (at a given time) violates the hypothesis of the independence of the variables that are statistically related. This bias (self-selection bias) is at the root of numerous scientific discussions (Manley et al. 2013; Cheshire et al. 2014) on the risk of overestimating neighborhood effects, and consequently on the low effectiveness of neighborhood based policies, whose motivation is simply to act on these neighborhood effects.

However, residential trajectories are not only considered through this measurement bias. They are also positively integrated when it comes to seeing whether these priority neighborhoods function as *"pits"* in which residents are *trapped for life* or whether, on the contrary, these neighborhoods function as *"airlocks"* by being a *temporary step* in the residential trajectory (ONPV 2017). The social mixing that can be brought about by residential mobility is at the heart of the reasoning behind polices of social housing allocation, but also of "natural experiments", the best known of which is the American *Moving to Opportunities* (MTO) program, conducted in the cities of Baltimore, Boston, Chicago, Los Angeles and New York in the 1990s with 4,600 low-income families with children living in extreme poverty (Briggs et al. 2010). Because residential mobility does not happen by chance, the goal here was to *facilitate moves* of randomly selected, voluntary *poor households*[10], in order to mitigate the harmful consequences of

---

10. Families who voluntarily participated in the experiment were randomly assigned to three groups, similar to experimental designs in medical research. The first group received a voucher to move into a low-poverty neighborhood and advice on how to make the best decision. The

collective poverty. These policies thus use residential mobility as an indirect way to combat the spatial concentration of poverty and its effects. Other policies aim, on the contrary, to *encourage the settlement of privileged populations* by providing a diversified supply of housing and amenities. In line with the reflections of Kirszbaum (2008), we can, however, discuss the effects of these policies, which seek to promote the inward mobility of more privileged social groups. They then consider diversity as an "exogenous" dynamic, in the sense that they seek to introduce a group into the residential space where another group dominates. These policies can then produce a gentrification that destroys the local social balance and, moreover, leads to the eviction of poor households, to the detriment of the objective of social mixing that is put forward. One solution might be to promote an "endogenous" social mix by stabilizing the most economically well-off households in priority neighborhoods. Finally, in this brief inventory of policies linking social mix and residential mobility, it is worth noting the legislative measure ("The Act on Extraordinary Measures for Urban Problems") introduced by the Dutch government in 2006. This measure allows local governments to refuse a residence permit in areas considered particularly vulnerable to persons who have lived in the metropolitan region for less than six years and who do not receive an income from work, pensions or student loans. Implemented in five Rotterdam neighborhoods (hence the more concise name, the Rotterdam Act, by which the measure is known), this measure that denies the right of a certain group of people to live where they want has generated widespread controversy (Uitermark et al. 2017). For all that, the general objectives are the same as those of policies that promote *inward mobility* of affluent populations into priority neighborhoods or *outward mobility* of poor populations: the aim is to counter a spiral of neighborhood decline by balancing the socio-economic profile of neighborhoods, that is, by preventing the proportion of poor and low-income households from being too high (van Gent et al. 2018). Ten years after its introduction, research has established that this exclusion measure has affected about 20,000 people (mostly young, male, single, and foreign) each year by weakening their access to the housing market. It has also been shown that this measure has led to an increase in the proportion of employed residents in the five targeted neighborhoods, but without improving local living conditions in these neighborhoods (van Gent et al. 2018) or achieving the unstated goal of reducing ethnic segregation (Ouwehand and Doff 2013).

Residential mobility and immobility are a *central lever* of neighborhood-based policies. In this sense, they lead politicians and researchers alike to explicitly incorporate time into their thinking, both in terms of individuals' life courses and the

---

second group received a voucher to move to a neighborhood of their choice; the third group received no special assistance. Comparing the situations of the three groups at the end of the experiment allows us to isolate the effect of public policy on initially similar individuals.

evolution of neighborhoods. But the thinking is still incomplete because, as the sociologist Sampson (2013, p. 12) notes, "what we need then is a life course of place and a more rigorous assessment of history in the form of prior neighborhood contexts and how they are revealed in the current lives of both individuals and neighborhoods".

7.3.2. Everyday dynamics

The temporal dynamics through which the interrelationships between the life-course of individuals and the geographical space in which they evolve are not reduced to residential trajectories: they also include the daily trajectories, not only of populations but also of the spaces they frequent. *While residential trajectories constitute a classic framework for analyzing neighborhood-based policies and their effectiveness, daily trajectories remain a less explored field.* The everyday attractiveness of priority neighborhoods and their functional mix often remain the poor cousins of neighborhood-based policies that focus on housing, its renovation and the social mix of the resident population.

Functional diversity is one of the objectives stated in the legislative texts: this objective leads public actors to develop commercial spaces and collective facilities in priority neighborhoods, and to develop tax exemptions to attract activities and jobs[11]. However, the attractiveness of priority neighborhoods on a daily basis is rarely measured in local neighorhood assesments: "The temporal dimension of space is seldom part and parcel of urban projects and planning documents. It would be appropriate for planners to take into consideration the various attributes of space in relation to the opening hours of services and to their attendance; planners should indeed question the cohesion of space's rhythms. These elements all condition the accessibility of places as well as their hospitality, their localization and the transportation systems allowing the public to go there" (Mallet 2014, p. 16).

7.3.2.1. Daily mobility and social mix in neighborhoods

One of the first questions that arises when analyzing the daily dynamics of priority areas concerns the *variation in the social composition of priority neighborhoods over the hours of the day*. While the definition of priority neighborhoods is mainly based on the residential concentration of poor households, it would be interesting to discuss the variations in the representativeness of priority neighborhoods at different times of the day, taking into account not the resident population but the population present.

---

11. One of the objectives of these measures is to fight against the "spatial mismatch" faced by residents of priority neighborhoods, who find themselves far from places of employment because they find it difficult to move or relocate to geographic areas where jobs exist (see Chapter 4).

Using a formalism specific to *time-geography*, Figure 7.1 illustrates the idea that the same priority neighborhoods (in the sense of areas containing a significant proportion of priority persons) do not emerge according to the time of day and the spatiotemporal trajectories of the populations.

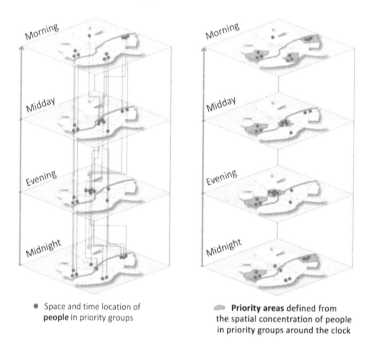

• Space and time location of people in priority groups

▬ **Priority areas** defined from the spatial concentration of people in priority groups around the clock

Figure 7.1. *Defining priority neighborhoods from concentration of priority people in space and time (source: Vallée 2017a). For a color version of this figure, see www.iste.co.uk/cottineau/inequalities.zip*

People-based interventions may not be very effective if they are implemented during the day in areas where poor people do not visit during the day, even if they live there at night. On the other hand, other areas would benefit from being the target of these actions, because a large number of poor people frequent them during the day, without actually living there. This brings us back to the question of the representativeness of priority areas, mentioned earlier in this chapter (section 7.1.2). If we look at the evolution of the *completeness rate* in the priority neighborhoods of the Paris region over the course of the 24 hours of the day (Figure 7.2(a)), we see a clear decrease in the values between day and night: while 27% of the poor population of Île-de-France is present in the priority neighborhoods between 10 p.m. and 6 a.m., this rate drops to 19% at 10 a.m. Actions that take place in priority neighborhoods during the day may therefore miss more than two-thirds (81%) of the poor population for whom these interventions may be intended. This drop in completeness can also be seen as a positive: it means that poor populations do not remain captive to priority neighborhoods. In fact, this decrease during the day should be seen in relation to the general decrease in social segregation observed in Île-de-France during the day (Le Roux et al. 2017). Looking in parallel at the evolution of the *efficiency rate* in the priority areas in the Île-de-France over the 24 hours of the day (Figure 7.2(b)), we see that this rate is close to 42% during the night (11 p.m.–6 a.m.). This efficiency rate tends to decrease – but not significantly – during the day (with a minimum value of 39% at 10 a.m.). The proportion of poor people in the priority neighborhoods of Île-de-France thus remains stable overall during the day. However, it should be noted that the absolute number of poor people in the priority neighborhoods decreases sharply as the population in the neighborhoods decreases (a decrease of about one quarter of the population between midnight and noon). By analyzing the completeness and efficiency rates of the daily concentration of poor people in and outside the priority neighborhoods, we have an empirical basis for discussing the efficiency of person-oriented actions. The decline in completeness rates during the day suggests that other neighborhoods not classified as priority neighborhoods, but with a high concentration of poor people during the day, would also benefit from neighborhood-based policies.

In the same vein, an analysis of the population present on a daily basis in the priority neighborhoods could make it possible to establish a *typology of these neighborhoods* according to their attractiveness (in terms of the increase or decrease in the population present during the day and the mix of activities carried out there), and also according to whether or not their social mix increases during the day. These typologies could inform planning policies (such as the viability of shops and services) and urban renewal and highlight the diversity of the areas concerned. Initial analyses are possible through Mobiliscope, an interactive geo-visualization platform of the population present in cities at different times of the day. With this tool, it is possible, for example, to compare daily variations in the number of people visiting four priority neighborhoods located in the French cities of Marseille, Toulouse, Lyon and Rouen (Figures 7.3(a) and (b)). We see that these four priority neighborhoods receive populations that do not live in these neighborhoods during the day, but that these non-resident populations are relatively more numerous in the neighborhoods of Grands Carmes (Marseille) and La Reynerie (Toulouse) than in the center of Vaulx-en-Velin (Lyon) and, above all, in the Les Hauts neighborhood (Rouen). While the majority of these non-resident populations come to these neighborhoods to work (but also to study, in the case of the Lyon neighborhood), their socioeconomic profiles differ: during the day, the share of non-residents with a high level of education is much higher in the priority neighborhoods of central

Vaulx-en-Velin (Lyon) and Reynerie (Toulouse) than in the priority neighborhoods of Grands Carmes (Marseille) and Les Hauts (Rouen). This type of analysis thus highlights the diversity of priority neighborhoods according to their attractiveness, their functional mix and the socioeconomic profile of the population that lives there.

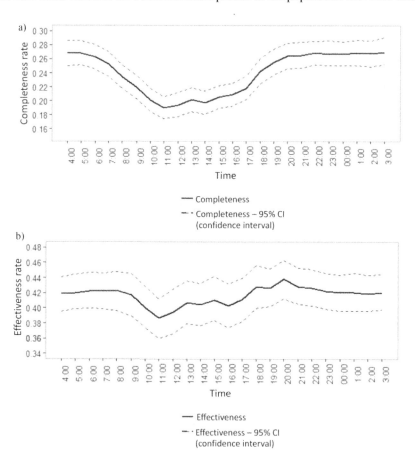

Definitions: The completeness rate corresponds to the number of people below the poverty line in the priority areas, compared to the total number of people below the poverty line in Île-de-France. The effectiveness rate corresponds to the number of people below the poverty line present in the priority areas, compared to the total population present in the priority areas of Île-de-France.

Figure 7.2. *Changes over a 24-hour period in (a) completeness rates and (b) effectiveness rates of "priority neighborhoods" in the Île-de-France region (source: (Vallée and Le Roux 2018), based on data from the "Global Transport Survey" (Enquête globale transport), 2010, DRIEA-STIF-OMNIL)*

A Critical Reading of Neighborhood-based Policies and their Geography

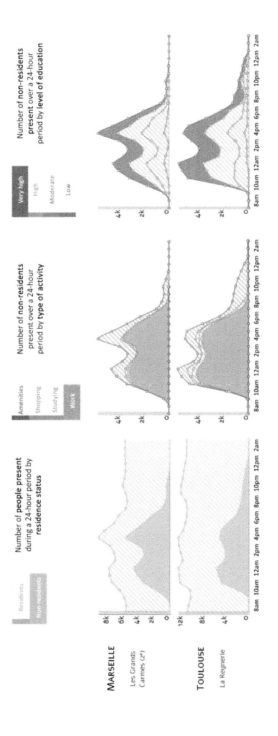

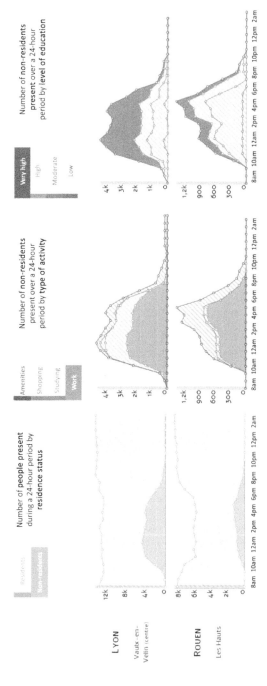

Figure 7.3. *(a) Hourly changes in the population of two "priority areas" in Marseille and Toulouse (b) Hourly changes in the population of two "priority areas" in Lyon and Rouen (source: Mobiliscope (v4), an open geovisualization platform of cities around the clock; https://mobiliscope.cnrs.fr). For a color version of this figure, see www.iste.co.uk/cottineau/inequalities.zip*

Since the definition of priority neighborhoods is traditionally based on the spatial concentration of poor or low-income households, we have focused our study on the socioeconomic profile of the individuals who live in and frequent the neighborhoods on a daily basis. However, this does not mean that other dimensions, such as gender or age, are ignored when analyzing the daily movements of individuals and the resulting variations in the composition of the population present in the neighborhoods.

A recent study (also based on French Mobiliscope data) shows that women – especially when they live in urban areas – spend significantly more time than men at home and in their neighborhood. However, a variation appears according to the time of day: the people who leave their homes while remaining in their neighborhood of residence are mostly women between 8 a.m. and 7 p.m., but mostly men from 7 p.m. onward and for the rest of the evening. This gendered occupation of space according to the time of day is observed throughout France but is more pronounced in the priority neighborhoods (Douet and Vallée 2021). It thus illustrates the fact that the spatiotemporal constraints to which certain individuals are subjected result from the combination of their socioeconomic position and their gender, and therefore refer to the intersectional mechanisms at work in the space and time of everyday life (see Introduction and Chapter 2). Taking them into account would allow neighborhood-based policies to move away from a fixed and segmented approach of the spatial distribution of priority populations.

7.3.2.2. Daily dynamics of neighborhoods and of neighborhood effects

Having discussed the temporal challenges that arise when trying to identify "priority neighborhoods" as those where populations in difficulty are concentrated on a daily basis (neighborhood-container reasoning), we now discuss the dangers of considering that neighborhood effects are fixed in time when we are applying neighborhood-agent reasoning.

The first danger is to ignore the daily mobility of populations, when this can modify the contexts to which populations are exposed during the day outside their neighborhood of residence (Shareck et al. 2014). If we take the example of access to services, it would be a mistake to think that all territories with a deficit in the healthcare provision are necessarily a priority: they become so if they concentrate on poorly mobile populations that do not have the opportunity to access care outside their neighborhood of residence. Ignoring multiple exposures can therefore distort diagnoses by wrongly giving a priority status to certain areas ("*false positives*") and, conversely, by excluding certain areas that should be included ("*false negatives*") from the list of priority areas.

The second danger is to assume that a neighborhood remains fixed in time, without, for example, taking into account changes in its social composition over the course of a 24-h day, or the opening and closing times of the services and facilities located there. In fact, *all of the "opportunity structures" of neighborhoods* (Macintyre et al. 2002) are *subject to daily variation* (Table 7.1).

The "opportunity structures" of neighborhoods	Daily variations
Physical environment (water, air, etc.)	For the same location, air quality is not the same at different times of the day, which is related in particular to the intensity of industrial pollution or vehicular traffic (Nyhan et al. 2016; Park and Kwan 2016).
Available facilities	Public or private facilities (schools, transport, health care, green spaces) are not open 24 h a day: they have opening and closing times. Moreover, the number of potential users (which determines their saturation) also varies during the day (Neutens et al. 2010).
Social norms	Because they are tied to the population present and their behaviors, the norms in a neighborhood may differ at different times of the day (Nuvolati 2003). Stigma toward smokers, for example, may be stronger or weaker at different times of the day depending on the population present, whether resident or transient (Glenn et al. 2017).
Reputation	The public and elected officials may view a neighborhood differently depending on the time of day. Certain spaces, qualified as safe places during the day, are perceived as dangerous at night – for example, if they do not benefit from public lighting (Mallet and Comelli 2017) – or during events that bring together a public whose profile is different from that of the resident population (soccer matches, places of prostitution, for example).

Table 7.1. *The daily rhythm of neighborhood "opportunity structures" – the daycourse of place – (source: Vallée 2017b)*

In analyses of place effects, it is, however, rare to take them into account, with the notable exception of work on air pollution (Park and Kwan 2018). If we take the example of neighborhoods lacking in services and facilities, we can see the interest in considering the cumulative amplitude of opening periods. Introducing a dose of daily temporality into accessibility measures can also be useful when relating a quantity of supply to a quantity of demand, that is, when relating the number of facilities to the population. In this case, demand is usually estimated from the resident population, without taking into account the population actually present at the time the facilities are in use (and open). In neighborhoods where the daytime population is greater than the resident population, this type of residential indicator tends to underestimate demand, and thus overestimate the level of accessibility. Conversely, in neighborhoods where the daytime population is lower than the resident population, this type of residential indicator tends to overestimate demand, and thus underestimate the level of accessibility. Finally, it should be noted that the use of the resident population to quantify demand and to calculate local accessibility indicators is all the more problematic when the spatial grid considered is small. This is another example of the importance of not giving in to the call for ever smaller numbers: when demand is estimated on the basis of the resident population alone, the elementary (and small) spatial grid is not very suitable because outgoing and incoming mobilities between these areas are neglected, even though there are many of them during the day. It is thus "implicitly assumed that exchanges and mobilities between the area under consideration and surroundings areas are non-existent [...] This is an acceptable approximation for large zonings, but it becomes awkward for small zonings" (Vergier and Chaput 2017, p. 20). When flow data are lacking, larger zonings, such as catchment areas, then have the advantage of presenting fewer differences between the present and resident population, because daily flows essentially take place within these areas.

In the context of neighborhood-based policies, it would be beneficial to consider both the multi-exposure of populations and changes in neighborhood attributes over the course of the 24 h of the day. Such an approach, inspired by time-geography (Hägerstrand 1970), would *match the temporalities of populations and territories with those of the policies to be pursued* (Vallée 2017a).

7.4. Conclusion

The originality of neighborhood-based policies is that they define specific intervention perimeters, in which they *link together the problem and its solution* (Estèbe 2001). But is not it illusory to hope to project the roots of the problem and the means of solving it onto a small number of small neighborhoods? By clarifying the different purposes at work in identifying priority neighborhoods, by discussing the simplistic vision of geographical space that arises when we focus on the extreme spatial manifestations of inequality rather than on the structural mechanisms at play, and by emphasizing the dynamic relationships that link neighborhoods and people over time, this chapter has sought to highlight the necessarily multiscalar dimension (both spatially and temporally) of the problem of social inequalities and the solutions to it. This multiscalar perspective is difficult to implement and should at least be integrated into the *evaluation of neighborhood-based policies*. Just as measures aimed at limiting social inequalities cannot be evaluated solely with regard to the poorest populations, but require an interest in society as a whole and in the social gradient that runs through it, it would be appropriate to monitor neighborhood-based policies and their evaluation not to focus solely on indicators relating to priority neighborhoods (and the population living there at a given time t), but to consider the whole territory and the mobilities, both daily and residential, between priority neighborhoods and other parts of the territory.

7.5. References

Andersson, R. (2004). Understanding the production and reproduction of poor neighbourhoods in Sweden. *Proceedings of the International Conference "Inside Poverty areas"*, Cologne.

Andersson, R. and Musterd, S. (2010). What scale matters? Exploring the relationships between individuals' social position, neighbourhood context and the scale of neighbourhood. *Geografiska Annaler Series B – Human Geography*, 92b(1), 23–43.

Bernard, P., Charafeddine, R., Frohlich, K.L., Daniel, M., Kestens, Y., Potvin, L. (2007). Health inequalities and place: A theoretical conception of neighbourhood. *Social Science & Medicine*, 65(9), 1839–1852.

Berroir, S., Cattan, N., Dobruszkes, F., Guérois, M., Paulus, F., Vacchiani-Marcuzzo, C. (2017). Les systèmes urbains français : une approche relationnelle. *Cybergeo*, 807.

Bourdieu, P. (1993). Effets de lieu. *La misère du monde*, 249–262.

Busquet, G. (2009). Le spatialisme et la pensée politique progressiste sur la ville. In *Faire territoire aujourd'hui*, Baudin, G., Bonnin, P. (eds). Éditions Recherches, Paris.

CGET (2017). Atlas des quartiers prioritaires de la politique de la ville [Online]. Available at: sig.ville.gouv.fr/Atlas/QP.

Cheshire, P.C., Nathan, M., Overman, H.G. (2014). *Urban Economics and Urban Policy: Challenging Conventional Policy Wisdom*. Edward Elgar, Cheltenham.

Crossick, G. (1993). Le quartier : caractéristiques économiques et sociales. *Mélanges de l'Ecole française de Rome. Italie et Méditerranée*, 105(2), 405–412.

Darriau, V., Henry, M., Oswalt, N. (2014). Politique de la ville en France métropolitaine : une nouvelle géographie recentrée sur 1300 quartiers prioritaires. Report, Insee, Paris.

Desrosières, A. (1994). Le territoire et la localité. Deux langages statistiques. *Politix*, 7(25), 46–58.

Douet, A. and Vallée, J. (2021). L'(im)mobilité quotidienne des femmes et des hommes. Rapport 2020 de l'Observatoire National de la Politique de la ville, 150–151.

Epstein, R. (2015). La gouvernance territoriale : une affaire d'État. La dimension verticale de la construction de l'action collective dans les territoires. *L'Année sociologique*, 66(2), 457.

Epstein, R. (2021). Un quart de siècle de rhétorique réactionnaire : l'effet pervers de la géographie prioritaire. In *Les cartes de l'action publique: pouvoirs, territoires, résistances*, Aguilera, T., Artioli, F., Barrault-Stella, L., Hellier, E., Pasquier, R. (eds). Presses Universitaires du Septentrion, Villeneuve-d'Ascq.

Epstein, R. and Kirszbaum, T. (2019). Ces quartiers dont on préfère ne plus parler. Les métamorphoses de la politique de la ville (1977–2018). *Parlement[s], Revue d'histoire politique*, 30(39), 23–46.

Estèbe, P. (2001). Instruments et fondements de la géographie prioritaire de la politique de la ville (1982–1996). *Revue française des affaires sociales*, 1(3), 23.

Estèbe, P. (2005). Les quartiers, une affaire d'État : un instrument territorial. In *Gouverner par les instruments*, Lascoumes, P., Le Galès, P. (eds). Presses de Sciences, Paris.

Frohlich, K.L., Potvin, L., Gauvin, L., Chabot, P. (2002). Youth smoking initiation: Disentangling context from composition. *Health & Place*, 8(3), 155–166.

Galster, G. (2012). The mechanism(s) of neighbourhood effects: Theory, evidence, and policy implications. In *Neighbourhood Effects Research: New Perspectives*, van Ham, M., Manley, D., Bailey, N., Simpson, L., Maclennan, D. (eds). Springer, Dordrecht.

Garnier, J.-P. (2010). *Essais sur la ville, la petite-bourgeoisie intellectuelle et l'effacement des classes populaires*. Agone, Marseille.

van Gent, W., Musterd, S., Ostendorf, W. (2009). Disentangling neighbourhood problems: Area-based interventions in Western European cities. *Urban Research & Practice*, 2(1), 53–67.

van Gent, W., Hochstenbach, C., Uitermark, J. (2018). Exclusion as urban policy: The Dutch "Act on Extraordinary Measures for Urban Problems". *Urban Studies*, 55(11), 2337–2353.

Glenn, N.M., Lapalme, J., McCready, G., Frohlich, K.L. (2017). Young adults' experiences of neighbourhood smoking-related norms and practices: A qualitative study exploring place-based social inequalities in smoking. *Social Science & Medicine*, 189, 17–24.

Hägerstrand, T. (1970). What about people in regional science? *Papers of Regional Science Association*, 24, 7–21.

Hancock, C., Lelévrier, C., Ripoll, F., Weber, S. (2016). *Discriminations territoriales. Entre interpellation politique et sentiment d'injustice des habitants*. L'Œil d'Or, Marne-la-Vallée.

Haynes, R., Daras, K., Reading, R., Jones, A. (2007). Modifiable neighbourhood units, zone design and residents' perceptions. *Health & Place*, 13(4), 812–25.

Jeannot, G. (2001). Diagnostic territorial et coordination de l'action publique. In *Le bricolage organisationnel. Crise des cadres hiérarchiques et innovation dans la gestion des entreprises et des territoires*, Coutard, O. (ed.). Elsevier, Amsterdam.

Kirszbaum, T. (2008). *Mixité sociale dans l'habitat : revue de la littérature dans une perspective comparative.* La Documentation française, Paris.

Kirszbaum, T. (ed.) (2009). I. Disperser ou enrichir : le dilemme de la déconcentration. In *Rénovation urbaine*. Presses Universitaires de France, Paris.

Le Galès, P. (1995). Politique de la ville en France et en Grande-Bretagne : volontarisme et ambiguïtés de l'État. *Sociologie du travail*, 37(2), 249–275.

Le Roux, G., Vallée, J., Commenges, H. (2017). Social segregation around the clock in the Paris region. *Journal of Transport Geography*, 59, 134–145.

Macintyre, S., Ellaway, A., Cummins, S. (2002). Place effects on health: How can we conceptualise, operationalise and measure them? *Social Science & Medicine*, 55(1), 125–139.

Mallet, S. (2014). The urban rhythms of neoliberalization. *Spatial Justice*, 6.

Mallet, S. and Comelli, C. (2017). Politiques d'éclairage public et transformations des espaces urbains : une approche critique. *Cybergeo*, 833.

Manley, D., van Ham, M., Bailey, N., Simpson, L., Maclennan, D. (eds) (2013). Introduction. In *Neighbourhood Effects or Neighbourhood-based Problems? A Policy Context*. Springer, Dordrecht/New York.

Maurin, E. (2004). *Le ghetto français*. Le Seuil, Paris.

Maurin, E. (2007). La ségrégation urbaine, son intensité et ses causes. In *Repenser la solidarité : l'apport des sciences sociales*, Paugam, S. (ed.). Presses universitaires de France, Paris.

Neutens, T., Schwanen, T., Witlox, F., de Maeyer, P. (2010). Evaluating the temporal organization of public service provision using space-time accessibility analysis. *Urban Geography*, 31(8), 1039–1064.

Nuvolati, G. (2003). Resident and non-resident populations: Quality of life, mobility and time policies. *The Journal of Regional Analysis and Policy*, 33(2), 67–83.

Nyhan, M., Grauwin, S., Britter, R., Misstear, B., McNabola, A., Laden, F., Barrett, S.R., Ratti, C. (2016). "Exposure track" – The impact of mobile-device-based mobility patterns on quantifying population exposure to air pollution. *Environmental Science & Technology*, 50(17), 9671–9681.

ONPV (2017). La mobilité résidentielle des habitants des quartiers prioritaires de la politique de la ville. Report, Observatoire National de la Politique de la Ville, Paris.

Ouwehand, A. and Doff, W. (2013). Who is afraid of a changing population? Reflections on housing policy in Rotterdam. *Geography Research Forum*, 33(1), 111–146.

Park, Y.M. and Kwan, M.-P. (2016). Individual exposure estimates may be erroneous when spatiotemporal variability of air pollution and human mobility are ignored. *Health & Place*, 43, 85–94.

Park, Y.M. and Kwan, M.-P. (2018). Beyond residential segregation: A spatiotemporal approach to examining multi-contextual segregation. *Computers, Environment and Urban Systems*, 71, 98–108.

Petrović, A., Manley, D., van Ham, M. (2019). Freedom from the tyranny of neighbourhood: Rethinking socio-spatial context effects. *Progress in Human Geography*, 44(6), 1103–1123.

Pickett, K.E. and Pearl, M. (2001). Multilevel analyses of neighbourhood socioeconomic context and health outcomes: A critical review. *Journal of Epidemiology and Community Health*, 55(2), 111–122.

Pinçon-Charlot, M. and Rendu, P. (1982). Distance spatiale, distance sociale aux équipements collectifs en Île-de-France : des conditions de la pratique aux pratiques. *Revue française de sociologie*, 23(4), 667–696.

Sampson, R.J. (2013). The place of context: A theory and strategy for criminology's hard problem. *Criminology*, 51(1), 1–31.

Shareck, M., Frohlich, K., Kestens, Y. (2014). Considering daily mobility for a more comprehensive understanding of contextual effects on social inequalities in health: A conceptual proposal. *Health & Place*, 29, 154–160.

Shortt, N.K., Rind, E., Pearce, J., Mitchell, R., Curtis, S. (2018). Alcohol risk environments, vulnerability, and social inequalities in alcohol consumption. *Annals of the American Association of Geographers*, 21, 1–18.

Slater, T. (2013). Capitalist urbanization affects your life chances: Exorcising the ghosts of "neighbourhood effects". In *Neighbourhood Effects or Neighbourhood Based Problems? A Policy Context*, Manley, D., van Ham, M., Bailey, N., Simpson, L., Maclennan, D. (eds). Springer, Netherlands, Dordrecht.

de Souza Briggs, X., Popkin, S.J., Goering, J.M. (2010). *Moving to Opportunity: The Story of an American Experiment to Fight Ghetto Poverty*. Oxford University Press, New York.

Thévenot, L. (1986). Les investissements de forme. In *Conventions économiques : 1985*, Piore, M.J., Thévenot, L. (eds). Presses universitaires de France, Paris.

Tissot, S. (2004). Identifier ou décrire les "quartiers sensibles" ? Le recours aux indicateurs statistiques dans la politique de la ville. *Genèses*, 54(1), 90.

Tunstall, R. and Lupton, R. (2003). Is targeting deprived areas an effective means to reach poor people? Report, CASE paper, London School of Economics and Political Science, London.

Uitermark, J., Hochstenbach, C., van Gent, W. (2017). The statistical politics of exceptional territories. *Political Geography*, 57, 60–70.

Vallée, J. (2017a). Challenges in targeting areas for public action. Target areas at the right place and at the right time. *Journal of Epidemiology and Community Health*, 71(10), 945–946.

Vallée, J. (2017b). The daycourse of place. *Social Science & Medicine*, 194, 177–181.

Vallée, J. and Le Roux, G. (2018). Quartiers prioritaires la nuit, quartiers prioritaires le jour ? *Proceedings du 4e colloque international du CIST (Représenter les territoires / Representing territories)*, 215–220.

Vallée, J., Le Roux, G., Chaix, B., Kestens, Y., Chauvin, P. (2015). The "constant size neighbourhood trap" in accessibility and health studies. *Urban Studies*, 52(2), 338–357.

Vallée, J., Le Roux, G., Chauvin, P. (2016). Quartiers et effets de quartier. Analyse de la variabilité de la taille des quartiers perçus dans l'agglomération parisienne. *Les Annales de Géographie*, 708(2), 119–142.

Vallée, J., Shareck, M., Kestens, Y., Frohlich, K.L. (2022). Everyday geography and service accessibility: The contours of disadvantage in relation to mental health. *Annals of the American Association of Geographers*, 112(4), 931–947.

Vant, A. (1986). A propos de l'impact du spatial sur le social. In *Espaces, jeux et enjeux*, Auriac, F., Brunet R. (eds). Fayard, Paris.

Vergier, N. and Chaput, H. (2017). Déserts médicaux : comment les définir ? Comment les mesurer ? Report, Les dossiers de la DREES.

Wacquant, L. (2008). *Urban Outcasts: A Comparative Sociology of Advanced Marginality*. Polity Press, Cambridge.

Wacquant, L. (2009). The body, the ghetto and the penal state. *Qualitative Sociology*, 32(1), 101–129.

Warin, P. (1997). L'impasse démocratique de la politique de la ville en France. *Swiss Political Science Review*, 3(3), 1–27.

Wilson, W.J. (1987). *The Truly Disadvantaged: The Inner City, the Underclass, and Public Policy*. University of Chicago Press, Chicago.

List of Authors

Philippe ASKENAZY
Centre Maurice Halbwachs
CNRS
ENS
Paris
France

Negar Élodie BEHZADI
University of Bristol
UK

Clémentine COTTINEAU
Centre Maurice Halbwachs
CNRS
Paris
France
and
Technische Universiteit Delft
The Netherlands

Lucia DIRENBERGER
Centre Maurice Halbwachs
CNRS
Paris
France

Verónica ESCUDERO
International Labour Organization
Geneva
Switzerland
and
Center for Effective Global Action
UC Berkeley
USA

Leïla FROUILLOU
CRESPPA-GTM
Université Paris-Nanterre
France

Serge PAUGAM
Centre Maurice Halbwachs
CNRS
EHESS
ENS
Paris
France

Laurence ROULLEAU-BERGER
CNRS
Triangle
ENS de Lyon
France

Julie VALLÉE
Géographie-cités
CNRS
Paris
France

Index

A

agency, 28, 45, 46, 50, 51
agent-based, 169, 170, 172
aggregation, 121
approach
 postcolonial, 28, 30, 31, 35, 36, 40, 50, 51
 relational, 194

B, C

body, 4, 20, 27, 31, 33, 34, 37–39, 41, 45, 48, 50, 66, 69
boundary, 37, 40, 111, 119, 127, 145
Bourdieu, Pierre, 2, 3, 7, 8, 16, 128, 194
capitalism, 47, 62, 69, 138, 141
cellular automata, 169, 170, 174, 175
circulations, 28, 35, 62, 75
Crenshaw, Kimberlé, 28, 32

D, E

digital space, 89, 91, 104
discontinuity, 71, 153, 159
discourse, 41, 42, 45, 67, 128, 131, 138, 140, 141, 143
discrimination, 44, 67, 93
diversity, 46, 48, 127, 137, 196, 197, 199
downgrading, 2, 65, 71, 78
ethnicization, 66, 69

F, G, H

feminist, 29, 48, 51
gender, 27, 29, 33, 38, 41–43, 49, 50, 62, 65, 72, 79, 100, 102, 112
Gini, 130, 153, 154, 156, 158, 173
hierarchy, 8, 31, 32, 34, 74
homogeneity, 32, 131, 168, 187, 188

I, J, L

immobility, 91, 93
information asymmetries, 102
injustice, 123, 137, 146
intersectionality, 28, 31, 49, 64, 65
jobs, 39, 85, 88–97, 100, 102, 106, 109–112, 126, 197

labor market, 63, 66, 89–93, 95, 98–100, 102–104, 106, 111
LGBTQI+, 49–51
Lorenz, 153, 154

M

mapping, 133, 153
microwork, 69, 110
migrations, 30, 33, 36, 62–66, 74, 76–78
mobility
    commuting, 88
    residential, 89, 90, 94, 111, 112, 195
mobilization, 189
model
    agent-based, 172, 176
    multilevel, 161, 162, 165
    simulation, 112, 152, 165, 169–172, 174, 177
monopsony, 95
moral order, 128, 129
multi-situated, 61
multiscalar, 164, 165, 167

N, P

neighborhood-agent, 188, 203
network
    professional, 103, 106
    social, 102
norm, 29, 188
Pareto, 153, 155
perception, 90, 122, 123, 125, 140, 143–145, 172
place effects, 4, 186, 193–195
poverty, 119, 121–126, 131, 132, 136–141, 143–146, 184, 186, 190, 193, 195

priority geography, 184, 186, 193, 197
public
    policies, 4, 5, 20, 42, 183
    statistics, 187, 191

R

relations
    of domination, 28, 45, 46, 51
    power, 27, 28, 30, 31, 33, 34, 38, 41, 51
    social, 2, 3, 27–29, 44, 49–51, 64, 78, 126
representations, 4, 5, 30, 41, 49, 123, 125, 126, 132, 136, 143, 144
Ripoll, Fabrice, 2–4

S

school
    system, 2, 8, 10, 12–14, 129
    trajectories, 1, 5, 6, 16, 18
segregation
    indices, 6, 11, 154–157
    school, 5, 6, 10, 18
    social, 193, 199
    spatial, 37, 90, 94, 119, 170, 185
self, 46, 121, 125, 128, 129, 134, 143, 144
social class, 12, 37, 46
sociospatial, 3
spatial
    dimension, 2, 5, 7, 8, 11, 12, 14, 16, 17, 19, 20
    mismatch, 88, 91, 92, 107, 197
structure
    social, 11
    spatial, 156, 160, 193
subaltern, 62, 68, 74

T, U, W, Z

transnationalism, 62, 63, 74, 76
unemployment, 42, 85–89, 92, 94, 97, 122, 141, 142, 162

wealth, 119, 131, 152–155, 176
van Zanten, Agnès, 5, 9, 10, 12, 15–17, 129

Printed and bound by CPI Group (UK) Ltd, Croydon, CR0 4YY
05/01/2023

03177944-0002